INCENTIVE-BASED BUDGETING SYSTEMS IN PUBLIC UNIVERSITIES

INCENTIVE-BASED BUDGETING SYSTEMS IN PUBLIC UNIVERSITIES

Edited by

Douglas M. Priest, William E. Becker,
Don Hossler, and Edward P. St. John

Edward Elgar
Cheltenham, UK • Northampton, MA, USA

Published by
Edward Elgar Publishing Limited
Glensanda House
Montpellier Parade
Cheltenham
Glos GL50 1UA
UK

Edward Elgar Publishing, Inc.
136 West Street
Suite 202
Northampton
Massachusetts 01060
USA

A catalogue record for this book
is available from the British Library

ISBN 1 84376 170 X

Printed and bound in Great Britain by Biddles Ltd, *www.biddles.co.uk*

CONTENTS

FIGURES AND TABLES

FIGURES

TABLES

ACKNOWLEDGMENTS

The editors wish to thank each of the authors who participated in the development of this book. Many of these authors presented their work at Indiana University in the spring of 2001, for which we as well as our students are especially grateful.

The quality of chapters in this book was raised markedly through the editorial assistance and final copy editing of Suzanne Becker. We all benefited from her expertise with the English language and knowledge of the editorial process. We are grateful to Delphine Sherwood for her patience and precision in the production of camera-ready copy. Delphine has made us all look better in print. Graphic Services at Indiana University prepared the camera-ready artwork under the direction of Suzie Hull, to whom we are grateful. Thanks are also expressed to Twanette Newton for her logistical support over the two-year life of this project.

Finally, the Office of the Chancellor, Indiana University Bloomington, and the *Journal of Economic Education*, through the sponsorship of the National Council on Economic Education, provided financial support for the development of this book. We gratefully acknowledge that assistance, without which this volume would not have been possible.

Douglas M. Priest
William E. Becker
Don Hossler
Edward P. St. John

LIST OF CONTRIBUTORS

William E. Becker, Professor of Economics, Indiana University; Adjunct Professor, School of International Business, University of South Australia; and Editor, *Journal of Economic Education*

Paul N. Courant, Associate Provost, Professor of Economics and Public Policy, University of Michigan

Cherry Danielson, Research Associate, Office of Policy Analysis, University System of New Hampshire

Kenneth R. R. Gros Louis, former Chancellor, Indiana University

Don Hossler, Professor of Educational Leadership and Policy Studies; Vice-Chancellor for Enrollment Services, Indiana University; and Editor, *CASE International Journal of Educational Advancement*

Marilyn Knepp, Associate Vice President for University Budget, Planning, and Administration, University of Michigan

Daniel W. Lang, Professor of Higher Education Management and Finance; Senior Policy Advisor to the President; and former Vice Provost for Planning and Budget, University of Toronto

Larry L. Leslie, Professor of Higher Education, University of Arizona

Ronald L. Oaxaca, Professor of Economics, University of Arizona

Michael B. Paulsen, Professor of Higher Education, University of New Orleans

Douglas M. Priest, Associate Vice-Chancellor for Budget and Planning; and Associate Professor of Educational Leadership and Policy Studies, Indiana University

Gary Rhoades, Professor of Higher Education, University of Arizona

Edward P. St. John, Professor of Educational Leadership and Policy Studies, Indiana University; Director Indiana Education Policy Center; and Consulting Editor for *Research in Higher Education*

Neil D. Theobald, Associate Professor of Education, Indiana University

Maynard Thompson, Vice-Chancellor for Budget and Planning, Indiana University

William Tobin, Director of Institutional Research, DePauw University

Robert K. Toutkoushian, Executive Director of Office of Policy Analysis, University System of New Hampshire

Edward L. Whalen, former Vice Chancellor for Administration and Finance, University of Houston System; and former Assistant Vice-President for Finance, Indiana University

John Douglas Wilson, Professor of Economics, Michigan State University

CHAPTER 1

WHY INCENTIVE-BASED BUDGETING SYSTEMS IN THE PUBLIC SECTOR AND WHY NOW?

Douglas M. Priest

William E. Becker

Don Hossler

Edward P. St. John

The genesis for this book stems from the ongoing interest of faculty and administrators in the growing use of incentive-based budgeting systems at large public universities. Our interest, in large part, stems from experiences with such a budgeting system at Indiana University and other large public institutions.

Thomas Ehrlich, as a relatively new president of the multi-campus system of Indiana University, initiated an incentive-based budgeting system in the 1988-1989 school year. This eight-campus system includes the two large campuses at Bloomington and Indianapolis. The Bloomington campus is the flagship research campus of Indiana University. The Indianapolis campus, like many urban commuter institutions, had transformed itself over a 20-year period from being a satellite regional campus of the Bloomington campus to a major research institution in its own right, replete with professional schools of medicine, dentistry, law, engineering, business, nursing, education, and public affairs.

Thomas Ehrlich came to Indiana from the private University of Pennsylvania. Penn had been using a variant of incentive-based budgeting called "responsibility center budgeting" (RCB) for several years. Forms of incentive-based budgeting, often described as "every tub rests on its own bottom," had been used at large private universities for decades. Ehrlich, however, put into motion the first implementation of RCB at a major public research university. This was a major departure from the incremental yearly budgeting process followed at most large public universities because academic units were now viewed as "profit centers," a concept not generally associated with public institutions.

As you read through our collection of chapters, you will see authors from different universities refer to budgeting strategies that are called RCM, value centered management (VCM), decentralized budgeting, and activity-based budgeting. In his edited book, Massy (1996) uses the term "values responsibility budgeting" while three of his co-authors, Strauss, Curry, and Whalen use the term revenue responsibility budgeting (1996). At a meta-level, all of these are variants of incentive-based budgeting systems. We have found that differences in what individual universities call their incentive-based budgeting schemes often reflect both differences in values, aspirations, priorities, and political realities of the campus on which they are executed, and efforts by senior administrators to make an idea their own by giving it a unique name and character.

When new budgeting systems are implemented the process becomes a case study in organizational change because a new budgeting system lays bare the realities of the campus on which the change is being implemented. By including chapters on budgeting theory, economics, finance, and case studies, this book is about both the use of incentive-based budgeting systems at public universities and the transformation process that occurs at public universities when an important new change initiative is being undertaken. As rapidly becomes evident reviewing the case studies at the University of Toronto, the University of Michigan, and Indiana University Bloomington, not all changes are welcome and not all are successful.

WHY INCENTIVE-BASED BUDGETING SYSTEMS?

Why Now?

As Wildavsky (1964) observed, the budgeting process cannot be isolated from the concerns of the campus in which it operates. To this observation we would add that budgeting systems at public universities cannot be separated from the larger economic and public policy environment in which they operate. In this context it is easy to see why public university administrators have toyed with incentive-based budgeting but yet have not universally accepted it. Public universities are in a period of fiscal duress. The percentage of their budgets that is derived from state support has been declining for several years. Public institutions are being forced to look for other sources of revenue to fund their operations (Massy, 1996; Roherty, 1997; Slaughter and Leslie, 1997; St. John, 1994). Except for an economic downturn in the early 1990s, revenues increased through most of the 1980s and 1990s. During this same time period, however, state revenues to public colleges and universities steadily declined. As a result of these trends, Geiger (2000) observed that public research universities seemed to gain ground on their private counterparts during the 1980s. However, since that time, Geiger suggests that public research universities have been losing ground with respect to fiscal health and a sense of mission and purpose.

Public universities also find themselves in an era of increasing demands for accountability. Public policymakers want to be reassured that public funds are being used wisely and being put to good purposes at public universities. A spate of publications emerged on assessment and benchmarking in higher education (see, for example, Gaither, Nedwek, and Neal, 1994 or Alstete, 1995). MacTaggart (1998) notes that between the 1970s and 1990s all but three states established governing boards to consolidate authority over public colleges and universities. In addition, staff and aides in state agencies, the executive branch, and in legislative offices "became more directly involved in both the substance and procedures of state higher education policy" (McGuiness, 1997, p. 23).

In addition, in many parts of the world public universities have entered an era where concepts associated with privatization and marketing dominate political ideologies about higher education (Clark, 2000; McTavish, 1998; Slaughter and Leslie, 1997). In response to a new higher education financial system in New Zealand, in which the country's eight public universities now must compete with one another, academics were told by administrators at the University of Auckland that they would face dismissal if they publicly criticized colleagues or the work of the institution, raising concerns about academic freedom (Cohen, 2002). Zemsky and Wegner (1997, p. 63) conclude the majority of colleges and universities "will be forced to adapt to an environment of heightened competition and from different types of educational providers."

The convergence of these trends has created environments on the campuses of some public universities where incentive-based budgeting systems have emerged as part of the solution to the challenges faced by public institutions. But others have shied away in part because of concern that unlike private institutions, public universities operate in a fish bowl – "profits" cannot be hid. Why should a state legislature provide additional funding to a university that is flush with cash reserves? Increasing competition within a university does not necessary follow as the way to meet increasing competition between universities.

Why Incentive-Based Budgeting?

Surprisingly, despite all of the attention that has been given to incentive-based budgeting systems and their advantages at public institutions, relatively few theoretical or empirical studies have been published on this topic. In this introductory chapter, we briefly highlight existing work to set the stage for this book.

Strauss, Curry, and Whalen (1996) suggest that incentive-based budgeting systems have the following advantages:

1. They create a more open budgeting system where information and ideas associated with the budget and institutional priorities are more openly exchanged.

This, they assert, is more consistent with the tenets of academic freedom and a collegial form of academic governance.

2. Decentralized budgeting gives departments and faculty greater responsibility for planning their entire academic operations. This too is consistent with the norm of local governance pervasive at research universities with strong and autonomous departments.

3. Decisions made and implemented at the local level are more likely to be based upon merit. They are likely to optimize opportunities at the local level because they are made by faculty who know their own situations best.

In Chapter 2 of this book, Whalen again looks at the advantages and disadvantages of incentive-based budgeting and concludes along with several other studies that incentive-based budgeting leads to efficiencies. That is, incentive-based budgeting systems lead institutions to maximize income and minimize expenditures (Hoenack, 1977, 1984, 1994; Massy, 1996; Robbins and Rooney, 1995; Whalen, 1991). Incentive-based budgeting systems eliminate the notion of "free goods" for faculty and departments and thereby lead to better resource use. Incentives for faculty to increase grants and/or increase credit hour productions may be examples of how this institution maximizes income. Charges for space and the concerns expressed by some academic administrators about the "taxes" they would have to pay for services rendered may make faculty and departments more likely to look for efficiencies in these areas.

Hoenack (1977; 1984) posits that incentive-based budgeting systems enhance cooperation, while others in this book (Wilson, Chapter 3; Lang, Chapter 6; and Becker/Theobald, Chapter 9) point to the pressures of competition between the units of a university that are expected to float on their own bottoms. As early as 1979 Strauss, Porter, and Zemsky reported that incentive-based budgeting increased competition among academic units. Hoenack also suggests that incentive-based budgeting systems provide students with more influence across institutions of higher education. On the other hand, Hossler, Kuh, and Bateman (1989), in their study, found that some faculty and academic administrators believed that students might be manipulated by schools or departments to enable these academic units to increase credit hour production.

In a study of the implementation of RCM at the Indianapolis campus of Indiana University, Robbins and Rooney (1995) indicated that not only is the academic units' autonomy preserved, but it is enhanced. Earlier Strauss and Salamon (1979) concluded that faculty members will design courses to maximize tuition income and that they will seek more sponsored research. The authors also found that incentive-based budgeting produces a greater desire for academic administrators who are good managers. This development challenges the public perception of university administrators who are often viewed as poor stewards of public resources.

Based on this brief review of the literature on incentive-based budgeting systems and the earlier study conducted by Hossler, Kuh, and Bateman (1989), we offer the following questions. These questions represent our central concerns about the compatibility and impact of incentive-based budgeting systems at public research universities.

1. To what degree are the assumptions and values of incentive-based budgeting systems compatible with the existing norms and values of public research universities? How are aspects of incentive budgeting systems affected or altered by the existing norms and values of a campus?

2. What kinds of financial information, and unit-based budget information are required for administrators to make incentive-based budgeting systems work?

3. What is the impact of incentive-based budgeting systems upon academic and nonacademic units? Are there variations in the effects of incentive budgeting across these units?

4. What influence do incentive-based budgeting systems have on the attitudes, behavior, and activities of faculty members?

5. What situational factors (i.e., student demand for courses, ability to generate external funds) are likely to influence the response of academic departments or individual colleges/schools to incentive-based budgeting?

6. How will the implementation of incentive-based budgeting influence the roles and responsibilities of administrators?

The remaining chapters of this volume include a range of treatments of incentive-based budgeting systems. The first set of chapters provides a broad view, focusing on the impact of incentive budgeting systems on institutions and on academic departments. As already mentioned, in Chapter 2, Edward Whalen makes an administrator's case for incentive-based budgeting. John Wilson, Chapter 3, explores the economic theory underpinning competitive markets. He raises concerns about the lack of appropriate market forces when academic units have to compete for students within a university. In Chapter 4, Larry Leslie, Ronald Oaxaca, and Gary Rhoades examine the impact of shifts in sources of revenue on faculty and departmental behavior.

The second set of chapters includes three case studies of efforts to implement incentive-based budgeting systems at public universities in the United States and Canada. The three institutions are Indiana University Bloomington, Chapter 5; the University of Toronto, Chapter 6; and the University of Michigan, Chapter 7. These case studies provide important insights into the use of incentive-based budgeting systems at public universities. In each of these case studies, the implementations of these new budgeting systems were not entirely successful. Indeed, Paul Courant and Marilyn Knepp report that at the University of Michigan much of the first effort at an incentive budgeting system was modified. On one campus of the University of Toronto, the new budgeting system was judged to be unsuccessful by Daniel Lang. At Indiana University, Kenneth Gros Louis and Maynard Thompson tell how some faculty members have recurring questions about the philosophical underpinnings of RCM and its use at a university. Incentive-based budgeting systems are not a panacea for public universities.

The last set of chapters looks at the impact of incentive-based budgeting systems upon faculty and campus performance indicators. It closes by reflecting on the evolution of various approaches to budgeting and the conditions under which implementation of select aspects of incentive approaches to budgeting might be successful within individual organizational cultures. Michael Paulsen and Edward St. John, in Chapter 8, consider how budget incentives might improve teaching. But William Becker and Neil Theobald, in Chapter 9, warn that any prediction of how a faculty member may or may not respond to a competitive reward structure versus a fixed merit standard, depends on the faculty member's position in the outcome distributions, how accurately the outcomes are measured, and the faculty member's behavior toward risk. They also provide the formula for converting merit scores into salary increases based on an absolute dollar and/or a percentage allocation system. Robert Toutkoushian and Cherry Danielson (Chapter 10) address the various outcomes that administrators might consider measuring as performance indicators in a decentralized budgeting system. Finally, Douglas Priest, Edward St. John, and William Tobin consider the evolution of incentive-based budgeting systems and conclude that given the general financial prognosis for public institutions, inventive-based budgeting, implemented in ways tailored to individual institutional circumstances, will be a useful tool that should be considered in a variety of possible formats.

REFERENCES

Alstete, Jeffery W. 1995. *Benchmarking in higher education: Adapting best practices to improve quality.* ASHE-ERIC Higher Education Reports, Report Five. Washington, D.C.: The ERIC Clearinghouse on Higher Education, George Washington University.

Clark, Burton R. 2000. Collegial entrepeneurialism in proactive universities: Lessons from Europe. *Change Magazine* 32 (1): 10-19.

Cohen, David. 2002. U. of Auckland threatens to fire academics who criticize their colleagues. <http://chronicle.com/daily/2002/04/2002041605n.htm> *Chronicle of Higher Education,* April 16.

Gaither, Gerald, Brian R. Nedwek, and John E. Neal. 1994. *Measuring up: The promise and pitfalls of performance indicators in higher education.* ASHE-ERIC Higher Education Reports, Report Five. Washington, D.C.: ERIC Clearinghouse on Higher Education, George Washington University.

Geiger, Roger L. 2000. Public research universities in an age of privatization. Presented at The Wells Archive: Exploring the World of Higher Education. September, 21, Indiana University Bloomington.

Hoenack, Stephen A. 1977. Direct and incentive planning within a university. *Socio-Economic Planning Sciences* 11 (4): 191-204.

Hoenack, Stephen A. 1984. *Economic behavior within organizations.* New York: Cambridge University Press.

Hoenack, Stephen A. 1994. Economics, organizations, and learning: Research directions for the economics of education. *Economics of Education Review* 13 (2): 147-162.

Hossler, Don, George Kuh, and Mark Bateman. 1989. An investigation of the anticipated effects of responsibility center budgeting at a public research university: The first year. Paper presented at the Annual Meeting of the American Educational Research Association, April, San Francisco, CA.

MacTaggart, Terrence J., and Associates. 1997. *Seeking excellence through independence: Liberating colleges and universities from successive regulation.* San Francisco: Jossey-Bass.

Massy, William F. 1996. Value responsibility budgeting. In W. Massy, ed., *Resource allocation in higher education*. Ann Arbor: University of Michigan.

McGuiness, Aimes C. 1997. The changing structures of state higher education leadership. In A. McGuiness Jr., R. Epper, and S. Arredondo, eds., *State postsecondary education structures sourcebook: State coordinating and governing boards*. Denver: Education Commission of the States.

McTavish, Duncan. 1998. Strategies management in further education colleges: A pilot study. *Scottish Education Review* 30 (2): 125-137.

Robbins, D. C., and Patrick M. Rooney. 1995. Responsibility center management: An assessment of RCM at IUPUI. *NACUBO Business Magazine* 28 (9): 44-49.

Roherty, Brian M. 1997. The price of passive resistance in financing higher education. In P. Callahan and J. Finney, eds., *Public and private financing of higher education: shaping public policy for the future*. Phoenix, AZ: The American Council on Education and Oryx Press.

St. John, Edward P. 1994. *Prices, productivity, and investment: Assessing financial strategies in higher education*, ASHE-ERIC Higher Education Study, no. 3. Washington, D.C.: George Washington University.

Slaughter, Shelia, and Larry L. Leslie. 1997. *Academic capitalism: Politics, policies, and the entrepreneurial university*. Baltimore: Johns Hopkins University Press.

Strauss, Jon, and Linda Salamon. 1979. Using financial incentives in academic planning. *Business Officer* 13 (November): 14-17.

Strauss, Jon, John Curry, and Edward Whalen. 1996. Revenue responsibility budgeting. In W. Massy ed., *Resource allocation in higher education*. Ann Arbor: University of Michigan.

Strauss, Jon, Randall Porter, and Robert Zemsky. 1979. Modeling and planning at the University of Pennsylvania. In Joe B. Wyatt, James C. Emery, and Carolyn P. Landis, eds., *Financial planning models: Concepts and case studies in colleges and universities*. Princeton: EDUCOM.

Whalen, Edward L. 1991. Responsibility center budgeting: An approach to decentralized management for institutions of higher education. Bloomington: Indiana University Press.

Wildavsky, Aaron. 1964. *The politics of the budgeting process*. Boston: Little-Brown.

Zemsky, Robert, and Gregory R. Wegner. 1997. Shaping the future. In P. Callahan and J. Finney, eds., *Public and private financing of higher education: Shaping public policy for the future*. Phoenix, AZ: The American Council on Education and Oryx Press.

CHAPTER 2

THE CASE, IF ANY, FOR RESPONSIBILITY CENTER BUDGETING

Edward L. Whalen

In the early 1970s a small number of distinguished, large, independent institutions of higher education adopted a decentralized form of administration that has come to be known as responsibility center management (RCM) or, somewhat more modestly, as responsibility center budgeting (RCB).[1]   Then, as today, the motivation for moving to this arrangement to structure decisionmaking and budgeting is to "balance the traditional independence of academic endeavor against the pressing need for more effective utilization of academic resources." (Strauss, et al., 1959, p. 148)   RCB consciously and explicitly adds effective resource use as an ingredient to the decision-making stew of a college or university. Given the motivation for its adoption, the case for RCB, therefore, lies in whether or not it results in more effective use of academic resources.

Since its inception nearly three decades ago, colleges and universities have not universally adopted RCB.   The number of institutions adopting it has increased, but RCB clearly is less pervasive than facsimile machines, cellular telephones, and personal computers whose introduction occurred during the same time interval. The omnipresence of those devices makes their case. If RCB had enjoyed similar widespread use, attempting to make a case for it would not be necessary. Its limited growth makes us wonder. Maybe (a) RCB does not result in more effective use of resources or (b) effective resource use is not an important or even desired consideration for colleges and universities.

Given the absence of empirical evidence for general acceptance of RCB, making a case for it leads to addressing three questions: What is RCB? What is required for its implementation?   Does it result in a more effective use of resources? The answers to these questions may show that it is suitable only for a limited number of institutions.   The costs or barriers to its introduction may exceed RCB's perceived and actual benefits. More effective resource use may fail to materialize under RCB.

WHAT IS RESPONSIBILITY CENTER BUDGETING?

The inclusion of RCB in this volume indicates that it is an incentive-based budgeting system that has been used in public universities. That hardly distinguishes RCB. All budgeting approaches provide to the heads of operating units incentives upon which they base their decisions. The problem with those incentives is that they often lead to unintended consequences: operating unit heads making decisions that do not serve well the interests of the institution.

Consider, for example, a budgeting and accounting system in which income from grants and contracts to cover general administrative costs does not accrue to principal investigators. Under such an arrangement, should it come as a surprise that principal investigators are inclined to improve their competitive position by waiving such costs in their grant and contract proposals. If resources made available to a school or college are not related to the amount of its classroom and laboratory instruction, doesn't it become likely that academic departments assign a low priority to teaching students? If support units find their budget allocations are related more to staff size rather than to the level of services provided, no one should be shocked when the number of employees engaged in administrative chores increase and support costs garner a larger share of the budget.

Resource use and operating unit behavior that is perverse from the standpoint of an institution's objectives are not confined to colleges and universities. Hoenack (1983, p. 38) observes in his study of economic behavior *within* organizations, "In general, resource diversions can result from an employee's producing outputs that are not demanded by his employer or from his failure to deliver demanded outputs, as well as from not applying inputs efficiently within his production domain. For example, an employee in an applied research laboratory may produce basic research for the purpose of furthering his personal professional reputation. Other employees may acquire general skills or make their personal accomplishments known to colleagues and potential employers at their employer's expense." Another example that comes to mind is contributing to and editing a book of readings on higher education administration.

If resource diversion besets organizations in general, colleges and universities are liable to be particularly vulnerable. "Large institutions have become unwieldy associations of quasi-independent schools and programs. Research centers complement academic departments, interdisciplinary degree programs supplement the traditional disciplines, and entirely new schools emerge to seek their niches in the organizational structure." (Strauss, et al., 1979, p. 147)

RCB is intended to reduce college and university vulnerability to resource diversion. Cost centers have been common features of business accounting for a long time. Such terms are used in two senses. "In the first sense, it is an *accounting entity* for the accumulation, allocation, and absorption of costs. In the second sense, it is a *responsibility center* set up for cost control." (Shah, 1981, p. 203) Cost centers usually consist of homogenous activities that are well defined, clearly identifiable, and mutually exclusive. Responsibility centers take the form of designated operating units within an organization that have someone in charge who manages them. Our concern is with responsibility centers that are concerned not only with costs but also with revenues generated by their activities.

Horngren, et al. (1996, p. 376) caution, "Do not confuse profit centers (accountability for revenue and expenses) with decentralization (freedom to make decisions). They are entirely separate concepts, although profit centers clearly are accounting devices that can aid decentralization. One can exist without the other." This last point is important. The formal structures and mechanisms associated with RCB often receive a lot of attention. Whereas such conventions become necessary in large and complex organizations, they do not capture the essence of RCB. RCB is embodied in a state of mind, an attitude, of both central administration and of center heads that they are empowered to make decisions. Just establishing responsibility centers is not sufficient. Decentralization of responsibility coupled with the authority to make decisions is also required.

The importance of RCB as an attitude as well as a system or approach became vividly apparent shortly after it was implemented at Indiana University-Purdue University at Indianapolis (IUPUI) in 1988-89.[2] A school dean found that student fee income for his school had exceeded budget expectations by $100,000. When he approached the chancellor for permission to hire an additional faculty member with the additional funds, he was told that the decision was entirely his. The money belonged to the school, and he was authorized to use it in whatever way he felt best promoted its program. In response, he exclaimed, "This is terrific! I understood responsibility center budgeting intellectually, but you have to experience it to really take it to heart. This is terrific!...Power. I have never had such power. I've been in charge of large federal agencies and served as dean at other schools, but this kind of discretion has not been available to me. It's almost scary." (Whalen, 1991, p. 145)

The trick of RCB is to provide managers of operating units designated as responsibility centers with a set of signals that lead them as if "by an invisible hand" to make decisions that are congruent with the interests of the entire institution as well as with the interest of their unit. RCB does so by allocating to each center all of the expenses that it incurs and attributing to it the revenue that it generates. In addition, at the end of each fiscal year, the center retains any surplus of revenue over expenses or any deficit of expenses over revenue. For management purposes, the centers become independent – but not autonomous – fiscal entities within an institution: little universities within a university universe.

Note that all of a center's expenses are allocated to it. Those expenses include not only such direct expenses as faculty and staff compensation, supplies, travel, equipment and telephone charges but also overhead costs for support services such as grounds and facilities operation and maintenance, academic and institutional support, and student services. All expenses are included.

Under RCB, a center with external grants or contracts receives the indirect cost recovery income associated with them. It also is charged with all their indirect costs. Indeed, those indirect costs get charged to the center regardless of whether those costs are covered by grant or contract income. Responsibility centers receive the tuition and fees that students enrolled in their courses pay. A link between serving the educational needs of students and the resources with which to carry out that task is thereby established. Resources are not allocated to responsibility centers providing support services based on their expenses but rather on the level of service provided and the value those served place on it.

Note also that although centers may operate as if they are independent, they are not autonomous. Center heads are assigned both the responsibility and authority to manage the internal resources of their respective units, but they must do so within the context of applicable university, state, and federal statutes and regulations. Moreover, a portion of the revenue they generate is "taxed" according to an established rate. The purpose of that exaction is not to cover overhead expenses but rather to leverage the leadership of the institution's central administration – president and provost. Based on the institution's strategic plan and priorities, the need to nurture vulnerable units, and units' plans to develop new programs, they allocate that exaction back to units.

> The fundamental principle being applied in this move toward distributed management is to get the decision-making at the level where information is available. At this level, individuals can still perceive, if not completely quantify, the combined effects of decisions and actions on understood, but ill-specified, objectives, and they can do so in the face of complex and overlapping constraints....As the direct beneficiary of its earned income, each school would presumably exploit every opportunity to increase...income as well as to weigh more carefully the relative merits of new programs. At the same time, once given responsibility for monitoring expense as well as generating income, the schools would learn to operate within a context of accountability rather than evasion. In sum, each school was to develop its own strategy for balancing its budget through income expansion on the one hand and cost reduction and selective reinvestment on the other. (Strauss, et al., 1979, pp. 148-149)

WHAT IS REQUIRED TO IMPLEMENT RCB?

While the principles of RCB appear to be straightforward, putting them into practice is not necessarily an easy proposition. "Institutional policies and practices are culture driven and culture bound." (Kuh and Whitt, 1988, p. 100) RCB, in changing the way decisions are made and how resources are allocated, can have a palpable effect on an institution's culture. Changing an institution's culture presents a challenge that is liable to be difficult to overcome.

Kuh and Whitt (1988, p. 101) observe,

> Institutional culture is difficult to modify intentionally. Anthropological perspectives suggest that institutional culture is immutable. Studies of efforts to

> change organizational culture have typically found that culture is not easily altered in intentional ways. Others are more optimistic and believe that administrators can signal the need to modify beliefs by the questions they ask, what they attend to, and how they spend their time...[and] by using a visionary interpretative leadership style.

These observations suggest that the outcome of an attempt to implement RCB may be either success or failure. Timing, circumstances, and personalities play a role.

Personalities

In my opinion, the three most important requirements for successfully deploying and effectively operating RCB are:

The governing board wants to use it.

The president of the institution wants to use it.

The chief academic officer wants to use it.

Those three requirements are listed in order of their priority and significance.

If the board is enthusiastic about RCB, the president and provost had better get that way. If the president is the prime mover for RCB, and if the board is supportive, the provost had better become enthusiastic. In the highly competitive and fine-tuned environment of higher education, no institution can afford to be a house divided at the top level of executive management. A board keen on RCB is unlikely to resign to accommodate an unwilling president. Only a president without backbone abides for long a recalcitrant chief academic officer.

RCB is an approach that helps translate an institution's plan into priorities, allocate resources that reflect those priorities, empower heads of academic and supporting units to use the resources allocated to them to accomplish the objectives assigned to them, and monitor their progress. It is essentially a *modus operandi* involving the president, provost, and responsibility center heads. As an approach, it has a certain style. Because people's styles, like their tastes, differ, RCB does not possess universal appeal.

Members of a governing board with a penchant for meddling in matters of administration will find little to like. RCB – properly structured – leads to defined roles for executive-level management along with everyone else. Under RCB, a board's focus will be on such strategic issues and such global concerns as academic programs, research thrusts, strengths and weaknesses relative to comparable institutions, areas for community service, their fiduciary responsibility, internal controls, and executive performance evaluation. The board's focus will not be on the cost of lawn mowing, a coach's salary, how much equipment is purchased, travel expenses, selection of architects, and the number of employees.

Presidents and provosts accustomed to making their allocation decisions based on the tears of fervent deans and department heads, the aggressiveness and belligerence of a request, threats of resignation, the appearance of sincerity, flattery, and feigned friendship will find RCB to be an unfamiliar environment. If they like being consulted on all matters of administrative detail in cheek-to-cheek conversations at cocktail parties and other social occasions, they may have to develop more engaging conversational skills when operating under RCB. If they view their role as one of keeping busy, busy, busy with involvement in the day-to-day trivia of departmental administration, RCB may leave them feeling as if they have suddenly lost their jobs. If they believe that all of the institution's resources are at their disposal to grant as boons to obsequious vassals in the feudal manner, RCB may appear to be a threat to their royal prerogatives.

On the other hand, presidents and provosts who view the heads of academic and supporting service units as partners in a magnificent collective endeavor with responsibilities differing only in scope will find much to like in RCB. So also will a president desiring to blend his or her vision for the entire institution with visions that heads of major units have for their assigned areas. RCB can provide relief from administrative minutia and enable a president to concentrate on those functions and duties that only a president can perform.

Similar blessings from a properly deployed RCB approach befall a provost. It provides a framework in which the overall academic objectives of an institution can be blended with the aspirations and initiatives of deans and department heads and a structure for measuring progress in accomplishing those objectives. Responsibility and authority for decisionmaking within major academic units are decentralized to the heads of operating units, freeing the provost from involvement in such matters and enabling him or her to focus on the overall academic mission of the institution and on recruiting the most able candidates to fill vacant deanships.

Given the right set of predilections, an institution's governing board, president, and provost should be kindly disposed to the concept of RCB. If any one of the three parties dissents, its potential contribution to an institution's performance will be compromised. In the implementation stage, those who fear the change will approach board members. If board members support the plaintiffs, the resulting distortions will prompt a deluge of such complaints as individuals seek arrangements that preserve their self-interest. The provost's engagement is essential to set the precedents that will determine how the approach will operate. Once established, RCB becomes somewhat more robust in the face of deviation from a common front among the three principal parties. The inertia of the status quo comes to the rescue. But no system manages itself, and continuous support from the top is required.

Institution Size

With likely resistance to culture change that a move to RCB entails and with the absence of assured success in attempting to put it in place, an institution's central administration must be possessed of a strong sense of urgency. One possible factor that can generate that sense of urgency is an institution's size. Zemsky, et al. (1978, p. 230) have observed, "The university has grown too complex for effective centralized control." Certainly the greater complexity associated with large institutions makes a rational and explicit approach to resource allocation an imperative.

I would argue that both large and small institutions could benefit from RCB. For large institutions, a formal and complete implementation of the approach is needed. Without the paraphernalia associated with RCB, a small college can capture to good advantage its benefits by empowering its department heads with responsibility and authority to manage their unit and providing them with adequate information to make sound decisions.

Nevertheless, if resistance to cultural change takes the same amount of central administration effort to overcome in a small institution as in a large one, adoption of RCB is liable to be limited to large and complex universities. Imperatives in managing complexity and potential payoff in the latter make the effort required worthwhile.

Changes in Patterns of Funding

Public colleges and universities are becoming increasingly state-assisted instead of state-supported institutions. Fading into memory are the days when all hopes hung on a university president and his or her entourage making a pilgrimage to the state capitol while the legislature was in session and then returning with a year's allotment of funds to parcel out among the colleges, departments, and support service units. While the ritual continues, state appropriation generally constitutes a proportionately smaller and declining share of total current fund revenue. Increasingly, public universities have had to rely on earned income from student tuition and fees, gifts, grants and contracts, endowment income, and the proceeds from sales of services to generate additional resources. Those sources of earned income are not obtained from the efforts of a central administration. Rather they are produced from the individual initiatives of the heads of operating units – initiatives that a RCB environment is intended to foster by the prospect of a responsibility center's retention of that income for its own use.

Technology and Information Access

RCB requires an information rich environment. Information that under centralized modes of operation is held by central administration has to be made available to responsibility centers on a timely basis. In order for central administration to perform its oversight role, information known to responsibility centers has to be shared with central administration.

Technological changes have made possible information sharing throughout an organization, but not all exploit the opportunities the new technology presents. The hazards of ignoring its potential is described by Thomas L. Friedman (1999) in his recent book, *The Lexus and the Olive Tree*. The title reflects the tension between cultural traditions and technology. At the Lexus luxury car manufacturing plant, 66 people and 310 robots produce 300 cars a day. The olive tree stands for the age-old traditions of culture and a sense of place.

The author, a foreign affairs columnist for *The New York Times*, contends that the end of the Cold War and technological advances have resulted in globalization and democratization of information, finance, technology. To describe what happens to those institutions – nations, companies – that do not adapt to those emerging circumstances, he coins a term: Microchip Immune Deficiency, MIDS. He defines MIDS as:

> A disease that can afflict any bloated, overweight, sclerotic system in the post-Cold War era. Microchip Immune Deficiency is usually contracted by countries and companies that fail to inoculate themselves against changes brought about by the microchip, and the democratizations of technology, finance, and information – which created a much faster, more open and more complex marketplace, with a whole new set of efficiencies. The symptoms of Microchip Immune Deficiency appear when your country or company exhibits a consistent inability to increase productivity, wages, living standards, knowledge use and competitiveness, and becomes too slow to respond to the challenges of the Fast World. Countries and companies with MIDS tend to be those run on Cold War corporate models – where one or a few people at the top hold all the information and make all the decisions, and all the people in the middle and bottom simply carry out those decisions, using only the information they need to know to do their jobs. The only known cure for countries and companies with MIDS is 'the fourth democratization.' This is democratization of decision-making and information flows, and the deconcentration of power in ways that allow more people in your country or company to share knowledge, experiment and innovate faster. This enables them to keep up with a market place where consumers are constantly demanding cheaper products and services tailored specifically for them. (Friedman, 1999, p. 62)

To countries and companies I could add universities.

RCB offers an approach to either curing or avoiding MIDS. Most institutions – regardless of their budgeting and management arrangement – have invested heavily in computer hardware and software and in telecommunication. Where both data input and retrieval have been decentralized, technology has been democratized. RCB gives universities and colleges an opportunity to democratize information meaningfully and to realize a payoff from that investment. Democratization of decisionmaking to the heads of responsibility centers requires that current and accurate management information be widely distributed, and increasingly this requirement poses less of a barrier to adoption of RCB.

Timing

Timing is an important requirement for implementing any good idea, and RCB is no exception. Circumstances have to be such that an institution is ready for change or at least willing to entertain the possibility of change. A widespread perception that the existing system of resource allocation and decisionmaking is defective, a change in university leadership, and cataclysmic events that require alteration of institutional goals and objectives constitute some of the circumstances that may make the culture of an institution more change-ready and amenable to experimentation.

RCB is a change agent.   And for higher education, as with any organization, change is necessary and inevitable.   Peter F. Drucker (1995) observed,

> Any organization, whether biological or social, needs to change its basic structure if it significantly changes its size. Any organization that doubles or triples in size needs to be restructured. Similarly, any organization, whether a business, a nonprofit, or a government agency, needs to rethink itself once it is more than forty or fifty years old. It has outgrown its policies and its rules of behavior.   If it continues in its old ways, it becomes ungovernable, unmanageable, uncontrollable.

Could he be talking (or writing) about us?

Maybe your institution has not doubled or tripled in size recently. But institutions of higher education come in a wide variety of sizes and degrees of complexity, at least in the United States. In the United States, most of institutions of higher education are small. Over 90 percent of them enroll fewer than 10,000 students. But the largest and most complex – the ones enrolling over 10,000 students and expending more than $100 million annually – account for around half of all enrollments and about three-fourths of higher education's annual expenditures. Despite differences in size and complexity, most institutions are governed in much the same way – alas, a way resembling those organizations with MIDS described by Thomas Friedman.

In a large college or university, individuals no longer recognize or appreciate the consequences of their actions for the total institution.   For individuals, including the heads of major operating units, the total costs and total revenues of their operations are unknown. Incentives, and therefore behavior, are just screwed up.

Although change is inevitable and although RCB offers promises of making large institutions more manageable, the need for change may not be perceived by those within an institution. Under such conditions, overcoming existing culture norms may prove to be insurmountable and make implementation of RCB difficult or impossible.

Recognition of Efficiency as a Priority

In March 1998, the Midwestern Higher Education Commission issued the results of a survey of state political and higher education leaders on issues of concern to its 10 member states. The survey was conducted to help shape an agenda for the Midwestern Higher Education Policy Summit scheduled for June 1998.   Survey questionnaires were sent to 3,000 political (e.g., state representatives) and higher education (chief executive officers of colleges and universities), and 34 percent responded. They were asked to rank nine issues in terms of priority.

> Political leaders ranked the issue of productivity and efficiency third on their priority list; education leaders put it next to the bottom. Many political leaders' comments focused on their concerns related to ensuring the public colleges and universities remain competitive in the higher education marketplace. Several of their comments referred either to the need to eliminate duplication in the system or concerns about quality assurance. It is also evident that a number of political leaders consider investing in computing and communications technology a means to increase the efficiency and effectiveness of the enterprise. But some higher education leaders are clearly concerned about the effects of other belt-tightening measures. "What can we sacrifice without sacrificing quality?" asked one. (Midwestern Higher Education Commission, March 1998)

That question indicates that at least one member of the higher education establishment is utterly clueless about using resources effectively and improving productivity. That higher education respondents collectively assign a low priority to using resources garnered from the public trust efficiently and productively should have made for a very stimulating discussion with legislative leaders at the summit meeting.

Estelle James (1990, p. 103) observed,

> This kind of experiment [RCB] seems even more rare at public institutions, which face the additional problems of not wishing to reveal to legislators the internal importance of and subsidies given to various activities and the possibility that any surplus generated by enhanced efficiency would be taken away by the state.

The survey results suggest that the rarity of RCB among public institutions is neither calculating nor sophisticated. Judging from the survey results, many of higher education's leaders just don't care whether resources are used productively and effectively.

The Requirements Summarized

A central administration enthusiastic about the potential of RCB for effective resource allocation and improved decisionmaking, the size and complexity of an institution, changes in patterns of funding, an information system that enables decentralized entry of and access to data, and a culture that is ready for change are among some of the requirements for implementation of this decentralized approach to institutional management. The list is not intended to be exhaustive but merely of sufficient length to suggest that adopting RCB is not as simple and easy as acquiring a facsimile machine, a cellular telephone, or a personal computer. Only a happy coincidence of circumstances at an institution makes putting RCB in place possible.

DOES RCB RESULT IN A MORE EFFECTIVE USE OF RESOURCES?

Have you noticed how people automatically work together to promote the common good when they operate in an incentive-based environment that gives them the impression – a correct one – that they are pursuing their own best interest. You should! Outside of college and universities, it is the system in which we live.

How the Rest of the World Operates

We live a charmed existence but generally do not appreciate the miracles around us. Say, you want to make a trip to a large city. It could be a business trip, or it could be for recreation. The decision is yours. If the distance is great, and your time is short, you will choose to fly there. Either through an agency or directly by telephone or Internet, you will find a wide assortment of routes, times, and fares to suit your situation. If you drive to the airport, you will find that provisions have been made for parking your car with varying degrees of proximity to the terminal and cost. If you so choose, the airline will take your luggage and see that it arrives at your destination when you do.

Once on board the airplane, you may find your self a bit cramped, but flight attendants will attempt to make you as comfortable as possible. Once the airplane reaches cruising altitude you will be propelled toward your destination at sustained speeds unattainable 50 years ago. The level of service you receive during the flight depends on your choice of airline. Invariably, the attendants will offer you beverages – not just one but a variety to suit your taste. Maybe you'll get something to eat: a snack at least; if you're lucky – or paid enough – even breakfast, lunch, or dinner – or something resembling it.

Upon arriving at your destination and retrieving your luggage, you may either rent a late model automobile or use a common carrier. If you choose the latter and select a taxi, one will be ready for you with little delay. Upon arriving at your hotel, you will be greeted warmly. The receptionist will appear glad to see you, smile, and greet you by name. Someone else will offer to help you take your luggage to your room. You will find it clean and in good order and suited to your particular needs.

In the evening, you may wish to dine out. If you are unfamiliar with the city, a concierge will be happy to offer a recommendation and make arrangements for you to get there. Vast arrays of cuisine options await your choice. The foods of the world are ready for your palate. Upon arriving at the restaurant of your choice, the maitre d' will welcome you like an old friend. If before dinner, you desire a suitable libation, it will be prepared to your specifications. The meal will be graciously served and delicious. And so it goes.

For those of you who are handsome or beautiful, rich and famous, it may come as a shock that those of us who are not also live that charmed existence. All those people we don't know treat us with respect and show concern for our well-being. The treatment we receive and have come to expect as commonplace is exceptional. Who is in charge of this great system? Who should we thank? The answer is no one and everyone. The system – in this case, the competitive market economy – sends signals to countless individuals operating independently to behave in that manner. It is in their best interest to become courteous, effective, and efficient. If they do a good job, they will be rewarded in a straightforward and easily understood manner. If they don't, they won't.

Of course, there is more to the system than a license to compete. Accompanying the market mechanism is a tradition of rule of law that aspires to treat all individuals equally, property rights that entitle people to own what they create, and political stability that assures people that the game will not change precipitously. In addition, mechanisms exist to transfer resources unrelated to economic productivity to persons and institutions out of a sense of equity and compassion and to accomplish societal objectives.

Inside the Academy

The world inside the academy operates very differently than the world outside it. Inside the academy – particularly in institutions with a research orientation – the relationship between good teaching and rewards for those who provide it usually is tenuous (at least not sufficient for tenure). The total costs and benefits of all activities – research as well as teaching – are not clear to those engaged in them. For example, office and research space often are perceived as free goods. They appear free to individuals, but they clearly are not free to an institution. As a result, individuals within an institution of higher education often are induced to behave in ways that are at variance with institutional welfare. When individuals in an institution operate at cross-purposes with the institution's best interests, it becomes in Drucker's words "ungovernable, unmanageable, uncontrollable."

RCB is an approach intended to address that problem. How does it work? In a sense, it internalizes some of the features of the economy that operates outside the hallowed, ivy-covered walls. At some risk of oversimplification, it empowers deans and heads of major support units and provides them with signals based on the value and cost of their program decisions.

Under RCB they get the same set of signals confronting university presidents. Their schools or colleges or divisions become financial management centers. Financial management centers become microcosms of the university. Like a university president, heads of responsibility centers are charged with academic, service, and management missions. Like a university, their units retain the revenue they generate from their activities. Like a university, they pay all the costs their activities incur – indirect as well as direct. Like a university, they function as separate financial entities, retaining their year-end balances – positive or negative. Like university presidents, heads of responsibility centers are expected to manage the resources at their disposal to maximize the effectiveness of their performance.

What's so great about making the major academic and support units of a megaversity into university-like entities? All that does is spread around the pain of being a university president to more people, doesn't it? Correct! RCB spreads around the pain – and the opportunity for initiative – and the challenge – and the exhilaration – and the incentives – and the responsibility with the authority. RCB automatically transforms deans and division heads into a president's allies. Each member of the management team operates in an environment in which all the benefits and consequences – at least, all the revenues and all the costs – are recognized. The megaversity is broken up into more manageable parts, which – although separate – nonetheless continue to operate as coordinated parts of a single institution.

Managing the Manager

RCB does not guarantee that wise decisionmaking and optimum resource allocation. RCB does not manage itself; it must be managed. The mantle of that responsibility falls to the central administration. Its role resembles that of government in the larger economy. It ensures that all responsibility centers operate under the same set of rules, that they are treated equally, that their property rights are respected inasmuch as revenue earned and balances retained by them are not arbitrarily taken away, that changes to the arrangement proceed in an orderly and participatory manner, that constructive competition and innovation are encouraged, and that harmful competition and dysfunctional practices are discouraged. Finally, to ensure that institutional priorities are addressed, RCB taxes revenue-producing centers a prescribed assessment for redistribution in differing proportions back to them.

Central administration's responsibilities include presiding over the arrangement with the consent of the governed and being attentive as much as possible to the reality that underlies the institution's operations. Costs and revenues must be properly defined and measured. Costs and revenues must be related correctly to activities designed to accomplish the institutions teaching, research and service mission and to the services that support them. The information must be used appropriately in decisionmaking.

The presidential election of 2000 reveals how difficult measuring reality can be. Counting votes seems far less complicated than measuring costs and revenues and assigning them to responsibility centers. All such measurements involve measurement error, and beyond a certain point the noise level swamps attempts to be more precise. What an RCB environment requires is not precision but accuracy "close enough to reflecting reality that it will not direct management into making a bad decision." (Hicks, 1999, p. 20) Like counting votes, politics may intervene in the way costs and revenues are measured and attributed to operating units. Attribution of overhead costs will tend to be arbitrary, but it need not be capricious. Full disclosure and involvement of all parties offers the best guard against biased assignment.

Leadership and Objectives

If you do not know where you are going and do not have a time when you have to get there, any road and any means of conveyance will do. In the same way, if an institution has no strategic direction, is in no hurry to develop one, and assumes that the status quo will last forever, putting RCB in place becomes an idle exercise. Moreover, unless an institution has a sense of direction and plans to move in that direction, no basis exists for judging the advantages of RCB. The criteria for evaluating this approach rest on whether it assists an institution's leadership and management to accomplish their objectives.

Under responsibility center management, leadership is no longer confined to the top echelon of university administration. A chance to lead is extended to each and every responsibility center head. Opportunities that could be overlooked from the lofty view at the top to set directions that better serve students, the community, alumni and – in the case of support service centers – members of the university itself can be perceived at the operating unit level. RCB provides avenues for communicating a vision for change both up and down the organization and for empowering those who will carry it out.

In short, the case for RCB depends on what the institution's leadership and management want to do. Will its adoption produce the results desired? Like beauty, its potential lies in the eyes of the beholders, in this case, the institution's governing board, president, and provost.

Gauging Effectiveness

Does RCB make a difference? Perhaps an early report will give some indication. IUPUI was the first Indiana University campus to adopt RCB in 1988-89. In 1995, the co-chairs of a review committee, David L. Robbins Sr., the vice chancellor of budget and fiscal affairs, and Patrick M. Rooney, associate professor of economics, reported on the outcomes of the then new approach. Among their findings they observed:

> • Academic units are given much more autonomy over their choices. Deans no longer have to 'beg' administrators for a new faculty or clerical position....Clearly, fiscal planning follows academic planning: the two are more closely interwoven . . . .
> • The campus administration and the Faculty Council's Budgetary Affairs Committee (BAC) peruse each unit's multi-year plan with the expectation that the unit will adhere to its academic priorities during the subsequent academic year. If the unit fails to follow its plan, the chancellor is unlikely to allocate additional funds....for this unit.
> • RCM [responsibility center management] successfully decentralizes decision-making from the central administration to the RCs [responsibility centers]....The deans and directors of each RC determine whether or not to decentralize RCM within their unit.
> • RCM better matches costs with benefits. Previously if a unit had a surplus at the end of the year, it spent those funds....

• Units are much more aware of their costs and those of the support centers to which they contribute. Because the academic units are the predominate income-generating units and the support centers are primarily financed by taxes on the academic units, the deans have begun to pressure the support unit directors to control their costs....The incentives to raise revenues are much stronger than under the old system, because the unit has full use of the funds it generates.

• Each unit can use its surpluses from a given year to fund multi-year projects, to accumulate for capital projects or seed money, or to protect against unforeseen contingencies. Likewise, any deficits are carried forward, which is an effective check against profligate spending.

• The dialogues that have transpired between the administration and the BAC...are much more informed because of the higher level of detailed information that RCM has provided. The discussions with schools, both among the faculty and between the faculty and their deans, have changed radically, due to the information-rich arena that RCM has induced. (Robbins and Rooney, 1995, p. 45)

Those observations suggest that RCB – or as the authors prefer to call it responsibility center management – has made complexity more manageable by compartmentalizing it into responsibility centers. Details of planning and budgeting have devolved to the heads of responsibility centers whereas dealing with issues of wider scope and with financial aggregates continues to reside appropriately with central administration. Achieving the particulars of the plan, monitoring results, controlling and meeting challenges as they come along rest with the center heads. Management in central administration oversees the results.

Several years after RCB began operating at IUPUI, I had occasion to visit with several of the deans and college administrators to talk over old times and see how things were going. Although the institution maintains its strong emphasis on sponsored research grants and contracts, the impression was given that good teaching now received more recognition. Schools and departments had come to value the contribution that student fee income makes to their total resources. Greater attention was being given to student recruitment, retention, and course availability. *Mirabile dictu*, students had benefited. One important constituency at least was being better served.

One of the deans told me that he had received an offer from his *alma mater* to return to that institution as dean of its school. Although he felt the school at his *alma mater* was more distinguished and more prestigious than his program, he chose to stay at IUPUI. RCB provided his reason. At IUPUI, he felt that RCB gave him the opportunity to make a difference, to exercise his initiative, to seize upon opportunities unencumbered by a meddling bureaucracy. What better endorsement can an approach to management of a complex institution of higher education have?

NOTES

1. I prefer the term responsibility center budgeting and shall use it throughout this paper. In a college and university environment, the idea of being managed is not usually

welcomed by the professoriate. Besides RCB sounds more cheery than the more solemn RCM.

2. IUPUI is a large urban campus shared by Indiana University and Purdue University with fiscal responsibility assigned to Indiana University.

REFERENCES

Drucker, Peter F. 1995. Really reinventing government. *Atlantic Monthly* (February) *The Atlantic On Line*. <http://www.theatlantic.com /polibig/reallyre.htm.>, available online 28 Mar. 2001.

Friedman, Thomas L. 1999. *The Lexus and the olive tree*. New York: Farrar Straus Giroux.

Hicks, Douglas T. 1999. *Activity-based costing: Making it work for small and mid-sized companies*, 2nd ed. New York: John Wiley & Sons.

Hoenack, S. 1983. Economic Behavior within Organizations. New York: Cambridge University Press.

Horngren, Charles T., Gary L. Sundem, and William O. Stratton. 1996. *Introduction to management accounting*, 10th ed. Upper Saddle River, NJ: Prentice Hall.

James, Estelle. 1990. Decision processes and priorities in higher education. In Stephen A. Hoenack and Eileen L. Collins, eds., *The economics of American universities*. Albany, NY: State University of New York Press: 77-106.

Kuh, George D., and Elizabeth J. Whitt. 1988. *The invisible tapestry: Culture in American colleges and universities*. Washington, D.C. and College Station, TX: ASHE-ERIC Higher Education Reports.

Midwestern Higher Education Commission. 1998. Survey results of state political and higher education leaders (March). Available online 27 Mar. 2001 <http://www1.umn.edu/mhec/summit/issues/htm>.

Robbins, David L. Sr., and Patrick Michael Rooney. 1995. Responsibility center management: An assessment of RCM at IUPUI. NACUBO *Business Officer* (March): 44-48.

Shah, Pravin P. 1981. *Cost control and information systems, A complete guide to effective design and implementation*. New York: McGraw-Hill.

Strauss, Jon C., Randall Porter, and Robert Zemsky. 1979. Modeling and planning at the University of Pennsylvania. In Joe B. Wyatt, James C. Emery, Carolyn P. Landis, eds., *Financial planning models: Concepts and case studies in colleges and universities*. Princeton: EDUCOM.

Whalen, Edward L. 1991. *Responsibility center budgeting: An approach to decentralized management for institutions of higher education*. Bloomington and Indianapolis: Indiana University Press.

Zemsky, Robert, Randall Porter, and Laura P. Oedel. 1978. Decentralized planning: To share responsibility. *Educational Record* 59-3 (Summer): 229-253.

CHAPTER 3

THE EFFICIENCY OF RESPONSIBILITY CENTER MANAGEMENT WITHIN STATE UNIVERSITIES

John Douglas Wilson[*]

In this chapter I investigate what economic theory has to say about responsibility center management (RCM) as a method of decentralized budgeting on state university campuses.[1] Under this system, the university is broken into academic and nonacademic units, which are given wide latitude over their resource-allocation decisions. The current chapter concerns the behavior of the academic units, which are interpreted as schools or colleges within the university (rather than individual departments). In its purest form, RCM essentially allows these units to keep the revenue that they generate, out of which they must finance the costs of their operations and pay fees to finance certain "public goods" such as the library. Sources of revenue include tuition, alumni contributions, and research grants, and the units may also receive fixed shares of the state appropriation. This chapter focuses mainly on the competition for undergraduate students that occurs under an RCM system. A purported strength of RCM is the visibility and simplicity of the rules for assigning revenues and costs to units. In particular, units are compensated for supplying credit hours, but little attempt is made to vary the compensation rate to reflect cost differences across different types of credit hours. Accordingly, this chapter considers an RCM system under which units are provided with a fixed "base allocation" and then compensated at a fixed rate per credit hour, which is uniform across students and credit hours.[2] The base allocation can be positive or negative, allowing the central administration to distribute resources across units and to adjust the compensation rate to elicit the desired level of competition across units.

An argument in favor of RCM is that it solves vexing information problems that confront the central administration in a large state university.[3] The basic idea is that the units themselves have the information needed to make superior decisions, and in the absence of incentives to lobby for subsidies, they will be driven by competition for students and other revenue sources to behave efficiently (as defined below). Thus, the argument for RCM appears to rest in large part on an appeal to the well-known efficiency properties of competitive markets. On the other hand, there are well-placed concerns about the desirability of introducing competition between units on a university campus.

The current chapter attempts to sort out these conflicting arguments. To accomplish this task, I examine what insights can be obtained from the types of models that economists have used to analyze competition in both private markets and markets for local public goods. The latter case is particularly relevant, because there are parallels between competition for households among communities in a metropolitan area and competition for students among units within a university. In both cases, perfect competition has been found to produce desirable outcomes, and I similarly show in the next section that competition among perfectly competitive units in a university can work similarly well. Even in this benchmark case, however, there is a critical distinction between RCM and the competitive markets normally studied by economists: units do not exercise control over the prices charged customers (students). Instead, they compete over educational attributes, such as curriculum matters and quality-enhancing expenditures. Furthermore, the uniform rates at which the central administration compensates units for credit hours are not similar to the rates that would be chosen by the units themselves. These uniform rates are found to distort decisionmaking within units.

Another distinction between RCM and competitive markets involves the role of profit maximization. The assumption of profit-maximizing behavior is more difficult to defend in the case of RCM than for firms in a market economy. I will address this issue as part of an extended discussion of strategies for modeling the behavior of units under RCM.

In addition to analyzing the benchmark case of perfect competition, I also investigate the much more realistic case of imperfect competition among units. Imperfect competition leads to important inefficiencies in a market economy, and I argue that it does the same in the case of RCM. I also further complicate the model by explicitly recognizing that each unit contains different types of students, as distinguished by abilities and educational preferences. One of the main points made here is that RCM leads to capricious decisions about which students "count" most in a unit's decisionmaking process.

Several of the inefficiencies described in this chapter may be viewed as the result of factors that economists refer to as externalities. In the current context, an externality occurs among units when the actions of individual units within the university benefit or harm other units. Because each unit does not itself face the full costs and benefits of its actions, its decisions cannot be expected to be optimal in any reasonable normative sense. Several types of externality problems are addressed in various sections of this chapter. In particular, externalities figure prominently in my discussion of "peer-group effects" and "signaling effects." Moreover, externalities become particularly important in a section that extends the model to explicitly allow each student to take courses in multiple units. For this case, I find strong parallels between RCM and the local public finance literature on fragmented metropolitan areas with multiple local public goods.

A separate section addresses the problems that arise because students are imperfectly informed. When students make their key decisions about which university to attend, which field to choose as a major, and which career to undertake, they are faced with uncertainties about their abilities and preferences. Units face incentives to take advantage of these uncertainties under RCM. I describe some of the inefficiencies that result from such incentives.

Another section considers the problems that arise when imperfectly-competitive units differ greatly in size. As a result of such differences, "market power" is unevenly distributed across units. In addition, decisionmaking processes within units are also influenced by size differences. I argue that large units are disadvantaged by RCM, resulting in a misallocation of resources between small and large units.

The following section briefly addresses the issues raised by the different treatment of in-state and out-of-state students by central administrations (and state legislatures), and the next section briefly addresses the incentives to conduct research under RCM. A final section offers some conclusions.

RCM WITH PERFECT COMPETITION: A BENCHMARK MODEL

In this section, I describe a model of perfectly competitive units. The model is taken from the literature in local public finance on competition for households between communities. In a seminal article, Tiebout (1956) argued that households can effectively "vote with their feet" by choosing the community with the most preferred bundle of public goods and taxes. Because these taxes must be paid to reside in the community and receive public goods, they serve as "prices" for the public goods. In a "Tiebout equilibrium," communities then have incentives to efficiently tailor their taxes and public good supplies to the preferences of their residents, and households efficiently sort themselves among communities according to their incomes and preferences for public goods.

There are important parallels between Tiebout's theory and student choices over units. Unfortunately, it is now known that Tiebout's theory holds only under strong assumptions. Similarly strong assumptions are required to show that RCM works well, at least in theory. I now sketch this "benchmark model," first assuming that units control their own tuition rates and then assuming an RCM system.

The Benchmark Model

The model assumes a fixed number of units, which for now operate with complete independence. Thus, they are free to set tuition rates and choose all of the attributes of their educational services. Each unit supplies credit hours, and each student enrolls in only one unit. Educational attributes include the types of credit hours offered (i.e., curriculum decisions), the quality of these credit hours, and the requirements imposed on students taking these credit hours (i.e., degree requirements and academic standards). Each unit keeps any profits generated by its activities, as measured by the excess of tuition revenue over educational costs. Its objective is to choose tuition and attributes to maximize profits. The concept of profits in the current context, along with the suitability of profit maximization as an objective, is discussed below.

The economy contains a fixed number of potential students. Each student decides whether to enroll in a unit or instead to undertake some other activity (e.g., work or attend another university). If a student enrolls in a unit, then he or she completes its academic requirements and obtains a university degree. All students prefer higher-quality credit hours and lower tuition, but they differ in their perceptions of quality. In particular, the model allows them to possess different preferences for many of the attributes chosen by units, such as curriculum issues and standards. For example, they may make different tradeoffs over the costs of learning and the benefits from future gains in income. I do not specify exactly how students differ in this model. Instead, I simply assume that there are a finite number of types of students, distinguished by how a student ranks combinations of tuition and educational attributes from least preferred to most preferred, and also by how the student ranks alternatives outside the university (which are treated as exogenous to the model). Economists often use utility functions to describe such rankings, where utility refers to a student's level of satisfaction or welfare. When the term utility is used in this chapter, it should be understood to encompass a student's views of how current educational activities are likely to affect his or her future social and economic conditions. Future outcomes are highly uncertain, a consideration that I explicitly address later. For now, utility can be interpreted as short for expected utility, taking into account the uncertain future.

Each student chooses the unit within the university or the outside alternative that yields the highest utility. By assuming that students are utility maximizers, I am assuming that they behave in a rational manner in the sense that their behavior can be predicted from knowledge of their preference rankings and budget constraints. This does not seem like much of a limitation, because I allow for a wide range of preferences. A more important restriction is that I evaluate the welfare consequences of RCM by assuming that social welfare depends positively on the utilities obtained by students.[4] To the extent that students make systematic errors concerning the relation between their current behavior and future earning potential, for example, the use of student utility functions to measure social welfare may be seriously flawed. My thinking here, however, is that it is too easy to criticize RCM simply by assuming students "don't know what's good for them." The current chapter describes potential problems with RCM that do not rely on this assumption.

The formal model unfolds in two stages. First, units choose their tuition rates and educational attributes, with the goal of maximizing profits. Second, potential students decide where to obtain credit hours, if any, with the goal of maximizing utility. A more realistic decision process would break the second stage into two separate stages, with students first deciding whether to attend the university and then, once enrolled, making a final decision about where to obtain credit hours. I later extend the model in this direction, but for now I sacrifice some realism in the interest of simplicity.[5]

Now comes the critical assumption of perfect competition. Units are perfect competitors in the sense that they do not possess any degree of market power. This means that they are utility takers on the market for students, and they are price takers on the market for the inputs required to produce credit hours.[6] In particular, each academic unit is able to attract as many students of a given type as desired, simply by offering them the tuition policies and attributes that generate the same utility that these students can obtain elsewhere, where "elsewhere" refers to a student's best alternative to enrolling in the unit. In an equilibrium for this system, each unit is indifferent about supplying another credit hour. Otherwise, it would either expand or contract its credit hours. To reach this equilibrium, the utility levels offered to different student types rise or fall until the total supply of students of each type equals the total demand, summed across units. In other words, these utility levels are similar to market-clearing prices in competitive markets for private goods: they adjust to equate supply with demand.

Given this model's similarity to private markets, the standard theorems on the efficiency of a competitive equilibrium can be applied to the current situation. First, the equilibrium is efficient according to the economists' definition of the term. In the present case, this means that there is no feasible change in the units' decisions that would make some individuals in the economy better off without making others worse off. Note that these individuals include all students (potential or actual) and their families, suppliers of inputs to the units, and recipients of any profit earned by the units. This conclusion tells us nothing, however, about whether profits are excessive in any particular sense.[7]

In fact, simple examples can be provided in which there are no profits. This will be the case under conditions of constant cost (e.g., providing 10,000 credit hours of a given type and quality costs ten times as much as providing 1,000 credit hours). When utility levels adjust in this case to leave each unit indifferent about providing another credit hour, units will actually be indifferent between any number of credit hours, which means their profits must equal zero. So in the constant cost case, all profits are competed away, leaving students with all of the gains from competition. Moreover, the possibility that a unit could not operate without making negative profits cannot be ruled out. Simply take the preceding constant-cost example and add a fixed cost. Perfect competition drives revenue down to the point where only variable costs are covered, leaving loses equal to the fixed costs. In this case, the unit would cease to operate unless the fixed costs were covered by a central administration. A similar possibility, modeled by Krause and Wilson (2000), is that fixed costs are required to operate particular fields of study within a unit. In this case, competing units may choose not to offer some fields because "ruinous competition" would lead these fields to generate negative profits. Given existing empirical evidence of increasing returns to scale in higher education, these possibilities cannot be dismissed. Once we turn to the realistic case of imperfect competition, however, units will be able to use their market power to generate positive profits.

A central authority, or center, could attempt to tax any profits that units do generate. The tax revenue could then be used to finance those units making losses, and in other ways that make students (and parents) better off. Thus, there is already a potential role for the positive or negative base allocations introduced in the beginning of this chapter. Any feasible redistribution of this type would need to be based on the center's imperfect observations of existing profits. But a unit could manipulate its profits simply by inflating costs in a way that benefited the recipients of profits (e.g., bigger offices and other perks). Indeed, with the center imposing no constraints on the use of profits, we might see an equilibrium where reported costs are no less than revenue in all units – a coincidence in appearance only. In fact, such behavior is commonly observed in universities, leading Garvin (1980, p. 38) to claim, "In general, the higher the income of the institution, the higher its per-student cost." But while Garvin takes this observation as evidence that university decisionmakers are not interested in maximizing profits, the arguments here suggest that profits, defined as revenue minus *minimized* costs, are maximized but then redistributed to faculty and administrators in the form of excess costs.[8]

Rather than attempt to directly tax profits, the center might want to take an indirect approach by taxing a variable that is indirectly tied to profits, such as various forms of revenue or costs generated by the unit. A problem with this approach is that the tax discourages the activities that generate these revenues and costs.

It appears that even in the idealized world of perfect competition, the center will find it desirable to place constraints on the behavior of units, so that it can redistribute profits while preventing the occurrence of runaway costs. For example, Cornell University specifies the average annual increment that faculty receive in their salaries, and this increment is constant across units. A more extensive discussion of profit maximization is undertaken below.

RCM

In contrast to the model just presented, units do not control tuition policies under RCM. Rather, tuition is collected by the center and distributed to units in the form of base allocations and a fixed "compensation rate" per credit hour. In theory, the system could be designed to replicate the efficient competitive equilibrium described above. In this case, the units would compete over their educational attributes, and their decisions about these variables would be the same as before. However, a fully efficient price system would be quite complicated, since it would normally require that the tuition and compensation rates vary across both the types of credit hours and the types of students. The basic idea is that each student should make his or her choices over educational services based on the actual costs of providing additional units of these services.[9] But these costs vary across credit hours and students.[10] For example, science courses are typically more expensive than humanities courses (e.g., the former require expensive labs), and large introductory courses are clearly cheaper. In addition, the effective cost of supplying a credit hour depends on the attributes of the student obtaining it (e.g., differences in demands placed on faculty time, or differences in desirable and undesirable forms of class participation). Finally, if we recognize that the provision of another credit hour imposes costs on noninstructional units within the university (e.g., the library), then tuition rates should exceed compensation rates to reflect these costs, again by amounts that generally vary across credit hours and students. More generally, the presence of costs that are external to individual instructional units justifies this excess of tuition over compensation rates, with any excess tuition revenue being returned to these units as part of the base allocations.

Large state universities typically charge effective tuition rates for undergraduates that vary little across different units, but these rates can vary significantly across students, as a result of financial aid packages and differences between in-state and out-of-state students. These rates are not those that would emerge from a model of competitive units with no intervention by the center, in part because the center uses admission standards to ration education, rather than relying solely on tuition as a rationing device. To separate the issues associated with tuition policies from the efficiency effects of RCM, we can ask how compensation rates should be set, treating as exogenous the tuition structure and admission standards chosen by the center. On this matter, the compensation rates under RCM are far from optimal, because they do not vary in a way that corresponds to cost differences.[11]

By confronting units with the wrong price signals, RCM has the potential to severely distort decisionmaking within the units. Units will have an incentive to find the cheapest way to generate credit hours, because all credit hours are equally valuable. This can lead, for example, to an inferior mix of expensive upper-level courses and lower-level courses, along with an inferior mix of regular and part-time or adjunct faculty used to teach them.

Returning to the issue of profits, note that an RCM system does allow the center to control the profits retained by a unit through variations in the base allocations. I have already noted the problems involved in such a system. Even with RCM, the center typically imposes constraints on units that prevent them from freely inflating costs as much as desired to hide profits, but such constraints may create their own inefficiencies.

This discussion raises the issue of whether RCM is the best way to create desirable incentive effects at a reasonable cost. In particular, why compensate units based only on how many credit hours they teach, when there are many other observable variables on which the compensation system could also be based?

(Average class size, for example.) An apparent virtue of RCM is its simplicity, but this virtue can become a liability when the simplicity of the RCM compensation system can lead to severe resource misallocations on a university campus.

Actually, some of the simplicity and transparency of actual RCM systems is more appearance than reality, once it is recognized that the compensation rates and base allocations do get adjusted over time to reflect changing circumstances and the acquisition of new information by the center. In particular, the base allocations are not so fully independent of the behavior of units. Rather, this behavior is a potentially important input into the center's decisions concerning the base allocations, although the relation between behavior and base allocations may not be fully understood by the units or even the center. The center faces a commitment problem: it might be better off if it could commit to a fixed system of base allocations and compensation rates, if the incentive effects from doing so are sufficiently desirable (i.e., units behave more efficiently because they know their profits will not be taken away). However, if such a system leaves a unit with unexpectedly high profits in the future, due perhaps to a surge in enrollment levels, then the center faces an incentive to renege on any such commitment and attempt to capture some of the excess profits. Unless adjustments in the base allocation occur infrequently, the incentive effects associated with RCM are greatly diminished, eliminating the distinctiveness of RCM as a resource allocation mechanism.

The subsequent sections of this chapter abstract from this dynamic process in an effort to identify other important ways in which the university environment departs from the benchmark model, producing additional inefficiencies under RCM. Many of these problems can be solved or reduced in importance through a well-designed system of compensation rates. But the design of such a system is typically either politically infeasible or requires the center to possess information about units that is not available. Due to this lack of information (or, alternatively, bad politics), the prices attached to different activities under any feasible RCM-type system are likely to produce large inefficiencies in university behavior. See, for example, Ehrenberg's (2000) revealing discussion of Cornell University's experience in this regard.

A CLOSER LOOK AT OBJECTIVES

The benchmark model assumes that RCM works by confronting units with a profit motive to improve their delivery of educational services. But is it reasonable to assume that units behave as though they maximize profits? To answer this question, we must first look further into the concept of profits in the current context. As defined above, profits are the excess of revenues over costs. These costs should be measured using the economists' definition of "opportunity cost." In particular, the cost of a factor of production, such as the labor supplied by professors, is measured by the minimum income that the owners of the factor must receive to induce them to provide the desired amount of the factor to the unit. Any payments above this minimum can be viewed as a distribution of profits to the factor of production. For professors and administrators, the minimum salaries needed to attract them to the university depend on many other characteristics of their positions, such as research facilities, course loads, and student abilities. In the benchmark model, these characteristics are also chosen to maximize profits, taking into account their relation to the minimum salaries needed to attract faculty with particular abilities.

Two complications arise here. First, whereas private firms distribute profits to the firms' shareholders, no such claimants formally exist in a university setting. The absence of such claimants allows university politics to influence how profits are distributed among administrators and faculty of different rank. These activities involve lobbying efforts that represent a separate source of inefficiencies, because they subtract from more productive activities.[12] A virtue of RCM is that such politics become less important on a university campus, because the units themselves are given less opportunity to lobby the center for funds generated by other units.

Second, restrictions are placed on the distribution of profits as monetary payments. I have already noted that the center has an incentive to impose such restrictions as a means of preventing units from inflating costs in an effort to hide profits. The point I wish to make here is that such restrictions have a potentially important impact on a unit's objectives. If profits are used to fund additional perks or educational policies favored by faculty and administrators, then units behave as though they care about maximizing some combination of these variables.

In fact, the variety of objectives posited in the literature on university behavior can be largely understood as a response to restrictions on the use of profits. James (1990) provides an informative review of decisionmaking within universities, highlighting the importance of research, graduate training and student quality as objectives. All of these variables tend to be valued by faculty, and James observes that institutes of higher learning can be viewed as labor-managed enterprises (p. 79).

More generally, the benchmark model can be enriched by positing the objective of "generalized profit maximization," under which constraints are placed on the distribution of profits and then the welfare of a set of members of the unit (perhaps not everyone) is maximized subject to these constraints. But as a modeling strategy, using the narrower objective of profit maximization enables us to capture some of the important incentive effects of RCM, without being sidetracked by tangential issues. Consequently, I continue to assume profit maximization for much of the subsequent discussion, but recognize that the basic arguments generalize to settings with more complex objectives.

The benchmark model also assumes an RCM system under which the unit is compensated at a fixed rate per credit hour. But revenue sources under actual RCM systems are more diverse. In particular, sizable shares of revenue typically come from research grants and alumni contributions. An RCM system allows the unit to keep much of these revenues, creating additional incentives. For example, units have a greater incentive to attract high-ability students when doing so increases future alumni contributions. The main focus of this chapter is on competition for credit hours, but I shall occasionally bring these other revenue sources into the analysis to explain university behavior.

IMPERFECT COMPETITION

The benchmark model assumes that units act in a manner similar to perfectly competitive firms. Whereas such firms are price takers in input and output markets, units are utility takers on the "market" for students. In other words, each unit can obtain all the students of a given type that it desires by providing them with the equilibrium utility, which is beyond the control of the unit. But just as an industry is perfectly competitive only if it contains a large number of firms offering a similar product, so too are units perfectly competitive only if there are a large number of them offering a similar product, either on the given campus or elsewhere in the economy. This is clearly far from the case. The units on a particular university campus offer unique products: different fields of study. Moreover, many attributes differentiate universities from each other, including location, cost, and a host of quality dimensions. For this reason, any given unit on a particular campus is effectively a "minimonopoly." Its products differ in important ways from the products offered elsewhere.

The dilemma facing a monopolist is that it can sell more output only by lowering its unit price or making the output more attractive to buyers. In the case of RCM, a unit attracts additional students only by changing the attributes of its educational services in ways that appeal to students.[13] But one unit's access to students depends on the behavior of other units. We need a model that recognizes such interdependencies.

The theory of "imperfect competition" provides such a model. The usual way to model imperfectly-competitive firms is to utilize the concept of a "Nash equilibrium." For RCM, the system of units is in this type of equilibrium when each unit correctly anticipates the educational attributes chosen by the other units and accordingly chooses the attributes that maximize its profits (or, more generally, its "payoff function"). For example, the arts and science school bases its decisions about how many sections of a particular course to offer on its prediction of how many are offered by the business school, among other factors.

It is well known that imperfectly competitive firms normally restrict output to create shortages that generate higher prices. The same phenomenon is at work here, except that it is the quality of educational services that is restricted, relative to the perfectly competitive case. Consider a particular component of quality, say the average size of the sections of a large introductory course. Presumably, reducing the size of sections by offering more of them attracts more students, generating more tuition revenue. To maximize profits, the unit keeps adding sections as long as the change in revenue, ΔR, from an additional section exceeds the added cost of offering this section. This revenue equals the rate at which the center compensates credit hours, denoted r, times the change in the number of credit hours, ΔN, generated by another section: $\Delta R = r\Delta N$. The costs resulting from the additional section consist of two components. The first is the additional direct costs involved in offering the section, holding fixed the number of students in the course. In other words, this term represents the expenditures on a "quality improvement." Let ΔC_F denote this cost. The second component is the cost of servicing the additional students that enter the unit as a result of this quality improvement: $c\Delta N$, where c is the cost of another credit hour. Putting these terms together, we find that sections should be added until the additional revenue generated by another section has fallen to the point where it equals the total additional cost of another section:[14]

$$r\Delta N = \Delta C_F + c\Delta N \qquad (3.1)$$

A central implication of this condition is that r exceeds c under imperfect competition, that is, the unit receives more revenue from another credit hour than it costs to supply this credit hour. This result contrasts greatly with our model of perfectly competitive units, in which each unit is able to attract as many students as desired by offering them the utility they can obtain elsewhere. In terms of our example, this means that there is no need reduce class size to attract more students. Rather, the unit simply lets students enter the course until $r\Delta N = c\Delta N$, which implies $r = c$. Because the cost c increases with educational quality, we therefore see that imperfect competition leads to quality levels below those chosen under perfect competition, holding fixed the compensation rate. This finding suggests that quality is underprovided, unless compensation rates are set higher than is typically the case.[15] But perhaps a more important observation – and one that is central to this chapter – is that a unit always benefits if another student takes credit hours in it. There must be a benefit because generating credit hours is costly. I have discussed one example of this cost, reduced class sizes, but there are many others. When the unit is fully optimizing its decisions, it will allocate its resources so that the cost of generating another credit hour does not depend on how it is done. This conclusion follows directly from a rearranged version of rule (3.1):

$$\Delta C_F / \Delta N = r - c \qquad (3.2)$$

where $\Delta C_F / \Delta N$ now equals this cost of generating another credit hour and $r - c$ is the net benefit.

An important implication of this finding is that units can be expected to continually explore new and cheaper methods of generating credit hours and then exploit them to the point where they no longer have a cost advantage over the existing methods.

As another example, consider a unit's grading policies. Grades serve multiple roles. On the one hand, they act as incentive devices to elicit desired levels of effort from students. On the other hand, they provide prospective employers with an imperfect signal of student knowledge or ability to acquire knowledge in a particular area. The value that different students place on these roles will vary, depending on considerations such as their expected performance in the course and their level of self-motivation. But student preferences for grades enter rule (3.2) only to the extent that they determine the relation between grades and the total number of credit hours that students desire to complete within a unit. In the extreme case where the unit bears no cost from changes in grade policies, rule (3.2) [and rule (3.1)] will be violated unless such policies have been designed to maximize credit hours (in which case a small perturbation in grade policies has a negligible impact on N: $\Delta N = 0$). If readers find it difficult to imagine that a unit would ever choose grade policies with the sole purpose of maximizing credit hours, even under an ironclad guarantee that the center would not renege on the RCM system, perhaps this is because there exist other considerations that can be represented by the cost term, ΔC_F. To the extent that credit-hour-maximizing grade policies interfere with teaching effectiveness, then they can be expected to have a variety of costs, perhaps including faculty dissatisfaction and reductions in future alumni contributions.

STUDENT HETEROGENEITY

Proponents of RCM argue that it induces units to act in the best interests of students. Rule (3.2) from the previous section suggests some validity to this claim. If a particular expenditure, ΔC_F, is found to be quite attractive to students, then it will attract a lot of them, that is, ΔN will be high. Units then have an incentive to increase this type of expenditure to the point where the dollar cost of supplying another credit hour, $\Delta C_F/\Delta N$, falls to the point where it equals the profit generated by this credit hour, $r - c$.

In a world where all students are alike, this rule would optimally allocate expenditures across different activities, simply because the change in credit hours, ΔN, could be expected to be proportional to the change in student utility from the given expenditures. In other words, RCM would induce units to allocate expenditures in a way that maximized student utilities.

But students are not identical. Instead, units typically contain students that differ greatly in terms of their abilities and preferences over the decisions facing a unit. This diversity creates two complications. First, the effective cost of offering another credit hour within the unit will generally depend on which student takes the credit hour. I have already noted that the rates at which units are compensated for credit hours should reflect such cost differences (e.g., "good students" pay less). Because RCM proposals typically do not allow for such variation, they create incentives for a unit to go after low-cost students [i.e., low "c" students in rule (3.2)].

Second, the students who receive a relatively large weight in a unit's decisionmaking process are those who exhibit the most "mobility" across units, measured by their responsiveness to changes in the unit's expenditures on various activities. It is these students who dominate the credit hour changes (ΔN) in rule

(3.2). For example, suppose that the business school has two types of students, those who will enroll there regardless of how it designs its courses (i.e., their strong preference to be business majors dominates concerns about the quality of their education) and those who are almost indifferent between the business school and the social science school. The business school will put more weight on the preferences of the latter type of student under RCM, because doing so attracts more of them to the unit. To design its educational offerings in this way, the business school must have some initial information about the preferences of students with greater mobility across units (but it need not know the identities of these students). Over time, however, the business school can use the observed response of enrollments to changes in its educational offerings to obtain more information about what initiatives are the most successful.

This determination of which students receive the most weight is not necessarily desirable from the viewpoint of welfare objectives such as economic growth in the state. To continue with the example, the students who strictly prefer the business school could be interpreted as possessing a strong aptitude for business, whereas the latter group is equally mediocre at business and social science. Catering more to the first group might then create greater welfare gains. But a unit might instead design its programs to be most appealing to the mediocre students, if they are the ones whose choices are most sensitive to the relative attributes of the different units.

This argument shows how competition for students under RCM can lead to a deterioration in academic standards, even if students are fully cognizant of the link between academic performance and future earnings. Again, the basic idea is that the unit caters to the preferences of weaker students if doing so increases the total number of students within the unit. Faculty may have preferences for teaching stronger students, but to the extent that RCM weakens such preferences by strengthening financial incentives, it may erode academic standards that tend to repel low-ability students.

Another possibility is that RCM distorts the degree to which units differentiate themselves from each other in an effort to satisfy the preferences of different types of students. In a recent paper, Debande and Demeulemeester (2000) use a formal model to address this issue. Although they are concerned with competition between different types of higher education institutions (one that is "academic-oriented" vs. one that is more "vocational-oriented"), their model is relevant for competition between units under RCM, because the institutions receive an exogenous fee per student and their objectives include profits. Students possess different ideal curriculums, and they differ in the importance they place on the quality of the curriculum. Under a set of assumptions that the authors associate with the U.S. situation, they show that competition leads to inefficiently similar curriculum choices and wide differences in quality. In other words, there is "academic drift" by the vocational-oriented institution and "vocational drift" by the academic-oriented institution. Such drifts are related to the problem of course duplication under RCM.

One way to circumvent the tendency of RCM to cater to mobile students would be to design separate programs for different types of students, such as separate honors programs. In this case, the unit could target its competition to different types of students, thereby more effectively influencing their decisions about where to obtain credit hours. But such targeting involves a cost tradeoff and also raises issues about whether it is desirable to mix students of different abilities in the same classes. The next section considers an argument for mixing students.

EXTERNALITIES

In the previous section, I described a mechanism by which competition for students can lead to deterioration in academic standards. This reasoning should be qualified, however, because there also exist reasons for why a unit might wish to design its programs to attract high-ability students. In particular, the presence of such students within a unit potentially gives rise to a phenomenon called "externalities." In economic theory, an externality occurs when the action of one individual or firm affects other individuals or firms, and there do not exist markets under which the resulting benefits or costs are efficiently priced.

An example of a positive externality in the present context is "peer-group effects," whereby the benefit that a given student receives from a particular course or program depends positively on the abilities of the other students in the course (or on their achievement levels). Simply stated, "good students" raise academic achievement among all students.[16]

On the other hand, the presence of high-ability students in a unit can be beneficial to low-ability students even if it has no direct impact on the latter's academic performance within the unit. The argument begins with the observation that employers possess imperfect information about the productivities of job applicants and must therefore rely on observations of past behavior. Thus, the amount of education obtained by a student serves as a "signal" of the student's innate abilities and, therefore, the student's productivity on the job, because students with relatively high abilities find education less costly and therefore obtain more of it. Because of the signaling effects of a college degree, for example, students who obtain this degree will be offered higher wages than students who do not go to college, even if attending college has no impact on productivity. In the present context, we can extend this story by observing that these signaling effects depend on the unit in which the student obtains his or her education. For example, a given student from a top-tier business program is likely to be a more attractive job candidate than a student from a lower-tier business program, even after controlling for the student's observable characteristics.

Externalities among students can lead to externalities among units. By generating a positive externality, a high-ability student lowers the cost of attracting other students to the unit. Similarly, a low-ability student may generate negative externalities, thereby raising the cost of attracting other students. Because compensation rates for credit hours are uniform across student types, they do not reflect these cost differences. As a result, a given unit may harm other units by attracting high-ability students, in the sense that reduced access to high-ability students lowers student utilities and profits in these other units.[17] In other words, attracting high-ability students creates a negative externality, and, similarly, attracting low-ability students has the reverse effect.   We shall encounter other examples of externalities among units in the later sections.

The final equilibrium allocation of students across units is difficult to determine without additional information. One possibility is that units alter their patterns of expenditures in a way that discriminates against different types of students, such as "honors courses" for high-ability students. Doing so diminishes the strength of peer-group effects and brings the costs of supplying credit hours to high- and low-ability students more in line with the common compensation rate. Given the presence of externalities, however, we cannot expect this equilibrium to possess desirable welfare properties. In the case of peer-group effects, low-ability students might receive a sufficiently large benefit from their interactions with high-ability students that offering fewer honors courses would be preferable.

The local public economics literature suggests another possibility: RCM may induce some units to specialize in attracting high-ability students, whereas others go for low-ability students. One particularly important contribution in this literature is Schwab and Oates (1991). Although their model applies to local public goods in general, education is a good example. In this case, peer-group effects might result from mixing the children of high- and low-income households, because children of households with higher earnings and education tend to perform better in school. But they observe that this efficient mixing of households can be achieved only if high-income households are charged lower taxes than low-income households when both reside in the same community. This tax structure is efficient, since it compensates high-income households for desirable peer-group effects. Without such tax differences, high-income families will attempt to segregate themselves into separate communities, since they have nothing to gain from mixing with low-income households. In the Schwab-Oates model, this outcome is inefficient, since it eliminates desirable peer-group effects.[18]

This reasoning suggests that some units may voluntarily use high admission standards under an RCM system, whereas others have low admission standards. A unit that "specializes" in high-ability students will not want to attract low-ability students, because doing so lowers the attractiveness of the unit to the existing high-ability students. Incentives to impose relatively stringent admission requirements are further strengthened by the existence of alumni contributions. To the extent that RCM allows units to keep these contributions, these units benefit from attracting those students who will ultimately give relatively large contributions. Other units forgo large contributions in favor of larger numbers of students, using lower admission requirements. Following the Schwab-Oates argument, these differential admission requirements may be quite inefficient, since they reduce desirable peer-group effects.

If, however, signaling effects are the source of externalities, then there is an efficiency argument in favor of a tendency for units to specialize in high- or low-ability students. Unlike peer-group effects, the benefit that low-ability students receive from being mixed with high-ability students does not take the form of increases in productivity in future careers. Rather, low-ability students benefit from the higher initial wages (or, more generally, better initial job placements) that come from their participation in a program with high-ability students, assuming employers have difficulty, at least initially, in distinguishing between students with different abilities who come out of the same program. In other words, mixing students of different abilities may cause more mismatches of jobs and workers. Such mismatches reduce the efficiency of the private sector. Thus, one benefit of specialization by units is that it reduces the mismatch. This reasoning suggests the need to carefully identify the sources of externalities on a university campus. Doing so is a tricky empirical task, however. As we have seen, for example, signaling effects and peer-group effects have similar implications for the behavior of units.

Finally, we come to the issue of how RCM should be modified, if at all, to eliminate or at least reduce externality problems. The usual prescription for eliminating externality problems in a market economy is for the central government to subsidize activities creating desirable externalities, and to tax activities creating undesirable externalities. For example, pollution emissions should be taxed. In the context of RCM, the compensation system could be designed to reward units that mix high- and low-ability students, if the result is desirable peer-group effects. But such a system is incomplete because it does not also reward the students for mixing; their tuition rates are not dependent on where they obtain credit hours. Moreover, there are significant practical problems involved in such a compensation scheme, most notably the problem of measuring ability.

To conclude, externalities are a potentially important source of inefficiency in an RCM system. Although RCM can be modified to reduce these inefficiencies, doing so places information requirements on the center that circumvent one of the main virtues of RCM: its simplicity.

REPUTATION AND FREE-RIDING

This section discusses another potential source of externalities among units. I start with the observation that not only does a single unit confer signaling effects upon its students, but so does the entire university. For example, if Harvard University had an undergraduate business program that was just as effective as Indiana University's business program, potential employers would probably still prefer Harvard business majors to Indiana business majors (again controlling for other attributes). But therein lies another externality problem. A unit's reputation depends in part on the reputation of the entire university, which is itself based on the collective reputations of all units.[19] Thus, when one unit undertakes actions to improve its academic programs, it benefits other units to some extent. Similarly, a unit can "free ride" on the reputation of the university as a whole by devoting fewer resources to its academic programs or letting academic standards deteriorate. (The issue of grade inflation is relevant here.) Over time, such deterioration will become known, but the time lag may be sufficiently long to preserve the free-riding incentives.

We thus have another mechanism by which RCM can lead to deterioration in academic standards, even when students fully recognize the link between their educational choices and future achievement. The argument is that some students are drawn to units that lower the amount of effort required to complete credit hours, since future wages do not fully adjust downward, at least in the short run. The attractiveness of these students to employers continues to depend in part on the reputation of the entire university.

This story becomes more convincing when we extend the model to allow students to take credit hours in multiple units. In this case, an employer would have to judge the effectiveness of multiple units in order to come up with an estimate of a student's productivity on the job. Undoubtedly, employers would use shortcuts, or rules-of-thumb, in formulating this estimate, and such shortcuts may enable individual units to cut academic standards without fully punishing students in terms of reduced future wages. This extension of the model raises a host of other issues, to which I now turn.

MAJORS VS. NONMAJORS

Students typically take courses in different units on a university campus. This consideration opens the door to important externalities that have not been considered previously. In this section, I extend the model to include two types of decisions for each student: in which unit to "enroll" (i.e., where to major) and in which courses to enroll. The model also recognizes the restrictions that a unit typically places on student choices over courses, particularly those taken outside of the unit. Thus, students are choosing their programs of study, subject to some potentially severe constraints. As before, students maximize utility, which now depends on where the student majors.

A basic message of this section is that RCM cannot be expected to possess desirable efficiency properties in this case. Units have become too interdependent, implying a host of welfare-reducing externalities. But this conclusion can be anticipated from the work in local public finance on overlapping jurisdictions. The basic idea is that households receive public goods and services not just from the town in which they reside, but also from the county, state, and various special districts (e.g., school districts). Each district is imperfectly competitive, because, at the very least, it has a monopoly on its location. In an important article, Hochman, Pines, and Thisse (1995) formally model a metropolitan area with many different types of public goods. After describing the optimal metropolitan area, they subdivide it into territories controlled by local governments. Each government chooses the supplies of various public goods, and also where to place the public good facilities, to which individuals must travel to consume the public goods (e.g., libraries, museums, parks, and schools). Individuals choose where to reside, taking into account travel costs to different public good facilities. Local governments are able to charge fees for the usage of public good facilities, and they seek to maximize their net surplus (NS), consisting of land rents and the excess of fee income over the cost of providing local public goods. This setup is similar to the models of RCM presented here, where units are also compensated for usage and seek to maximize profits.[20] In addition, the spatial aspect of the model implies a form of imperfect competition, since each public good offered by a local government has a unique attribute: the location of the facility.

Given the similarities to RCM, it is particularly interesting that Hochman, et al. (1995) find that, "...if a Nash equilibrium among NS-maximizing local governments exists, it is inefficient" (p. 1235). They explain,

> Actually, to make the socially optimal decision, any club (local government, in this case) must capture the full increment of the land rent it generates by supplying its LPG [local public good]. Of course, one can conceive of designing a mechanism which allows such a distribution of the ALR [aggregate land rent]. However, implementing such a mechanism requires the intervention of the central government. But then the scope of decentralizing the optimum through local governments is much smaller than envisaged by Tiebout (1956) and the proponents of fiscal federalism (p. 1236).

Similarly, the units in an RCM system fail to make optimal decisions in part because their decisions affect profits in other units. For this reason, a unit's profits fail to accurately reward it for good decisions; a portion of the reward is passed on to other units. Put differently, RCM creates wasteful "profit-shifting motives," whereby units engage in activities designed to shift profits from other units to themselves.

Hochman, et al. obtain their negative conclusions even though they work with the assumption of utility-taking communities. This case corresponds to perfectly competitive units, which were found to behave efficiently in the benchmark model. But that model assumes away any important interactions between units. In the present case, interdependencies between units produce externalities, leading to inefficiencies even in the case of perfect competition.

To take an example, consider two units, business and computer science. Assume that business sends students to computer science to take "elementary computer science." Assume that cost considerations make it desirable to mix computer science majors and business majors in the same course. We can expect computer science to design a curriculum that is most appropriate for their own majors. Curriculum improvements in this course may allow it to reduce costs elsewhere in the program without losing majors. There is a limit to how inappropriate the curriculum can become for business students; at some point, the business school would be induced to teach computer science in-house. But until that point is reached, the computer science department has room to increase its own profits by moving its curriculum in favor of these students at the expense of business school students. Doing so increases its profits at the expense of business school profits, which fall because the business school must compensate with improvements elsewhere in its program or risk losing students.

Moving to the much more realistic case of imperfect competition, it becomes even easier to produce examples of inefficient behavior. Units now have market power, and their ability to control the programs taken by their majors provides yet another way for them to exploit this power. Now a unit can increase its majors only by making the programs for majors more attractive (assuming tuition is not under its control). But instead of doing so, it may simply choose to force its majors to take more credit hours within the unit, rather than other units. The number of majors may decline, but the rise in the credit hours per major may result in a net gain in total credit hours.

The imperfect-competition case is related to the industrial-organization literature on "tied sales." For example, if a consumer is willing to buy at most 100 units of a good from a firm at a given price per unit, then the firm may be able to increase profits by telling the consumer that he or she has the choice of only 50 or 150 units at this price.[21] In other words, the consumer is forced to either buy more than desired or less than desired, and the firm can structure the choice so that the consumer chooses more than desired. Similarly, an academic unit can tell a student, you have the choice between majoring or not majoring in the unit, but if you major you must take most of your courses in the unit. By limiting choice, the unit increases profits. This mechanism falls apart in perfectly competitive markets, because other firms enter the market and make profits by offering somewhat better choices.

Hochman, et al. conclude that optimal allocations can be supported only by metropolitan-wide governments. For RCM, this corresponds to a system of universities, each operated by a single central administration, rather than subdivided into units. However, central administrators and metropolitan-wide governments face similar informational and political problems.

Another approach is to design alternative incentive mechanisms that improve upon RCM while retaining a large degree of decentralized decisionmaking. One possibility is the University of Michigan system, where each academic unit is compensated for the number of students that major within the unit, rather than credit hours.[22] But this creates the opposite problem: units will generally wish to save on costs by sending their students to other units to take courses. Once again, we have an externality problem that arises from a flawed compensation system. By cutting back on its course offerings, a unit imposes additional cost on the other units, which must now teach additional students.

A potential solution to this problem is to base compensation on both credit hours taught and students majoring in the unit. Alternatively, Ehrenberg (2000) describes a proposal at Cornell University to reduce course-duplication incentives by making the compensation rate per credit hour depend negatively on the size of the course (and therefore correspond more closely to the marginal cost of instruction). These proposals are far from perfect, but they represent practical alternatives that deserve consideration.

INCOMPLETELY INFORMED STUDENTS

Students face considerable uncertainty about their own abilities and preferences, and units possess incentives to exploit this uncertainty under RCM. This section discusses some insights that emerge from an RCM model that accounts for this uncertainty.

The models discussed to this point do not distinguish between competition for students not yet enrolled in the university and competition for students already on campus. This distinction matters because students base their choices among universities on incomplete information about the academic units within the universities. Once on campus, they gather information about these units, and many do not choose a major until they have been enrolled in the university for a year or more.

Given this incomplete information, we can expect changes in the academic policies and expenditures of a unit to affect differently the decisions of students already on campus and those deciding whether to enroll in the university. To take an example that I know well, it is rarely the case that a high-school student decides before attending college to major in economics. Thus, quality improvements in the economics major may increase the quantity or average ability of students admitted to the university, simply by improving the overall reputation of the university, but many of these additional students are likely to major elsewhere.

This is another externality problem. A unit's quality improvements raise the overall quality of the university, causing additional units to benefit in terms of additional, or more-able, students. This problem is similar to the one discussed in the previous section: a unit is no longer appropriately rewarded for increasing quality, because other units capture part of the benefit in the form of higher profits. To take an example, a weak economics department will benefit from being in a strong school of arts and science, because the school will tend to attract strong students, some of whom ultimately decide to major in economics.

This reasoning suggests that the incentives created by RCM are not sufficiently strong. But we have already seen that this is generally the case as long as units are imperfectly competitive. As previously suggested, attempts to raise compensation rates to create better incentives may create other distortions, because compensation rates are uniform and do not reflect cost differences across different courses and students.

Another possibility is that units with particularly strong reputations are in a position to exploit imperfectly informed students by recruiting them before they arrive on campus. If only one unit engages in extensive marketing efforts to recruit students directly out of high school, then the other units are placed at a "competitive disadvantage." The welfare effects of such marketing efforts are unclear. On the one hand, these efforts have the potential to benefit all units by bringing more high-ability students to campus, not all of whom ultimately major within the unit doing the marketing. On the other hand, they distort the allocation of students across units, with too many going to the unit engaged in the marketing.

This last concern may be exacerbated by the ability of the unit to keep the students it has recruited from switching majors once they arrive on campus. For example, a unit might introduce excessive course requirements within the unit, making it impossible for the student to explore other intellectual interests outside of the unit. Such requirements might also artificially raise "switching costs," by diminishing the student's ability to take courses that fulfill the degree requirements in other units.

To summarize, a unit can cut down on competition within the university by recruiting students directly out of high school and then making it difficult for them to switch majors. Incentives to engage in this behavior may be accompanied by genuine improvements in educational quality within the unit, but educational quality elsewhere on campus may suffer if other units perceive that their enrollments are less sensitive to quality improvements.

ASYMMETRIC UNITS

When competing for students, not all units are on an equal footing. One major difference between units at Indiana University, for example, is that they differ greatly in size. The College of Arts and Sciences teaches more than half of the credit hours on campus. This difference in size has important effects in our model of imperfect competition. Large units tend to have a greater degree of market power. If not the "only game in town," they are at least one of the few games in town from the viewpoint of many of the students choosing where to major. Put differently, students as a whole tend to be less responsive to changes in the educational attributes offered by large units, simply because the very largeness of a unit implies fewer alternatives outside of the unit. This statement is obvious in the extreme case where the entire university is the unit (i.e., centralized budgeting), but is also applies to large units like Arts and Sciences.

This reasoning explains why we might expect small units to have a competitive advantage under RCM. The small units simply have a greater incentive to make themselves more attractive to potential students. Once again, there are parallels to this result in the public economics literature. When small and large countries compete for scarce capital by reducing the taxation of capital (or offering subsidies), small countries have a greater incentive to lower their taxes, because the amount of capital invested there is more responsive to the after-tax return on capital (i.e., the elasticity of capital investment is greater in small countries). See, in particular, Wilson (1991) and Bucovetsky (1991). The same forces are at work in the case of competition for students under RCM. Allocating resources across a university campus based on differing degrees of market power is not conducive to efficiency. We can expect too many students to major within the small units, with too few remaining in the large units.

These arguments assume that decisionmaking within a unit does not depend on the unit's size. In other words, each unit still seeks to maximize profits (or some generalized concept of profits, as previously discussed). But the possibility that a unit can be treated as though it has a single, well-defined objective becomes less tenable as unit size increases. With increased size, the opportunities to support money-losing departments also rise. Departments within the unit recognize this situation and so devote an increasing share of their time and resources to lobbying the unit's administrators for subsidies financed by effectively taxing other departments. Deans could counteract this trend simply by making their departments mini-RCM-units, with budgets formally tied to credit hours. But the temptation to pursue other objectives, such as "prestige maximization," becomes too strong, making deans susceptible to lobbying pressure by department heads. With departments recognizing the presence of cross-subsidies as an alternative revenue source, their incentives to compete for students are diminished. In effect, the dean is using a centralized budget system within the unit, thereby short-circuiting RCM incentives. The existence of a positive base allocation, which is independent of enrollments, provides the dean with some freedom to behave in this manner. This argument reinforces my previous claim that large units are at a competitive disadvantage under RCM.

One solution to the problem of "asymmetric competition" is to reduce the degree to which units differ in size, but doing so may involve additional costs and conflict with other educational goals. More generally, there is not only the issue of how similar to make units in size, but also how many units to create. On the one hand, creating more units brings us closer to the case of perfect competition. On the other hand, efficiency-reducing externalities are likely to become more widespread as the number of units increases. An important task for future research is to study this tradeoff.

OUT-OF-STATE STUDENTS VS. IN-STATE STUDENTS

Let us now distinguish between in-state and out-of-state students. State legislatures typically behave as though the former contribute a lot more to state welfare than do the latter.[23] In particular, out-of-state students are charged high tuition rates relative to in-state students. The university effectively acts more like a profit-maximizing firm with respect to out-of-state students, suggesting a relatively small weight is being placed on the welfare of these students per se.

This difference in tuition rates suggests that the university should also distinguish between in-state and out-of-state students when it compensates units for credit hours. Indiana University, for example, now rewards units for bringing additional out-of-state tuition revenue to the campus. If we continued to assume that the compensation rates are uniform across all students, then no such reward would exist.

It is not clear, however, that this reward should exist. To exercise its market power over out-of-state students, the center should inhibit units from raising the cost of educating another out-of-state student to the point where it equals the tuition paid by this student. Keeping compensation rates low accomplishes this task. On the other hand, a justification for charging low tuition to in-state students is that educating them confers externalities on the state economy. In other words, in-state students do not capture all of the benefits of their education; some of these benefits accrue to the state economy in the form of increased economic development. As a general rule, the tuition rates paid by these students should fall short of the cost of educating another student, with the difference reflecting the values of the externalities captured by the state. But to induce units to invest in education-enhancing activities until this excess-cost condition obtains, the center may find it necessary to compensate credit hours at a rate exceeding the tuition rate per credit hour.[24]

To summarize, these arguments suggest that units should be compensated for the credit hours taken by out-of-state students at rates that fall short of these students' tuition rates, whereas the reverse is the case for in-state students.[25] Since out-of-state tuition is substantially higher than in-state tuition, however, the relation between the relative compensation rates is theoretically ambiguous. Once again, we see that it is difficult to design a set of prices that causes units to compete efficiently for students.

RESEARCH

The research undertaken by academic units is financed in multiple ways under RCM. To the extent that research and teaching are complementary activities, research increases the quality of educational services, thereby generating revenue through additional credit hours. In addition, research activities receive outside funding. Alternatively, there can be self-financing of research by existing faculty, in the sense that they are willing to sacrifice income in order to engage in research activities (perhaps with the goal of increasing future income). Finally, the profits generated under an RCM system can be funneled into research, especially if the center places constraints on the use of the profits units obtain under RCM and allows research to be an "approved use." [26]

Rey (2001) develops a formal model that nicely captures this last possibility. Although she considers competition for students between two universities, the model is relevant for RCM, since university funding is assumed to come from a constant subsidy from the state for each student taught (plus a fixed subsidy). An interesting aspect of the model is that each university benefits from attracting high-ability students, because less teaching is required to raise their productivities a given amount, thereby leaving more funds for research.

Whether the use of RCM reduces research activities then depends on the details of the RCM system, such as the way in which the center continues to regulate units, including the extent to which they are allowed to keep the profits earned under RCM. The answer also depends on what we mean by "the absence of RCM," which is not uniform across university campuses.

Another issue is how RCM affects the composition of research, such as basic and applied research. Once again, the answer will vary across different variants of RCM, and also depend on how incentive effects within universities interact with incentive effects created by government programs and regulations.[27] In any case, it would be difficult to evaluate the welfare implications of any conclusions about how RCM affects research, because there remains considerable debate about what research, and how much, should be conducted on university campuses. Research funding is often justified on the grounds that it creates positive externalities for the state and national economies, but these externalities are difficult to quantify.

CONCLUSION

By harnessing the forces of competition, RCM is supposed to induce units to function more efficiently. But even in my benchmark model of perfect competition, which assumes away important interdependencies among units, RCM introduces important inefficiencies by compensating units for credit hours at rates that do not vary with the cost of offering these credit hours. Moving to the realistic case of imperfect competition, we have also seen that RCM favors activities that tend to benefit students who exhibit a high degree of mobility across units. This criterion for favoring students is unlikely to possess favorable welfare characteristics. To the extent that units differ in size, they will also differ in their ability to compete under RCM, giving rise to additional misallocations of resources on the university campus.

Once important interdependencies among units are recognized, profits cease to serve as a reliable guide to the desirability of particular activities or policies, even under conditions of perfect competition. Actions undertaken by one unit affect other units in important ways. I have described many instances of this externality problem. Externalities are well-known in the literature on local public economics, where competition for households by independent governments has already been extensively studied. At this point, the implications of externalities for the observable behavior of units seem to be highly dependent on the nature of the externalities under consideration, and may not even be uniform across units. For example, competition for high-ability students can lead to increased academic standards, whereas the incentives a unit faces to free-ride on the reputations of other units can lead to reduced academic standards. I have also described an equilibrium where units respond differently to peer-group effects, with some "specializing" in attracting high-ability students and others going after low-ability students.

Separate problems arise as a result of students being poorly informed. RCM presents a host of opportunities for units to take advantage of this lack of information, and units typically differ in their abilities to exploit informational deficiencies.

These conclusions should not be viewed as a justification for scrapping RCM in favor of centralized budgeting. But they do lend support to the view that central administrations should remain active in guiding educational and research priorities on campus, while constraining the allowable behavior of units in important ways. The analysis also suggests the need to explore compensation schemes that are more complex than those under RCM.

In theory, centralized budgeting could eliminate the problems associated with RCM; central administrators could simply allocate funds in an efficient manner across units, and impose the appropriate restrictions on the use of these funds. But the theory breaks down in the face of likely informational asymmetries, whereby central administrators lack critical information about individual units and their departments. In addition, centralized budgeting leaves central administrators with some discretion concerning which objectives to pursue (although state legislators and trustees may limit this discretion), making them susceptible to the lobbying efforts of individual units. My previous discussion of the problems associated with large units within an RCM system applies here.

In practice, an RCM system does allow for some discretion on the part of central administrators. First, not all university funds need be distributed according to an RCM formula; some may be withheld for discretionary use.[28] Second, I have already noted that the base allocations received by units would not remain constant over time in response to large enrollment shifts. However, an identifying feature of RCM is that both the size of discretionary funds and the speed at which base allocations can be adjusted are limited. In other words, RCM may be viewed as a limited commitment device, under which the central administration faces severe constraints on its ability to exercise discretion over the allocation of resources on a university campus. The rules that replace this discretion are relatively simple and transparent, but they create the multitude of inefficiencies discussed previously. On the other hand, placing severe limitations on discretion has advantages. In particular, unit and department administrators face weaker incentives to engage in wasteful activities designed to influence central administrators. Similarly, the latter are better able to resist forces working against desirable changes within the university, with less fear of political backlash, because "their hands are tied." In effect, the center can implement an initial resource allocation decision through the RCM system of base allocations and compensation rates for credit hours, and then reduce political problems by giving up discretion over a subsequent time period.

Thus, the choice between RCM and centralized budgeting need not be viewed as dichotomous. Instead, one can envision a continuum of systems, distinguished by the degree of discretion afforded central administrators. The current chapter has focused on what economic models tell us about the particular resource allocation rules that replace discretion under RCM, but the study of how much discretion should be allowed necessarily involves an investigation of the political processes that operate on university campuses, and how they are affected by limitations on discretion. The desirability of RCM may ultimately involve tradeoffs involving both economic and political concerns.

NOTES

*I would like to thank Guenter Krause, Bill Becker, Ronald Ehrenberg, Don Hossler, Douglas Priest, and Edward St. John for helpful comments and suggestions.

1. Whalen (1991) provides a detailed description of RCM and extols its virtues. (He was also a driving force behind the implementation of RCM at Indiana University.) See also Cross's (1996) brief, but highly informative, description and history of the system, highlighting some of its fundamental problems. While emphasizing the relevance of the economic theory for RCM, he notes the dearth of academic literature on RCM per se.

2. Actual RCM systems do allow some variation in compensation rates, such as between undergraduate and graduate students, across different professional schools, and between in-state and out-of-state students. Although some of the analysis in this chapter also applies to graduate students, readers will also notice several differences. I initially do not distinguish between in-state and out-of-state students, but I later discuss how compensation rates might optimally differ between them.

3. Although the focus of this research is on state universities (reflecting the author's own background), much of the discussion is also relevant to private research universities, where RCM models are actually more prevalent.

4. I later distinguish between in-state and out-of-state students in the measurement of welfare.

5. The two-stage process modeled here can be interpreted as being repeated throughout time, allowing the decisionmakers to learn the relevant information required to make informed decisions.

6. These inputs include both labor inputs (faculty, administrators, staff) and capital inputs. I exclude student inputs in this statement. As Rothschild and White (1995) emphasize, students are also inputs into the production of their own education. In the current model, the units may be viewed as exercising at least partial control over student inputs, and students take such control into account when evaluating the relative desirability of different units.

7. More generally, the economists' definition of efficiency ignores income distribution problems by assuming that it is possible to costlessly redistribute income across individuals. The current chapter discusses the problems involved in attempting to redistribute the profits earned by units, but other attempts to redistribute income, such as through federal or state income taxes, also entail social costs.

8. In addition to inflating costs, a unit might also wish to reduce revenue in ways that benefit faculty, such as through restrictive admission standards. But this particular type of behavior is strongly discouraged by an RCM system.

9. This claim assumes that obtaining an education does not confer "externalities" on the economy, as defined below. I also defer until later in the chapter the special considerations involving out-of-state students.

10. In fact, it is possible for the cost of one type of credit hour to depend on what other types of credit hours are offered (e.g., once a professor is hired to teach a particular course, his talents can also be used in other courses). In this case, an efficient compensation structure would have to reflect such interdependencies. For simplicity, I do not pursue this issue further.

11. One potential qualification to this and similar claims in the chapter is that fixing tuition rates at nonoptimal levels places us in the theory of the second best, where it is sometimes desirable to violate standard efficiency prescriptions to offset inefficiencies that exist elsewhere in the economy. But to the extent the university can

use admission standards as a rationing device, it can circumvent the distortionary effects of nonoptimal tuition policies. In any case, most of the analysis in this chapter essentially assumes that nonoptimal tuition policies do not provide an important justification for unit behavior that deviates widely from first-best efficiency rules.

12. See Masten's (2000) discussion of political processes within universities.

13. This statement should be qualified by noting that some monopolists can increase the demand for their products by limiting consumer choices (perceived or actual) for alternative products. Microsoft, for example, has been accused of engineering its operating system so that its own applications software works better than the corresponding software sold by competitors. In the present case, for example, a unit might design its degree requirements to limit the ability of students to take courses in other units.

14. More precisely, the number of sections is increased to the highest value where the left side of (3.1) remains at least as great as the right side. In other words, (3.1) is an approximation, because the number of sections is a discrete variable.

15. Compensation rates under RCM are lower than tuition rates if the center follows the common practice of withholding some tuition revenue for "discretionary funds."

16. Epple, Romano, and Sieg (2000) use a model with peer-group effects to analyze competition among colleges and universities.

17. The exact combination of reduced utilities and profits depends on the market structure and production technologies. Even under conditions of perfect competition, the externality problem persists. A single unit may have a negligible impact on utilities obtained elsewhere, but if several units increase the average abilities of their students, then the remaining units will suffer.

18. In fact, an equilibrium will not exist if the high-income families do not have access to exclusionary zoning policies to prevent low-income families from entering their communities. Our analysis of RCM implicitly assumes that an equilibrium allocation of students across units does exist.

19. Similarly, Garvin (1980) models the "prestige" of a university as depending on the prestige of each of the individual departments within the university.

20. In Hochman, et al. (1995), land rents are similar to profits from the viewpoint of residents owning land.

21. This strategy assumes consumers are not able to easily buy and sell units of the good among themselves, thereby circumventing the firm's restrictions on choice.

22. See Courant and Knepp (2001).

23. Groen and White (2000) investigate the relative preferences of state governments and universities for in-state and out-of-state students.

24. We cannot say for sure that this condition is necessary, unless we know the level of costs that credit hours impose on noninstructional units.

25. One qualification to this conclusion is that some out-of-state students do remain within the state after graduation, creating the possibility that they too confer positive externalities on the state economy. On the other hand, out-of-state students tend to have higher average abilities than in-state students, suggesting desirable peer-group effects. The former consideration implies higher compensation rates, whereas we have seen that the latter suggests lower compensation rates.

26. I am reminded of a conversation I had with an administrator at IU, who emphasized that the introductory economics courses taught by the economics department "make everything else possible." The term "everything else" can be viewed as including research.

27. See, for example, Jensen and Thursby's (2001) analysis of the incentives created by the Bayh-Dole Act, which gives universities the right to retain title and license inventions coming out of federally funded research.

28. An example of this practice is the Chancellor's Discretionary Fund at Indiana University.

REFERENCES

Bucovetsky, Sam. 1991. Asymmetric tax competition. *Journal of Urban Economics* 30 (September, no. 2): 67-181.

Courant, Paul N., and Marilyn Knepp. 2001. Budgeting with the UB model at the University of Michigan. University of Michigan, unpublished manuscript.

Cross, John G. 1996. A brief review of "responsibility center management." University of Michigan, unpublished manuscript.

Debande, Olivier, and Jean Luc Demeulemeester. 2000. Quality and variety competition between higher education institutions, unpublished manuscript.

Ehrenberg, Ronald G. 2000. Internal transfer prices. In R. G. Ehrenberg, ed., *Tuition rising: Why college costs so much*. Cambridge, MA: Harvard University Press.

Epple, Dennis, Richard Romano, and Holger Sieg. 2000. Peer effects, financial aid, and selection of students into colleges and universities: An empirical analysis. Carnegie Mellon University, unpublished manuscript.

Garvin, David. 1980. *The economics of university behavior*. New York: Academic Press.

Groen, Jeff, and Michelle J. White. 2000. In-state versus out-of-state students: The divergence of interest between public universities and state governments. University of Michigan, unpublished manuscript.

Hochman, Oded, David Pines, and Jacques-Francois Thisse. 1995. On the optimal structure of local governments. *American Economic Review* 85 (December, no. 5): 1224-1240.

James, Estelle. 1990. Decision processes and priorities in higher education. In Stephen A. Hoenack and Eileen L. Collins, eds., *The economics of American universities*. Albany: State University of New York Press.

Jensen, Richard, and Marie Thursby. 2001. Proofs and prototypes for sale: The licensing of university inventions. *American Economic Review* 91 (March, no. 1): 240-259.

Krause, Gunter, and John D. Wilson. 2000. Responsibility center budgeting within a university. Michigan State University, unpublished manuscript.

Masten, Scott E. 2000. Commitment and political governance: Why universities, like legislatures, are not organized as firms. University of Michigan Business School, unpublished manuscript.

Rey, Elena Del. 2001. Teaching versus research: A model of state university competition. *Journal of Urban Economics* 49 (March, no. 2): 356-373.

Rothschild, Michael, and Lawrence J. White. 1995. The analytics of the pricing of higher education and other services in which the customers are inputs. *Journal of Political Economy* 103 (June, no. 3): 573-586.

Schwab, Robert M., and Wallace E. Oates. 1991. Community composition and the provision of local public goods: A normative analysis. *Journal of Public Economics* 44 (March, no. 2): 217-238.

Tiebout, Charles M. 1956. A pure theory of local public goods. *Journal of Political Economy* 64:416-24.

Whalen, Edward L. 1991. *Responsibility center budgeting: An approach to decentralized management for institutions of higher education.* Indianapolis: Indiana University Press.

Wilson, John D. 1991. Tax competition with interregional differences in factor endowment. *Regional Science and Urban Economics* 21 (November, no. 3): 423-452.

CHAPTER 4

REVENUE FLUX AND UNIVERSITY BEHAVIOR

Larry L. Leslie

Ronald L. Oaxaca

Gary Rhoades

In this chapter, we examine incentive-based budgeting systems by focusing primarily on the context of those systems. We report on a study having a broad purpose: how shifting revenue patterns within public research universities affect their internal operations.[1] In the course of considering this question, we observed the effects of university administrators who were attempting to cope with those reductions by introducing or expanding various financial management techniques. Most of those efforts involved some form of incentive-based budgeting systems. Of course, incentive-based budgeting systems involve shifting resources in one way or another; therefore, our results do relate to the theme of this book.

In our study, we considered the effects of the revenue shifts at three institutional levels. We examined: 1) institution-level shifts in revenues and in resulting institutional-level activities; 2) institution-level policies developed to deal with shifting revenues; 3) the consequences or effects of variations in revenue patterns upon academic departments, *en toto* for our sample and by field of science (FOS)[2]; and 4) the consequences for faculty members' individual productivity. This listing specifies the organization of this chapter.

Our examinations included several sources. The findings related to institutional revenues shifts and institutional effects were taken from Hasbrouck (1997), whose work was completed for her Ph.D. dissertation at the University of Arizona. The results related to the effects of institutional policies developed to cope with changing revenues come from the NSF study cited in note 1. The department-level findings come from three sources, two of which are University of Arizona Ph.D. dissertations completed as parts of the larger NSF study (Ward, 1997; D'Sylva, 1998); the third source was the larger NSF study itself. The data dealing with individual faculty members also were collected as part of the larger NSF study.

EFFECTS AT THREE LEVELS

We utilize data from these sources to shed light on fundamental questions:

1. To what extent do those who provide resources to public research universities determine how those resources will be spent; that is, how and to what extent do universities respond to resource providers?
2. How is the work of the principal production unit of the university, the academic department, affected by its changing revenue patterns, including incentives and disincentives, and by its (hypothesized) search for new revenues? And to what degree is this effect on the department's work a function of the kind of department that it is, that is, its FOS?
3. How are individual faculty members affected by the changing financial environment and by incentives?
4. Are particular financial management strategies, in particular incentive-based management systems, effective in helping public universities cope with their changing financial environments?

In each of these questions, we will search for clues as to the effects of incentive-based budgeting systems on university behaviors: institutional, departmental, and faculty member.

Resource Dependency

Each of the empirical works cited above and our search for answers to these questions were in considerable part guided by notions of resource dependency (RD) (Pfeffer and Salancik, 1978), which holds that the internal activities of organizations are influenced importantly by the desires or demands of external resource providers. Put directly, the theory holds that "He who pays the piper calls the tune." RD asserts that organizations are destabilized either by declines in major revenue sources or in critical resources (Pfeffer and Salancik, 1978).   Organizations respond by pursuing, leveraging, and substituting alternative revenue sources. A reduction of as little as 10 percent, or even less, can lead to organizational destabilization, resulting in urgent responses aimed at regaining fiscal equilibrium.

The University Level

Slaughter and Leslie (1997) purported to show that both destabilization and efforts to regain fiscal equilibrium characterized public higher education institutions in the United States and three other countries in the early 1990s. Using descriptive statistics, they demonstrated that relative support by state governments, the major providers of funds for most U.S. public universities, had declined substantially over the decade of the 1980s and that these institutions had made up for their losses by substituting revenues from other sources (Slaughter and Leslie, Chapter 3). Further, after demonstrating that universities changed their internal resource allocation patterns in predictable ways during the decade, they argued that resource dependency clearly was suggested. They made no claim, however, that they had "proven" the theoretical connections posited by resource dependency.

Hasbrouck (1997) set out to test those connections. Utilizing HEGIS and IPEDS[3] FY1982-1983 and 1992-1993 financial data for 175 U.S. public, four-year institutions, she employed causal models to test the relationships between shifting revenue and shifting expenditure patterns, reasoning that how money was spent by functional category (e.g., teaching, research) was a good test of whether a benefactor's expectations were being met, that is, whether the resource provider was "calling the tune."

Hasbrouck's answer to this question was in the affirmative. Her overall finding was that it was possible to predict accurately variations in how universities spent their money from variations in who supplied the revenues. For example, she showed that *expenditures* for instruction – the area commonly held to be of greatest interest to state legislators and students – were predicted consistently and strongly by state appropriations and by tuition and fee *revenues*. The single and modest exception was that gift, grant, and contract income, which funding agents intended largely for research, was used to a modest degree to "cross-subsidize" instruction. In summarizing her findings, Hasbrouck (1997, p. 8) reinforced resource dependency explanations: "Were a particular revenue source to decline either absolutely or relatively, one would presume that expenditures for that revenue's related activity might also decrease."

Within the Departments and Within FOS

Whereas institution-level results provide important background information, it is within the academic departments, centers, and institutes where the university production activities of teaching, research, and service largely are carried out. At first glance, one might assume that if causal relationships between changes in sources of revenues and changes in expenditure functions can be demonstrated institutionally, then those same relationships must exist within the organization's production units; however, as those familiar with university accounting systems know, this is not necessarily the case. In fact, the relationship between what is happening at the two levels is not a simple and direct one.[4] Indeed, Ward (1997) and D'Sylva (1998) suggest that within departments relationships between revenue sources and expenditures may be very modest.

The work of Ward and D'Sylva. As part of our larger NSF study, Ward (1997) and D'Sylva (1998) analyzed different national data sets to examine effects of shifting revenue patterns at the department, center, and institute level.[5] Ward (1997) found that research-active departments produced slightly more student credit hours (SCH) than less-research-active departments but offered slightly fewer class sections. Overall, he concluded that departmental instructional variables, such as percentage of tenure/tenure-track faculty within the department and instructional spending variability, were far more important in explaining instructional productivity than was volume of departmental research activity.

D'Sylva (1998) compared departmental "rates of return"[6] to instructional productivity, research productivity, and departmental quality with the income production (allocation) function of departments. His reasoning was as follows:

> If changes in the institution's resource dependencies drive internal resource allocations, then the rate of return [sic] for these variables should reflect the priorities of those upon whom the universities are dependent. Alternatively, if internal factors drive this process, then the optimization of inputs with respect to the utility function of the institutions will dictate the relative return for the outputs of teaching, research, and departmental quality. (p. 91)

D'Sylva's *overall* result was that departmental returns to teaching exceeded those to research by a margin of more than five to two, suggesting that research was subordinate to teaching as a departmental motivator.

D'Sylva's FOS results were the first of the larger study to suggest that departments clearly differed in ways that were important to our research questions. In short D'Sylva found that in most cases the FOS outlier was the Life Sciences; for most of our questions, the Physical Sciences, Mathematics, Engineering, and the Social Sciences were more similar to each other than they were to the Life Sciences. For example, only in the Life Sciences was the return to research greater than that to teaching although this result simply may have reflected the relatively large enrollment growth across the Life Sciences during the period examined. If enrollments increase within a field and university resource allocations to the field do not keep pace, all else equal, the observed "return" to teaching will be relatively less in this field than in fields where enrollments do not grow.

One thing is very clear from these two studies. Departmental dynamics are different from those at the university level, as reported by Hasbrouck (1997).

Departmental adjustments to revenue losses. Our field work centered on interviews with department heads and individual faculty members within 11 public, AAU[7] universities. We interviewed heads regarding departmental resources, changes in resources, and about productivity issues identified as possibly being related to the revenue changes. Central to the interviews with faculty members were time budget analyses (TBA) showing how faculty members spent their time.[8]

Through the interviews we came to understand better the various reasons for the lack of strategic departmental responses to the fiscal stress experienced in virtually all institutions. For example, Physical Science and Math departments were often backward looking, apparently because of the 1990s declines in research monies available to them. Department heads bemoaned these changes which, as one Physics head observed, "came with the end of the Evil Empire." Thus, Physical Science heads tended to pine away for the good old days of large, defense-related R&D grants and contracts and to give less attention to new opportunity structures. By contrast, in the Social Sciences, where the relative reduction of federal support in the 1980s had been from a much smaller base, department heads seemed unable or unwilling to visualize a place for the social sciences in a more entrepreneurial university. Of course, there were some social science departments that sought external research funding for the conventional purpose of advancing their research reputations, but on the whole there was almost a fatalism, in the social sciences, that resulted in a lack of strategic orientation. The interviews, then, helped us to understand why many departments failed to respond aggressively to the difficult financial times that most universities, and departments, were experiencing. In the end we could not be sure whether departmental inaction, where we found it, was in a sense self-imposed or whether the financial difficulties experienced were too modest to invoke action on their part.

The interviews with department heads focused on how departments responded to changing revenue patterns, that is, how changing revenues had affected departments. Whereas Ward (1997) and D'Sylva (1998) looked for effects of changing revenue patterns in objective data contained in national data sets, in the interviews we asked heads for their insights into the often subtle outcomes of changing department revenues.

Our econometric analysis controlled for four major variable groups: 1) FOS, that is Engineering, Life Sciences, Mathematics, and Physical Sciences, relative to Social Sciences/Education;[9] 2) existence of substantial[10] reductions in revenues from grants and contracts, from institutional funds, from sales and services, from state (or tuition) support, and from all other sources taken together; 3) changes in the extent to which power resides within the central administration; and 4) institutional affiliation (relative to Park State University).[11] We examined the effects of these variables on five categories of outcomes, three of which are pertinent to this chapter: 1) the substitution of departmentally self-generated funds for state funds; 2) changes in undergraduate teaching loads; and 3) changes in overall teaching loads. For the purposes of the analyses for this chapter, we had between 131 and 133 (departmental) observations. We employed a number of econometric techniques in analyzing the data.[12] We discuss a select set of these results here.

Because the resource dependency issue was raised in connection with relative declines in state funding of public universities, we examined (logit probability models) departmental substitution of self-generated funds for state (including tuition) funds for four categories of expenditures: equipment, instruction, graduate student support, and a residual category "Other" consisting of operations, secretarial, travel, and miscellaneous. The resource dependency-related question was whether revenue declines in major categories or in critical areas induced organizations to seek alternative sources of supplies of factors of production.

First, we examined the effects of our explanatory variables on the probability that a department would resort to substitution for *any* category of expenditure. The estimated model correctly predicted 95 (71 percent) of the outcomes. In 83 cases (62 percent), the department heads indicated that their departments resorted to revenue substitution in at least one category of expenditures.

Although this result suggested widespread declines in state support[13] and thus the potential for resource dependency effects to be experienced, it said nothing about the *amount* of revenue lost, nor of the extent to which departments were in fact destabilized; that is, a unit could have lost some support without being affected importantly. How sizeable was the effect? Substantial revenue reductions in state support had a statistically significant and positive effect on the probability that the department would substitute self-generated revenues for state funds. At the sample mean and holding other factors constant,[14] a 10 percent rise in the probability of a substantial reduction in state support was associated with a 2.3 percent rise in the probability of substituting self-generated funds. This is a substantial, though not huge value. Probably the most likely explanation of this result is that many departments did not respond aggressively to state-funding declines: Either the revenue decline was not sufficient to cause major revenue-compensating behavior at the unit level, or the departments were *unable* to raise substantial, new funds. If the former was the case, unit destabilization could not be said to have occurred and various RD effects would not have been expected; if the latter was the case, unit destabilization and various RD effects *may* have occurred.

When we examine the categories in which departments are willing to draw upon their own funds as shortfalls occur, we gain some additional insights into departmental financial dynamics. There are at least two ways to represent these effects. First, we can compare the relative propensities of substitution for each of the several categories. Here (Table 4.1) we see that department heads report the greatest subsidization of Other expenditures, followed by equipment, graduate students, and instruction.

What can we learn from these substitutions? First, although the question predicate is substitution of self-generated funds for activities previously paid for from state funds, we must recognize that various granting agencies may permit some classes of expenditures but not others, or they may permit greater latitude in certain expenditure areas; therefore, we cannot assume that the data in Table 4.1 necessarily reflect only departmental decisions to subsidize the activities. For example, departmental subsidization of *any* item in the Other category, presumably would yield a positive department head response to this category. We know that almost any agency will authorize grant funds for items in the Other category (such departmental operations as telephones and copying) and most will

Table 4.1: Departmental Substitutions of Self-Generated Funds for State Funds

Function	Number (and Percentage) of Funds, by Function
Other	70 (53)
Equipment	62 (47)
Graduate Students	60 (45)
Instruction	37 (28)

Note: Other function includes secretarial, operations, travel, and miscellaneous.

finance travel and secretarial help, which also are components of the Other category. Grantors generally are somewhat less likely to pay for equipment but almost all are willing to pay for graduate student support. Probably very few willingly subsidize instruction directly although many allow faculty buyouts for instruction, and when those funds are used to hire replacement instructors grant funds are used indirectly for instruction. Further, in most universities the departments can generate revenues from special instructional efforts, such as summer school, workshops, and courses offered at night and on weekends. The point is that if grant or contract (or other) terms permit funding of one spending category but not another, all else equal, the department is more likely to fund the former category than the latter. Having said all of this, the data are still interesting. It is noteworthy, for example, that self-generated funds are used to support instruction, a finding that is consistent with Hasbrouck's only identified cross-subsidy at the institutional level. Our general impression from the data is that the departments do in fact show expense preferences roughly in accordance with the data in Table 4.1 and that the tendencies of departments to substitute their own funds for state funds when budget shortfalls are experienced are indeed widespread, extending as they do to approximately half of all departments (Table 4.1). Put another way, the data offer few surprises to us as we reflect upon departmental behavior during the recent period of relative declines in state funding. From the standpoint of assumptions that seem to drive many policy makers, however, the findings are very surprising, for they show that, contrary to the prevailing perspective about universities sacrificing instruction to pursue research, the reverse often holds in that many departments are subsidizing instructional activities with self-generated funds (research grants and contracts are a principal source of such funds).

Another way to view the department heads' responses is through the magnitude of effects. In Table 4.2 we show the percentage increase in the probability of departmental revenue substitution for a given category, taken at the sample mean, assuming a 10 percent increase in the probability that there would be a substantial reduction in state funding, and holding constant all variables in the equations. Put directly, as state support declines, what is the probability the department will make up the loss in a particular category? For this, we may look to Table 4.2.

In all categories, as state support (including tuition revenue) declines, department heads say they are making up for the shortfalls from money the department has generated itself, such as through grants and contracts or special instructional programs. Again, the effects are substantial if not huge. Specifically

Table 4.2: Change in Departmental Subsidization of Various Functions for a
10 Percent Increase in the Probability of a Reduction in State Support

Function	Percentage Change
Equipment	3.4
Other	2.2
Instructional	0.9
Graduate Students	0.7

Note: Other function includes secretarial, operations, travel, and miscellaneous.

a 10 percent increase in the probability that there would be substantial reduction in state support is associated, at the sample mean, with a 3.4 percent increase in the probability of revenue substitution to purchase equipment. For departmental subsidization of the Other category, the instructional program, and graduate student support, the corresponding values are 2.2, 0.9, and 0.7 percent, respectively (Table 4.2). Regardless of the category, declining state funds are compensated for by departments from their own funds.

What can be made of these results? For example, can we say that the recent declining state support destabilized production units and caused them to seek alternative external support? Yes, but not to the extent anticipated. What of response to incentives and disincentives? To this question, we can conclude, indirectly, that departments can and do respond; that is, as resources are reduced, such as through across-the-board cuts, departmental responses are noted. These responses, however, are not one-for-one substitutions. Substitution is evident in only about one-half of the departments and is of only moderate magnitude, where it occurs. It may be that the (state) revenue reductions were not of a sufficient magnitude to generate the effects we anticipated. Either the revenue declines were not sufficient to destabilize most departments and thus did not lead to major revenue-generating behavior, or the departments were unable, unwilling, or did not know how to raise substantial new funds. Our general sense from the interviews was that departments did not respond aggressively to the state-funding reductions. Of course, *institutional* revenue declines may not have been passed on, in full measure, to the departments; to some degree the universities may have buffered the departments from the reductions.

Were FOS differences apparent from these interviews? Quite consistently. For example, using the Physical Sciences as the comparison or base field (the field left out, the field constrained to have a zero coefficient), Engineering departments were 16.7 percent more likely to substitute their own funds when state budget declines were substantial. Engineering departments, relative to Physical Science departments, were about 25.5 percent more likely to substitute self-generated funds for instruction. In regard to substitution of departmental funds to support graduate students, Engineering, Life and Social Sciences were all more likely to substitute than were the Physical Sciences, by margins ranging from more than 20 to almost 40 percent. The recent reported declines in funding opportunities in the Physical Sciences may have contributed importantly to reduced support of graduate students.

How did the Ward (1997) and D'Sylva (1998) results compare with results from the department head interviews? Ward reported minor shifts in departmental outputs, such as instruction, as departments generated funds from research. The revenue substitution for state funds revealed in our interviews, of course, did not necessarily suggest corresponding changes in departmental *outputs*; neither did D'Sylva's findings regarding relative returns to instruction and research. In short, our results did not necessarily conflict with Ward's findings even though important internal, financial dynamics were evident within departments.

Another way to view instructional productivity is through teaching loads. Our department head interview data relate changing revenue patterns to these loads. Of course, any revenue change may be viewed as an incentive or a disincentive. Put another way, whether revenue changes are imposed by management or occur naturally, such changes conceptually may be considered as incentives.

Whereas Ward (1997) had observed effects of changing revenues on student credit hours produced and numbers of class sections offered, we asked heads whether over the past five years teaching loads had changed in their departments. We considered both the effects on *undergraduate* and overall teaching loads,[15] the former, of course, being the area of primary interest to most state policymakers. The interviews suggested some increases in both undergraduate and overall teaching productivity over the five years. While most heads reported no change in loads, about 41 percent reported increased undergraduate loads and 31 percent reported increased overall loads. These findings, too, would seem to be at odds with the public perception regarding faculty work.

Partially balanced with load reductions, however, were some departmental field effects. Other things equal, Engineering departments were *less* likely, relative to Social Sciences departments (the omitted group), to increase undergraduate teaching loads and were *more* likely to lower these loads.[16] We note that this was a period of decline in undergraduate engineering enrollments, nationally, which may suggest that the load changes merely were an artifact of the enrollment trends rather than of departmental *decisions*. On the other hand, Life Sciences departments were more likely (than the Social Sciences) to experience both increased undergraduate and overall teaching loads and were less likely to experience reductions in these loads. The "effects sizes" were very similar to those for Engineering. Here, increases may have reflected changing student demand, as well, because Life Science enrollments increased during this period. In sum of these results, it should be noted that no connection was found between revenue amounts, by category, and loads, thus lending further support to Ward's findings.

Individual Faculty Member Responses to Revenue Changes

From analyses of these first two levels of public research universities, we see that institutional effects of revenue shifts are not necessarily translated into departmental effects. The remaining question is whether effects occur at the level of the individual faculty member, the primary production worker of the public research university. Directly put, does a changing financial environment affect the individual and his or her work? Specifically, is there a causal connection between receiving external financial support and one's academic work, that work being measured in faculty time allocations to the various role components, controlled for quality of output?

To answer these questions we utilized time budget analysis (TBA), a technique for gaining accurate assessments of how individuals spend their time, and we collected research productivity and teaching performance data.[17] Combined with time sampling techniques, the TBA yielded data on how 417 faculty members spent their time during an average week. Faculty time allocations were broken down into six instructional categories (e.g., undergraduate/graduate, in class; contact out-of-class; preparation for class); six categories of research (e.g., publicly funded or privately funded, internally or externally supported, research administration); and four categories of service (e.g., public or private consulting, professional service, public service). Also measured were joint production activities, that is when two or more different outcomes of production were realized, simultaneously.[18] Including weekends, the average faculty member worked 57 hours per week and 10 hours per weekday (11 hours when we consider joint production), 7 hours per weekend. Of the 10 hours, 4.2 hours were spent on instruction, 3.2 hours on research, and 2.5 hours on service. Approximately 75 percent of the day was spent on research and teaching, with teaching accounting for 42.4 percent of the day. For our basic analysis, to control for quality of outputs, we interacted instructional time with teaching evaluations and research time with several measures of research production (the number of various publications and of research grants obtained). Service was captured by the total time allocated to service activities interacted with seniority at one's institution.

Although we examined a host of variables associated with faculty members' time allocations and outputs (e.g., we composed salary models that estimated the effects of allocations and outputs on salaries[19]), our primary concern here was how faculty time allocations were affected by receiving external revenues, which may be viewed conceptually as faculty incentives.[20] What we found was that faculty members who received external grant and contract funding spent less time on instruction and more time on research and service than did those who were not so funded.[21] Having external funding led to a reduction of about 1 hour per day on instruction, and an increase of about 1 hour on research and 0.8 hours on service, yielding a net increase of about 0.8 hours per academic work day. These results certainly were consistent with resource dependency theory and with Hasbrouck's (1997) central finding that expenditure patterns were largely predictable from revenue source patterns.

Field effects are again noted. Other things equal, being in an Engineering department is associated with spending 1.5 hours per day more on instruction and 0.8 hours less on research than is the case within Physical Sciences departments. In interpreting such findings, one should note the quite different instructional production functions employed across the various fields. For example, Physical Science professors tend to teach, relatively, very large (but fewer) classes in a lecture format, compared to Engineering professors, who spend more time working out solutions to assigned problems, solving problems in order to grade examinations, and in the grading itself.[22] Obviously, overall instructional productivity is affected by these different instructional approaches, which vary strikingly across all five FOS.

INSTITUTIONAL POLICIES AND EFFECTS

In keeping with the larger purposes of this book, we conducted analyses to determine whether the financial management strategies employed by the 11 public research universities had differing effects on university outcomes. In our original work, we had identified many joint institutional effects, which meant simply that the (dummy) variables used to identify the 11 universities *collectively* did explain differences in many university outcomes. A finding of joint effects, however, does not permit us to identify the *sources* of the effects; that is, *which* institutions account for the joint effects findings, let alone which institutional policies might explain the effects.[23]

Some of the more pertinent joint (institutional) effects were as follows. Jointly, the institutional variables were statistically significant in explaining changes in overall teaching loads; that is, collectively, the university in which a department was located contributed to explaining changes in teaching loads. Another result dealt with changes in power and authority relationships. RD theory suggests that power and authority in universities becomes more vested in central administration and in production units; presumably some power and authority flows to these levels from intermediate level administrators, such as college deans (Slaughter and Leslie, 1997). The finding related to this proposition was that departments in universities perceived by heads to have increased centralization of power were more likely to have greatly increased overall teaching loads and were less likely to have reduced these loads.[24] Such findings suggest that institutions may be able to leverage increased emphasis on instruction at the department level (a result supported in subsequent analyses below). Of course, assuming causality is problematic, in part because the measure of centralization is department head perception; nevertheless, the hypothesis may be worthy of further exploration.

Department heads and faculty members identified important institutional policy changes, *incentives and disincentives,* during our interviews; for example, we were informed of centrally established incentives to increase enrollments and SCH production; of incentive-based allocations of indirect cost recovery funds, not to mention administrative exhortations aimed at generating more grant and contract revenues; and occasionally of the granting of reduced teaching loads to faculty engaged in university service work, such as serving on important university committees.

Because of the small sample size, we faced difficulties identifying which institutions and which policies accounted for the jointly significant effects.[25] We approached the joint significance questions in three different ways: simple reporting of the descriptive statistics, including "expected values"; reporting on selected comments made by the department heads in the interviews; and developing models to test the interaction between the institutional variable and the FOS variable.

Descriptive Data

First we need to describe some of the variables of primary relevance to our purposes here. When we conducted our interviews, the most powerful impressions gained were that the entrepreneurial environments of two universities were notably different from those of the other nine universities. One of the universities was known to have employed responsibility centered management (RCM), which, in simple (and *relative* to non-RCM universities) terms, permits units to capture the revenues that they earn (usually net of some institutional tax), such as through student enrollments and research grants, but requires the units to cover their costs with these revenues.[26] In discussing the implications of resource dependency, Slaughter and Leslie (1997) had predicted evolution in the direction of RCM kinds of approaches to financial management. The second university perceived to have a notably different environment was located in a state that historically had substantially underfunded higher education *and* had implemented a limited form of RCM. Of the remaining nine institutions, seven had either implemented some form of university-wide reallocation of funds or were preparing to implement an RCM variation. Moreover, each of these remaining institutions was experiencing relatively moderate financial stress (compared with the second university).

In Table 4.3 we provide some basic descriptive information regarding grant and contract activity and faculty time allocations. It is important to note that not all of the 11 universities possess all five of the FOS and that we do not always meet our quota of three faculty interviews per department; most notably for the financial implications, not all have engineering. Therefore, because there are great variations in the grant and contract activity among the five FOS, the data in Table 4.3 are useful primarily as a point of departure; the table does not compare "apples and apples."

To illustrate the information in this table, note that Center State U, which is the university that instituted RCM, ranks last (11th) in the number of grants and contracts received, at 1.17 per faculty member and that Forest State U, which has experienced historic, major underfunding, ranks only ninth at 1.68 grants/contracts per faculty member. Most universities, however, probably would attach greater importance to the amount of research dollars generated by the grants/contracts. On this measure Center State U is ranked a much higher fourth at $438,000 per faculty member in the sample, and Forest State U ranks first at $587,000. The latter also ranks first in mean faculty time spent on instruction and

Table 4.3: Grant and Contract Activity and Faculty Time Use (Actual Values)

	-1	-2	-3	-4	-5	-6	-7	-8	-9	-10	-11	-12
State University	G/C Number	Dev. from Mean %	Rank	G/C Amount	Dev. from Mean %	Rank	Instruction & Research	Dev. from Mean %	Rank	Total time	Dev. from Mean %	Rank
Lake	1.91	-2	6	290.18	-28	10	441	-10	10	594	-2	8
Breadbasket	1.95	1	5	350.13	-13	8	478	-2	6	634	4	4
Timber	2.37	22	2	371.30	-7	6	397	-19	11	456	-25	11
Prairie	2.05	6	4	358.43	-10	7	495	1	4	616	1	5
Forest	1.68	-13	9	587.18	47	1	661	35	1	770	27	1
Mountain	2.44	26	1	309.30	-23	9	526	8	2	654	8	2
Mineral	2.35	21	3	494.50	23	3	459	-6	8	639	5	3
Center	1.17	-40	11	438.28	9	4	466	-5	7	582	-4	9
Winter	1.64	-15	10	517.69	29	2	509	4	3	615	1	6
Park	1.86	-4	8	402.76	1	5	445	-9	9	527	-13	10
Eastern	1.90	-2	7	285.51	-29	11	492	1	5	600	-1	7
Average	1.94			400.48			488			608		

Notes: G/C number: present number of grants and contracts per faculty member. G/C amount: present grants and contracts amounts in thousands per faculty member. Instruction & research: minutes spent on instruction and research per day per faculty member. Total time: minutes spent on instruction, research, and service per day per faculty member. Dev. from Mean: the deviation of the actual value from the sample mean, which is located at the last row of the table. Rank: the rank order of the university among the 11 universities in the column to the left.

research and in faculty members' total time devoted to academic work.

The data in Table 4.4 are standardized for curricular differences in the distribution of faculty actually interviewed among the 11 universities, specifically for variations in the FOS each possesses. For this table, adjusted values are calculated to reflect what the data relationships in Table 4.3 would be if each university possessed all five FOS and if equal numbers of faculty were interviewed in each FOS.[27] For example, whereas Center State U still ranks 11th in number of grants/contracts per faculty member, instead of being 40 percent below the mean (Table 4.3, column 2) it is now 36 percent below the adjusted value (Table 4.4, column 2), because its expected grant and contract number is reduced to 1.84 grants/contracts per faculty member (Table 4.4, column 1) from the 1.94 unadjusted value reported in Table 4.3 (column 1). In regard to the G/C amount, Center State U moves from fourth position in dollars generated from this source (Table 4.3) to second and is now 25 percent above the adjusted value. In short the grant and contract money generated at the university that utilizes RCM is relatively high. Similarly, Forest State U moves from ninth to fifth on the comparison of the number of grants and remains first on the dollar comparison – by an even wider margin. In time devoted by faculty members to instruction and research, Center State U moves from seventh to sixth; Forest State U remains first. The Forest State U case, in particular, seems to suggest a resource dependency effect: major revenue problems are associated with relatively successful efforts in generating external funds from grants and contracts.

These two universities were singled out because one appeared to provide the clearest test of a fairly radical financial management technique, RCM, and the other illustrated the effects of substantial state underfunding *and* RCM. Based upon the data in the Tables 4.3 and 4.4, it does appear that major revenue difficulties are associated with relatively high levels of grant and contract work and large expenditures of faculty time (Forest State U). The relationships among the data for Center State U, which employs RCM, suggest that the technique is associated with relatively large grant and contract revenues per faculty member. Although this is the only striking relationship, it is an important one. For deeper insight into the policies and practices of the universities we turn to our interview data.

The Interview Data

We asked department heads whether there had been introduced unique or distinctive *university* initiatives – financial management techniques – that affected the department. Also, at the end of the interviews, we asked whether there was anything else regarding revenue stream changes that they would like to point out. Combined with questions about university-imposed pressures to increase external revenues, effects on departmental autonomy, and changes in institutional power relationships, we gained a good understanding of the effects of institutionally imposed, finance-related incentives and disincentives.

Before a brief statement of department head reactions to these financial in-

Table 4.4: Grant and Contract Activity and Faculty Time Use ("Expected" Values)

	-1	-2	-3	-4	-5	-6	-7	-8	-9	-10	-11	-12
	Expected G/C Number	Dev. from Expected Value %	Rank	Expected G/C Amount	Dev. from Expected Value %	Rank	Expected Instruction & Research	Dev. from Expected Value %	Rank	Expected Total Time	Dev. from Expected Value %	Rank
State University												
Lake	1.92	-1	7	381.56	-24	10	484	-9	9	607	-2	7
Breadbasket	1.99	-2	8	431.00	-19	8	491	-3	7	614	3	4
Timber	2.06	15	3	437.00	-15	7	484	-18	11	608	-25	11
Prairie	1.98	4	5	381.36	-6	6	489	1	4	614	0	5
Forest	1.61	23	1	316.01	86	1	476	39	1	595	29	1
Mountain	1.99	16	2	401.34	-23	9	492	7	2	616	6	2
Mineral	2.03	16	2	408.41	21	3	491	-6	8	616	4	3
Center	1.84	-36	11	351.28	25	2	478	-2	6	600	-3	9
Winter	2.12	-23	10	426.81	21	3	492	3	3	619	-1	6
Park	1.87	-1	7	375.57	7	5	487	-9	9	609	-13	10
Eastern	1.98	-4	9	399.90	-29	11	490	0	5	614	-2	7

Notes: Calculation of "expected" value: Given the fact that the distribution of SME (Science, including Social Science, Math, and Engineering) departments and faculty members interviewed is not the same across the 11 universities, direct comparison of their absolute value is problematic. For example, if University A has more Engineering faculty members interviewed than University B, we would expect that A generates more grant and contract money than B because Engineering faculty generally generate more grant and contract money than those in other fields. In order to calculate the "expected" value, we first calculate the average values of an outcome variable in each SME field across the 11 universities and the distribution of the SME departments and faculty members interviewed in each university. Then, the average values are weighted by the distribution of SME departments and faculty members interviewed to generate the table of "expected" values. Taking Grants and Contracts amount as an example, given the performance of different fields, we would expect higher "expected" values from those universities with higher proportion of Engineering and Physical Science faculty interviewed. At both Forest State University and Center State University, *no* Engineering faculty members were interviewed. This largely explains why the "expected" values of these two universities are quite low. Moreover, compared with Forest State University, at Center State University more Physical Science and fewer Other (low performance field) faculty members were interviewed. This largely explains why Center State University has a higher "expected" value than Forest State University. Dev. from "Expected" Value: the deviation of the actual value (Table 4.3) from the "expected" value (Table 4.4). Rank: the rank order of the university among the 11 universities in the column to the left.

terventions within each university, we offer a few generalizations. The first is that all but one of the 11 universities were employing some form of financial incentives, disincentives, or both. The second is that, by a vast margin, the heads spoke more of fears and of guarded optimism, of the potentials for harm or good resulting from these interventions, than of any realized positive or adverse effects of the interventions, *per se*. Both the fears and the tentativeness of the responses may have had to do with the relative newness of many of these initiatives. Also, no doubt some of the negativism or reservation simply was normal resistance to change or fear of the unknown. Some department heads had adopted a wait and see, or an "it's too soon to tell" attitude, as the initiatives had not been in place for more than one budget cycle. Others pointed to the turnover of deans, provosts, and presidents and the related effect on the initiatives: if the administrator who had established the initiative was departing, the future of the initiative was unclear. Regardless, in fact most of the strategies employed by central administrators were perceived by heads as not having a great deal of effect on departments, other than in creating burdensome record keeping. As we listened to the frequent complaints and fewer praises of the interventions, we usually could not separate out the (alleged) effects of the intervention from the head's personal values, reactions to the additional work involved, perceived threats to the "nature of the university," or perceptions of changes in departmental autonomy. A third generalization is that most responses were more negative than they were positive. The fourth was that heads' negative reactions resulted primarily from what one head described as the "wasted effort and bureaucratic paperwork" that these interventions required. There were statements about extraordinary investments of time for the limited benefits that might actually have accrued. Other causes were the perception that the head's department wound up a "loser" as a result of the resource reallocation process and that there were important negative, unintended consequences of the interventions. The minority of heads, who were favorably disposed toward the intervention strategies, cited as their reasons the gaining of resources and occasionally the inherent merits of the interventions when judged on effectiveness and efficiency grounds. Another generalization was that the greatest negative response from heads were to the *planned,* not the realized, implementation of RCB.

Finally, it appeared that the implementation *strategy* for the intervention was more important than the particular intervention itself. The response to an intervention might have been only slightly negative or even almost neutral in one university whereas the same technique might have generated extreme hostility in another institution, even if the magnitude of the intervention in the latter was less than in the former (e.g., a larger budget reallocation). It appeared that the perceived legitimacy of the intervention was important to acceptance, as was the political skill with which the intervention was introduced. Following is a brief synopsis of institutional incentives employed or planned and department head views of the effects within the 11 universities.

Forest State U. In the context of an historic statewide pattern of significant reductions in state appropriations, which already had led to an institution-wide effort to increase class loads, department heads cited a "productivity formula" that had been introduced at the university level and that was essentially a form of RCM. The overriding emphasis of this formula, which involved setting production targets, was on credit hour generation, particularly at the undergraduate level. Thus far, the formula had been utilized primarily at the college level although some heads expected deans to begin using it for allocations as well. The allocation of teaching assistant positions in particular was linked to the formula, and although not officially the case, heads had a sense that the allocation of faculty lines and state monies also were connected to department undergraduate credit-hour production.

Some of the complaints surrounding the productivity formula had to do with the fact that although the formula was intended as an incentive for enrollment growth, enrollment *declines* had occurred, consistent with a statewide pattern. The result was that the RCM system was seen as ineffective, inappropriate, and punitive. It was seen as causing internal competition for existing students, particularly in general education. Further, there was a clear sense that professional schools were winning out in this competition, relative to arts and sciences. The push was for units to take as many students as possible.

In addition to implementing an RCM system focused on student credit-hour production, the central administration encouraged departments to connect more closely with the private sector and to engage in entrepreneurial research. Few department heads or faculty, with the exception of those in computer science, reported a positive response to these encouragements, blaming the lack of any connection to resource allocation.

From the interviews it seemed that department heads and faculty were too busy scrambling for general education credit hours to undertake entrepreneurial research initiatives; it also seemed that many departments lacked any strategic sense of how to position themselves in this competitive environment. There was far more evidence of fiscal stress and disequilibrium than of entrepreneurial responses to financial incentives.

Center State U. At Center State, whose implementation of RCM was probably greatest, the prevailing institutional initiative identified by department heads was a "teaching capacity model." As at Forest State U, the overwhelming emphasis was on instructional productivity at the undergraduate level, although the model included numbers of department majors as well as credit hour production. As at Forest State U, the incentive system thus far had been implemented more at the college than at the departmental level although at least one college was in the process of developing a related college incentive plan (CIP), which was a more comprehensive model, in that it would include thesis students, doctorates produced, quality rankings, and grant monies.

Problems identified by department heads were similar to those identified at Forest State U. Despite an incentive system aimed at encouraging instructional productivity, university enrollments were declining, and competition for the declining numbers had developed among colleges and departments, leading to an internal redistribution of students. Moreover, units worked politically to change general education requirements so that they could attract more students, and they reduced or eliminated difficult prerequisites for their degree programs. Again, department heads held that the professional schools were winning the competition, employing such strategies as hiring part-time faculty to teach language and programming courses that in the past would have been offered in arts and science departments.

As at Forest State U, department heads at Center State U indicated that the central administration was encouraging departments to develop closer ties with the private sector and to pursue entrepreneurial research opportunities. In both cases there were virtually no reports of collective efforts to engage in entrepreneurial research. Perhaps the RCM incentives dissipated most of the entrepreneurial energy. Or perhaps such efforts only involved individuals.

As at Forest State U, we were struck by the relative lack of strategic activity at Center State U. There were clear incentives to be found in the RCM model; however, few departments displayed strategic efforts to position themselves in the new resource allocation environment, or in the new national environment for entrepreneurial activity, even in Life Sciences. Although a sense of hard economic times was common, an entrepreneurial sense of how to organize collectively to replace threatened or reduced state revenues was seldom found.

Park State U. Department heads at this institution cited both university strategic planning and reallocation efforts as well as state board of regents' interventions in the area of faculty workload and undergraduate instruction; however, heads indicated that reallocation efforts largely were ineffective. In one sense, entrepreneurial activities seemed to be similar to those at the other universities – extant but limited in the area of initiatives aimed at commercializing research, more evident in instructional areas. In sum, at Park State U and elsewhere, we found a relative disconnect between the incentive structures of central administration and the entrepreneurial initiatives of the departments.

Several years prior to our visit to the campus, Park State U engaged in a university-wide review of academic and support units. *Ad hoc* faculty committees were asked to identify and reallocate resources to "strong" departments. There was no particular focus on entrepreneurial research or on instructional productivity at the undergraduate level. Instead, the focus was more on enhancing the university's position in national academic rankings. Afterward, the consensus was that despite the extraordinary amount of time and effort invested in the review activity, little systematic resource reallocation had occurred. Rather, there was a sense that allocation was driven more by private deals than by public deliberations and established criteria. In the eyes of most, the university had experienced a series of sporadic efforts tied to changes in senior administration.

Department heads spoke as much about the ventures of the state board of regents as they did about university initiatives. As at Eastern State U (below), a state-level body had directly exercised pressure on the university to increase faculty course loads and instructional productivity, particularly at the undergraduate level. In contrast to Eastern State U, Park State U had not followed upon this state intervention, either systematically or effectively.

Despite rather negative perceptions by department heads, we found a pattern of modest entrepreneurial initiatives similar to that found in universities that had implemented RCM; that is, we found some evidence of initiatives to link university research more closely to the private sector, but less than our theory had promised. We also found some evidence of initiatives in the area of undergraduate education, of revising undergraduate programs and courses to make them more attractive to students and to make them more technology intensive. Finally, we found some initiatives to develop masters-degree programs that would both attract students from the private sector and provide businesses with employees.

Prairie State U. From the department heads' perspective, the primary institutional strategy introduced in this university in the name of effectiveness and efficiency was a 4 percent reallocation of departmental funds. For reasons that we only partially came to understand, the heads at Prairie State U reacted less negatively to this 4 percent reallocation than did their counterparts at another university, where the reallocation was only 1 percent. Several possible explanations surfaced in our interviews. The head of a meteorology department pointed out that reallocations had been common-place for several years in the university; he commented that "the new reallocation probably w[ould] have little effect in this department." A Life Science department head clarified that the chancellor pushed for only a 1 percent reallocation and that it was the deans who had increased the figure to 4 percent. Perhaps the fact that three-quarters of the money could stay within the heads' colleges was also of major importance to the heads' reactions. Another head, from an Engineering department, characterized the reallocations as "nothing substantial," and the head of a Physical Science unit observed that the reallocations were to the "signature science programs," which he appeared to have believed was not a bad strategy. A head from the Mathematics area said that in his field the reallocations were "coming, but not here yet."

Criticism of the reallocation was strongest in the Social Sciences, which often viewed it as unfair – as a "deck stacked against us," in the words of one head. There were also several criticisms about the process and the implicit costs. As the head of a combination Life Sciences and Engineering department said, "The money is going to process, not enhancement."

Two other Prairie State U initiatives were cited by *at least* two heads. Several heads objected to the enhancing of a university branch campus located in the major metropolitan center of the state. "This takes money out of the system," explained a Life Science head. Niching, the concentrating of departmental efforts in the area "where we can be the best in the world" (Physics and Astronomy head), was also cited as an institutional, finance-related strategy.

Mountain State U. The overriding institutional initiative at this institution was this same "niching"; however, the consequences at Mountain State U were seen as much greater than were those of the 4 percent reallocations or the niching at Prairie State U. What was unclear was whether the particular intervention or its implementation strategy largely explained the difference. Representative reactions to niching were, "A good idea that went too far" (a head from a department in the Math area), "It's crazy; it drains faculty and administration time" (a head from Physical Science department), and "There's a dissonance between the assigned niche and the department's strengths" (a Social Science head).

In spite of the strong feelings expressed, niching did not appear to be having a major effect on most departments at Mountain State U. As put by a Life Science head, "We are doing our own thing and doing it successfully; the U environment is not much of a factor." Intimating that university leaders were not very skillful in deploying or choosing financial interventions, a Physical Science department head observed that "The central administration controls the money but does not employ resources in ways that matter that much, such as RCM."

Timber State U. Although our department head interviews were limited in number at Timber State U, which was our pilot institution, the major finding there was clear cut: everyone was talking and thinking about the upcoming implementation of RCB, which was to be driven heavily by enrollment flows (changes). Whether viewed positively or negatively, clearly the opinion at Timber State U was that RCB would change departmental behaviors in major ways, good or bad. We wondered whether the effects possibly could be as great as those anticipated by Timber State U department heads.

The heads' expectations ranged from fairly positive, through neutral or undecided, on to very negative. The head of an Engineering department said that RCB was "not intrinsically bad; it has some pluses." "The trick will be to balance teaching loads and the associated money with the money from research grants," reflected a Physical Science department head. Another Physical Science head, whose views were mixed, concluded that RCB would yield more rational budgeting and would help meet infrastructure costs. In contrast he also believed that "the professional schools w[ould] be helped and the liberal arts hurt." He thought that research emphases would change "from theoretical to experimental," and he stated his "fear that we are substituting algorithms for wisdom with RCB." Another head, from a Life Science department, believed that interdepartmental cooperation would be hurt, that "the model [had] been inter-departmental cooperation, and now would become competition." "This is terrible (for higher education)," he lamented.

Lake State U. Lake State U was the university where reactions were more negative to a 1 percent reallocation than they had been to the 4 percent reallocation at Prairie State U. Perhaps a contributing factor was that the 1 percent had come to be labeled a "takeback" whereas the term "reallocation" had been used at Prairie State U. Another reason may have been that the Lake State U president had come from a business background, resulting in the interventions he imposed being characterized by faculty members and heads as "simply business practices" – hardly a positive recommendation in most university communities. As at Prairie State U, there were complaints at Lake State U about the paperwork and the bureaucracy, but in greater numbers and with greater vehemence. The head of an Engineering department maintained that "management [was] the new role of the faculty." The most serious and consistent complaint, however, was that the 1 percent was a great financial burden to the departments. According to the heads, no departmental funds were protected at Lake State U, meaning that the cuts had to come largely from already stressed operations budgets. This "drops operations by $10K per year," said one head, who argued that so many unit costs were fixed (e.g., salaries) there was little real choice about where the cuts could be found. There were a few positive comments about the takebacks, but at least some relatively neutral ones. "We are more autonomous, but still have to be accountable to those who provide the dollars," remarked a Life Science department head in a statement that seemed to us literally to *define* resource dependency. "We got it back for [increased] enrollments," said a Physical Science department head explaining how the 1 percent money could be regained. Perhaps not realizing the full implications of his statement, a department head in an economics area seemed to be critical of the 1 percent takeback in saying, "There is no way to cut this much, so you hustle that much more for dollars." A Mathematics area head cited also the negative and interacting consequences of the university guaranteeing tuition prices be held at a certain level for a given number of years, which he saw as having a cumulative, dilatory effect when coupled with the 1 percent takeback. Another Mathematics area head summed up the prevailing sentiment at Lake State U when he said, "the market economy prevails on campus."

Eastern State U. Department heads at Eastern State U spoke most often about a university-wide graduate program review. Conducted by a blue ribbon, *ad hoc* academic committee that rated each academic unit on a five-point scale, the reviews were aimed at identifying centers of excellence to be targeted for a 1 percent budget reallocation. The process was unique among our sample in its overriding focus on traditional measures of research excellence: the explicit goal was to advance the institution's position in national research rankings by investing in no more than 10-12 percent of the university's *graduate* programs. This focus was neither the entrepreneurial research emphasis that we had expected nor the undergraduate instructional productivity strategy that we found generally in other institutions.

The push for increased accountability and productivity in *undergraduate* instruction came directly from the state. There were state audits of individual departments, based on a standard state teaching load that essentially required a significant increase in teaching for some faculty, particularly those who were not research active.

The university also encouraged faculty to engage more in entrepreneurial research although, again, response by departments was limited, even in the Life Sciences. Instead, many departments were taking advantage of the university's geographical location by tapping into public sector opportunities.

Whereas a few department heads were supportive of the institution's reallocation efforts, more were critical, even those faring well in the process.

There was a sense that the university was avoiding difficult choices, that departments and faculty simply were being asked to do more of everything as resources declined. One Life Science head reported that his area was under enormous pressure to teach more, as university enrollments had declined and his college was the only one experiencing enrollment growth. He criticized the central administration and the graduate program review process and indicated that he did not anticipate any substantial reallocation to take place, because of the pending departure of the provost. Even so, he stated that despite the Life Sciences' mediocre ranking it was targeted by the strategic plan for enhancement. Heads in two other favored units spoke of the adverse effects the central administration's activities were having even on good departments.

Mineral State U. At Mineral State U a 0.9 percent takeback was identified by department heads as the major, centrally imposed strategy for enhancing campus effectiveness and efficiency. Although the protests at Mineral State U were not as strident nor numerous as those at Lake State U, where the 1 percent takeback occurred, they were fairly common and were sometimes impassioned. The generally more moderate reactions at Mineral State U may have resulted in part from the fact that the takebacks or reallocations were tied to a strategic planning effort, which seemed to have contributed perceived legitimacy to the process. Almost certainly, another factor was a tuition surcharge that increased university revenues and thus reduced the sting of the takeback, at least for some departments. On the other hand, a negative aspect of the takeback, from the Mineral State U heads' perspective, was the perception that the money involved would be used for (central) administrative purposes.

Again, the full range of opinions was evident. The head of a Physical Science department referred to the 0.9 percent as "a big-time sink," and from another Physical Science head, we heard, "Nickel and dime reductions every year are eating us up." More parsimoniously, an Engineering head characterized the entire effort simply as "a failure." Toward the other end of the response continuum, the efforts of central administrators were seen as resulting in "much, much independence" for departments successful in raising new money (from a Physical Science head), and an Engineering head reported that even with the takeback his department had "gotten new faculty lines because of [the unit offering] so many service courses." In another realm, a head in the Life Sciences stated that the university had been successful in moving its focus from agricultural sciences to life sciences, "where the money is." A head from an applied area of the Social Sciences was pleased with the 0.9 percent effort, modestly boasting that his unit had "been on the good side of budget reallocation." Another Social Science head reported that his unit had been "strengthened."

Winter State U. Although there were special state efforts to enhance salaries and the productivity of tenured professors at Winter State U, special university financial management strategies were not evident. A university wide "data bank" had been created, but was not yet being utilized in decisionmaking, according to the department heads. Also, some selective resource allocations had been made to a few departments that had increased enrollments; these appeared to be more *ad hoc* than systematic. The most representative response by heads to our question about university financial initiatives was "nothing significant."

Breadbasket State U. As was true at Timber State U, the *anticipated* deployment of RCB was the most discussed financial management issue among Breadbasket State department heads. Although the euphemism used on campus was "budget reform," most everyone knew that RCB was the real issue. As at Timber State U, anxiety levels were very high, and the usual range of views was found. "RCB substitutes dollars for judgment," lamented a department head in a Math area. "Is RCB a hoax? We don't have control of costs, what with unions and [with] so many [fixed] costs, so it's a joke!" – this from an Engineering department head. And from another Math area head: "Resources will not change with enrollments, so how will enrollment swings be handled?" As strong as these reservations were, there were as many statements of guarded optimism. "RCB is coming and with it increased departmental autonomy," said a Life Science head. From an Engineering head: "Funding may not change but we will get a better handle on what departments really cost." He continued, "Productivity will drive dollars" and "Staff differentiation will occur." And then there were statements of uncertainty and urging caution. "The implications are not yet clear," observed a Life Science head. And from a head in the Social Sciences, "RCB will apply to colleges, not departments, and there will be a 'hold harmless' clause for five years." This head was saying that he thought that many worries were overstated or at least premature.

Two other finance-related issues were mentioned secondarily by Breadbasket State U department heads. One was a planned billion dollar fund-raising campaign; the other was continual declines in state support. In regard to the latter, testimony was offered in support of resource dependency principles when a Social Science department head called the University "un-American" because "Minority shareholders (that is, the state) call the shots!" He was referring to the high degree of state control compared with the relatively small share of university revenue coming from the state.

University/FOS Interactions

The third means by which we explored the effects of institutional policies was through additional econometric analyses. For these analyses, we interacted the institutional variable with the FOS variable. Those results are illustrated in Table 4.5, which shows the number of grants and contracts per faculty member by university and FOS.[28] Our left-out group was the Mathematics area at Center State U, which was relatively very low in terms of grant and contract awards per faculty member (thus all coefficients in the table are positive). The first university by FOS entry in the table is for Engineering at Lake State U. Compared with Center State U's Mathematics area (FOS), Engineering units at Lake State U on average (and as always, all else equal) have 3.457 more grants per faculty member, a value that is significant at the .006 level. Scanning down through the tabled values, we note a high of three significant interactions at Mountain State U and at Mineral State U (.10 level). Our other university of particular interest, Forest State U, shows one significantly different FOS. There are other notable results in Table 4.5. For example, a closer look reveals that the pattern for the Engineering FOS shows significant differences in most cases, a finding that speaks to why it is important to adjust the values in Table 4.3.

For grant and contract amounts per faculty member (Table 4.6), our left-out group and relatively very low group is the Math FOS at Mountain State U. Now, Forest State U, along with Mineral State U, show significant differences: For example, Math and Physical Sciences FOS grant and contract amounts per faculty member at the these universities average $745,000 and $1,056,000 more, respectively, than in the left-out group. Further, of the significant values all but two are in Physical Science or Engineering FOS.

We look at one other set of interactions in this chapter: faculty time use (Table 4.7). Selecting a few examples, we see that compared to the left-out group (Math FOS, Timber State U, based on total time use), total time "worked" by faculty members in the Math FOS at Prairie State U averages almost 431 minutes or in excess of 7 hours more per day.[29] Instruction time within Forest State U's Life Sciences averages 470 minutes more; research time within Forest State's Physical Sciences averages 338 minutes more; and service time within Engineering at Timber State U averages 106 minutes less. A simple scanning of Table 4.7 suggests very strongly that there are very different departmental production functions among the five FOS, at least as indicated by the greatly varying expenditures of faculty time, both in total and by function: teaching, research, and service.

DISCUSSION

Clearly, the effects of shifting revenue patterns among these 11 public research universities vary importantly by level – institutional, production unit, and faculty member. Institutionally, revenue shifts result largely in corresponding shifts in how the universities spend their money; the exception is some modest substitution of what presumably are largely research-related revenues (gifts, grants, and contracts) for instruction although some revenues from the gifts, grants, and contracts category no doubt are in fact intended for instruction (e.g., special education "training grants"). Perhaps the most important implication of the institution-level results is that as states reduce, proportionally, their support of public research universities, the public interest may be jeopardized. The new resource providers likely will insist that their own wants be served. As long as tuition and fees are the major substitutes for state funds, the risk to the public interest should be minor because students' interests preponderantly are consistent with those of the state; for example, the primary concern of both is undergraduate instruction. Always the issue is what the substitute resource providers demand and

Table 4.5: Number of Grants and Contracts – Interaction Effect Model

	coeff.	*t* ratio	*p* value		coeff.	*t* ratio	*p* value
Constant	0.466	0.476	0.634				
PLNRET	-1.312	-3.857	0	MTENG	2.268	1.993	0.047
FULLPROF	0.13	0.493	0.623	MTLS	3.934	3.404	0.001
ASSOCPRF	-0.125	-0.418	0.676	MTMATH	0.455	0.352	0.725
LKENG	3.457	2.76	0.006	MTPHS	2.134	1.843	0.066
LKLS	2.514	2.238	0.026	MTOTH	0.378	0.327	0.744
LKMATH	0.781	0.674	0.501	MNENG	2.343	2.086	0.038
LKPHS	1.406	1.249	0.212	MNLS	2	1.751	0.081
LKOTH	0.343	0.284	0.777	MNMATH	1.072	0.86	0.39
BBENG	3.083	2.768	0.006	MNPHS	3.358	2.902	0.004
BBLS	0.642	0.47	0.638	MNOTH	1.149	0.947	0.344
BBMATH	0.78	0.673	0.501	CTLS	0.577	0.489	0.625
BBPHS	2.163	1.899	0.058	CTPHS	0.799	0.663	0.508
BBOTH	0.011	0.009	0.993	CTOTH	0.5	0.368	0.713
TBENG	2.561	1.882	0.061	WTENG	1.328	1.179	0.239
TBLS	2.404	1.763	0.079	WTLS	1.39	1.236	0.217
TBMATH	0.382	0.317	0.751	WTMATH	0.194	0.15	0.881
TBPHS	2.795	2.366	0.019	WTPHS	2.294	2.016	0.045
PRENG	1.859	1.578	0.116	WTOTH	0.032	0.024	0.981
PRLS	2.224	2.001	0.046	ETENG	3.086	2.71	0.007
PRMATH	2.132	1.652	0.099	ETLS	0.948	0.817	0.415
PRPHS	0.613	0.493	0.622	ETMATH	1.178	0.948	0.344
PROTH	0.764	0.632	0.528	ETOTH	0.398	0.337	0.736
FRLS	2.345	1.886	0.06	PKENG	1.906	1.391	0.165
FRMATH	1.074	0.862	0.389	PKLS	2.094	1.731	0.084
FRPHS	1.583	1.311	0.191	PKMATH	1.25	0.919	0.359
FROTH	0.001	0.001	1	PKPHS	2.636	2.359	0.019
N	401			PKOTH	0.382	0.335	0.738
R2	0.262						

Table 4.6: Grants and Contracts Amount – Interaction Effect Model

	coeff.	t ratio	p value		coeff.	t ratio	p value
Constant	235.993	1.099	0.273				
PLNRET	-354.719	-2.728	0.007	MTOTH	138.904	0.338	0.736
FULLPROF	225.224	2.236	0.026	MNENG	197.539	0.496	0.62
ASSOCPRF	36.767	0.322	0.747	MNLS	723.106	1.779	0.076
LKENG	936.948	2.077	0.039	MNMATH	286.162	0.638	0.524
LKLS	360.973	0.906	0.365	MNPHS	996.53	2.414	0.016
LKMATH	158.275	0.384	0.702	MNOTH	447.154	0.99	0.323
LKPHS	260.485	0.653	0.514	CTLS	-32.856	-0.078	0.938
LKOTH	21.618	0.05	0.96	CTMATH	520.729	1.053	0.293
BBENG	578.573	1.47	0.143	CTPHS	709.789	1.642	0.101
BBLS	222.523	0.447	0.655	CTOTH	61.979	0.125	0.9
BBMATH	276.732	0.672	0.502	WTENG	1241.41	3.098	0.002
BBPHS	429.081	1.077	0.282	WTLS	239.804	0.601	0.548
BBOTH	97.33	0.217	0.828	WTMATH	361.08	0.772	0.441
TBENG	204.865	0.414	0.679	WTPHS	577.967	1.429	0.154
TBLS	407.809	0.825	0.41	WTOTH	71.785	0.145	0.885
TBMATH	79.436	0.184	0.854	ETENG	528.451	1.308	0.192
TBPHS	556.478	1.322	0.187	ETLS	138.389	0.335	0.738
PRENG	738.201	1.758	0.08	ETMATH	53.497	0.119	0.905
PRLS	281.679	0.716	0.474	ETPHS	508.523	1.235	0.218
PRMATH	257.536	0.552	0.581	ETOTH	40.166	0.096	0.924
PRPHS	71.551	0.161	0.873	PKENG	823.088	1.648	0.1
PROTH	318.293	0.733	0.464	PKLS	509.968	1.172	0.242
FRLS	506.33	1.129	0.26	PKMATH	873.229	1.766	0.078
FRMATH	744.613	1.662	0.097	PKPHS	328.526	0.836	0.404
FRPHS	1056.37	2.45	0.015	PKOTH	394.056	0.966	0.335

Table 4.6: Grants and Contracts Amount – Interaction Effect Model (Continued)

	coeff.	t ratio	p value
FROTH	16.103	1.099	0.273
MTENG	497.921	-2.728	0.007
MTLS	252.238	2.236	0.026
MTPHS	287.771	0.322	0.747
N	397	2.077	0.039
R2	0.152	0.906	0.365

Note: For grant and contract amounts per faculty member (Table 4.6), our left-out group is the Math FOS at Mountain State U. Now, Forest State U, along with Mineral State U, show significant differences: for example, Math and Physical Sciences FOS grant and contract amounts per faculty member at the these universities average $745,000 and $1,056,000 more, respectively, than in the left-out group. Further, of all significant values all but two are in Physical Science or Engineering FOS.

Table 4.7: Faculty Time Use – Interaction Effect Model

	Instruction			Research			Service			Total		
	coeff.	t ratio	p value	coeff.	t ratio	p value	coeff.	t ratio	p value	coeff.	t ratio	p value
Constant	218.87	2.75	0.01	34.71	0.38	0.7	67.46	1.1	0.27	321.04	3.19	0
STEVCTHI	16.77	0.65	0.52	-57.5	-1.96	0.05	4.95	0.25	0.8	-35.78	-1.09	0.27
STEVCTMD	23	0.95	0.34	-35.87	-1.31	0.19	-1.41	-0.08	0.94	-14.27	-0.47	0.64
RSTCHGRD	16.17	0.62	0.53	40.34	1.37	0.17	-17.45	-0.88	0.38	39.07	1.19	0.23
RSTCHBTH	35.49	1.24	0.22	46.65	1.44	0.15	-36.19	-1.65	0.1	45.95	1.27	0.2
GCEXTYES	-76.52	-3.32	0	64.1	2.45	0.01	48.22	2.73	0.01	35.8	1.23	0.22
PLNRET	-42.28	-1.27	0.2	-105.19	-2.79	0.01	-13.83	-0.54	0.59	-161.3	-3.83	0
WEEK	-6.41	-0.21	0.84	22.06	0.63	0.53	-8.59	-0.36	0.72	7.06	0.18	0.86
FULLPROF	-37.08	-1.46	0.14	29.91	1.04	0.3	38.46	1.98	0.05	31.29	0.98	0.33
ASSOCPRF	4.83	0.17	0.87	-22.89	-0.69	0.49	12.63	0.57	0.57	-5.43	-0.15	0.88
LKENG	204.48	1.91	0.06	13.06	0.11	0.91	81.05	0.99	0.32	298.59	2.21	0.03
LKLS	34.6	0.37	0.71	50.08	0.48	0.63	60.8	0.85	0.39	145.47	1.24	0.22
LKMATH	69.65	0.73	0.47	188.06	1.73	0.08	19.41	0.26	0.79	277.12	2.29	0.02
LKPHS	67.83	0.73	0.46	108.19	1.03	0.3	62.82	0.88	0.38	238.84	2.04	0.04
LKOTH	38.11	0.37	0.71	259.66	2.25	0.03	17.75	0.23	0.82	315.52	2.45	0.01
BBENG	115.87	1.27	0.2	197.08	1.9	0.06	38.7	0.55	0.58	351.65	3.05	0
BBLS	-84.59	-0.72	0.47	270.23	2.03	0.04	186.94	2.08	0.04	372.58	2.51	0.01
BBMATH	64.42	0.66	0.51	52.57	0.48	0.63	20.11	0.27	0.79	137.1	1.12	0.27
BBPHS	194.88	2.1	0.04	106.51	1.01	0.31	60.51	0.85	0.4	361.9	3.09	0
BBOTH	9.35	0.09	0.93	113.43	0.94	0.35	14.99	0.18	0.85	137.77	1.03	0.3
TBENG	154.06	1.3	0.19	77.69	0.58	0.56	-106.48	-1.17	0.24	125.27	0.84	0.4
TBLS	216.02	1.83	0.07	125.29	0.94	0.35	-90.95	-1.01	0.31	250.36	1.68	0.09
TBPHS	134.8	1.36	0.18	59.13	0.52	0.6	-55.46	-0.73	0.47	138.48	1.1	0.27
PRENG	113.07	1.16	0.25	24.67	0.22	0.82	-8.91	-0.12	0.91	128.83	1.04	0.3
PRLS	189.11	2.07	0.04	95.41	0.92	0.36	13.58	0.19	0.85	298.1	2.58	0.01
PRMATH	57.38	0.49	0.62	254.28	1.92	0.06	119.33	1.33	0.18	430.99	2.92	0
PRPHS	135.47	1.28	0.2	7.55	0.06	0.95	-33.66	-0.41	0.68	109.37	0.81	0.42

Table 4.7: Faculty Time Use – Interaction Effect Model (Continued)

	Instruction			Research			Service			Total		
	coeff.	t ratio	p value	coeff.	t ratio	p value	coeff.	t ratio	p value	coeff.	t ratio	p value
PROTH	65.86	0.64	0.52	238.74	2.06	0.04	46.73	0.6	0.55	351.33	2.72	0.01
FRLS	469.92	4.46	0	24.95	0.21	0.83	-43.19	-0.53	0.59	451.69	3.39	0
FRMATH	145.52	1.39	0.17	131.67	1.1	0.27	3.33	0.04	0.97	280.52	2.11	0.04
FRPHS	175.63	1.73	0.08	338.1	2.94	0	47.96	0.62	0.54	561.69	4.37	0
FROTH	137.65	1.39	0.17	144.47	1.29	0.2	5.99	0.08	0.94	288.1	2.3	0.02
MTENG	212.37	2.25	0.02	31.6	0.3	0.77	42.11	0.58	0.56	286.08	2.4	0.02
MTLS	35.82	0.37	0.71	140.81	1.28	0.2	51.08	0.69	0.49	227.71	1.86	0.06
MTMATH	54.99	0.5	0.62	211.85	1.7	0.09	-2.99	-0.04	0.97	263.85	1.9	0.06
MTPHS	64.41	0.67	0.51	218.17	1.99	0.05	-37.82	-0.51	0.61	244.76	2	0.05
MTOTH	94.77	0.98	0.33	116.39	1.07	0.29	50.24	0.68	0.5	261.4	2.14	0.03
MNENG	175.93	1.91	0.06	83.69	0.8	0.42	105.59	1.49	0.14	365.2	3.13	0
MNLS	45.46	0.48	0.63	24.06	0.22	0.82	169.78	2.32	0.02	239.3	1.99	0.05
MNMATH	235.12	2.22	0.03	145.31	1.21	0.23	-47.18	-0.58	0.56	333.25	2.49	0.01
MNPHS	51.86	0.54	0.59	158.08	1.44	0.15	10.6	0.14	0.89	220.54	1.81	0.07
MNOTH	142.44	1.4	0.16	98.17	0.85	0.4	47.05	0.6	0.55	287.66	2.23	0.03
CTLS	222.95	2.26	0.02	79.49	0.71	0.48	-37.13	-0.49	0.62	265.32	2.13	0.03
CTMATH	88.91	0.69	0.49	81.18	0.55	0.58	91.11	0.92	0.36	261.2	1.59	0.11
CTPHS	57.46	0.56	0.57	67.46	0.58	0.56	1.72	0.02	0.98	126.64	0.98	0.33
CTOTH	65.46	0.56	0.58	168.31	1.27	0.21	-36.04	-0.4	0.69	197.74	1.33	0.18
WTENG	142.65	1.54	0.12	177.96	1.69	0.09	-11.56	-0.16	0.87	309.05	2.64	0.01
WTLS	78.67	0.85	0.39	82.54	0.79	0.43	0.42	0.01	1	161.64	1.38	0.17
WTMATH	34.19	0.31	0.76	186.82	1.49	0.14	-54.73	-0.65	0.52	166.28	1.19	0.23
WTPHS	78.22	0.81	0.42	253.5	2.33	0.02	60.98	0.83	0.41	392.7	3.23	0
WTOTH	213.09	1.82	0.07	77.67	0.58	0.56	-17.75	-0.2	0.84	273	1.84	0.07
ETENG	265.04	2.74	0.01	125.26	1.14	0.25	-15.14	-0.2	0.84	375.16	3.06	0
ETLS	-5.67	-0.06	0.95	320.41	2.83	0	-12.94	-0.17	0.87	301.8	2.39	0.02

Table 4.7: Faculty Time Use – Interaction Effect Model (Continued)

	Instruction			Research			Service			Total		
	coeff.	t ratio	p value	coeff.	t ratio	p value	coeff.	t ratio	p value	coeff.	t ratio	p value
ETMATH	113.03	1.07	0.28	123.26	1.03	0.3	-12.46	-0.15	0.88	223.83	1.68	0.09
ETPHS	29.76	0.31	0.76	118.26	1.09	0.28	66.47	0.9	0.37	214.49	1.77	0.08
ETOTH	-65.77	-0.66	0.51	208.72	1.85	0.06	28.22	0.37	0.71	171.17	1.36	0.17
PKENG	180.27	1.52	0.13	248.84	1.85	0.06	-19.65	-0.22	0.83	409.46	2.73	0.01
PKLS	113.18	1.11	0.27	189.47	1.64	0.1	17.44	0.22	0.82	320.09	2.48	0.01
PKMATH	-43.23	-0.37	0.71	52.12	0.39	0.7	-5.24	-0.06	0.95	3.64	0.02	0.98
PKPHS	96.03	1.06	0.29	211.18	2.05	0.04	-42.45	-0.61	0.54	264.76	2.3	0.02
PKOTH	-41.87	-0.44	0.66	40.08	0.37	0.71	8.13	0.11	0.91	6.34	0.05	0.96
N	397			397			397			397		
R2	0.242			0.211			0.184			0.256		

Note: We looked at one other set of interactions in this chapter: faculty time use. Selecting a few examples, we see that compared to the left-out group (Math FOS, Timber State U, based on total time use), total time "worked" by faculty members in the Math FOS at Prairie State U averages almost 431 minutes or in excess of 7 hours more per day.[29] Instruction time within Forest State U's Life Sciences averages 470 minutes more; research time within Forest State's Physical Sciences averages 338 minutes more; and service time within Engineering at Timber State U averages 106 minutes less. A simple scanning of Table 4.7 suggests very strongly that there are very different departmental production functions among the five FOS, at least as indicated by the greatly varying expenditures of faculty time, both in total and by function: teaching, research, and service.

whether those demands are compatible with the public interest.

Whereas the focus of our analyses is income from grants and contracts in relation to patterns of university expenditures, there are many other revenue categories and many more subcategories of revenues and expenditures that bear examination. For example, what do corporate resource providers demand for their funding, in contrast with what public agencies demand? What university priorities are affected by the sales and services the universities offer in the marketplace? What do universities "give" for what they "get" in the way of contributions to endowments? Yes, resource dependency effects are evident at the institutional level. What are the consequences?

Resource dependency relationships also are evident at the individual faculty member level, where we observe shifts in how faculty allocate their time as they receive grants and contracts, even when we control for quality of outputs. True, such faculty members work more hours, but how do these shifts affect departmental dynamics and the universities and their various clientele in the long run? For example, do faculty members who take on these tasks and thus work extra hours in the short run produce less in later years? Do they "burn out"? Do they retire early? Are they more likely than others to shift careers, later on? Or do they maintain a record of high productivity throughout their working years? In another vein, are the resources garnered by these individuals so important to the university that inordinate power over the conduct of university affairs is gained?

What was most interesting to us as we reviewed our findings was how substantial institutional and individual effects did not necessarily or directly translate into resource dependency behavior of the sort that we expected at the production unit – the department level. In retrospect this result should not have surprised us, but it did. Whereas the effects at the other two levels were noted, the departments turned out to be the great mediators of the demands of external resource providers that were observed at the institutional and faculty member levels. The explanation now seems quite simple. It is in the departments that the final work of the university takes place, where teaching, research, and service occur. Regardless of all the financial and related turmoil surrounding and within them, the departments have several jobs to do. First and foremost, they must teach their courses and serve their students. They may have to reconfigure their resources, but they get this job done. It is their most basic work and they view it as such. This work completed, they turn their attention to other demands, such as those set by the government agencies that offer the research grants and by the corporations that tender the contracts. Is it any wonder that incentives and disincentives have only modest effects? Very likely, *the* question is how administrators can penetrate the departmental structure in order to be successful in changing their universities.

What goes on within these departments as they deal with all the competing interests – the need to increase instructional productivity, publish more, and generate more funds while allowing faculty flexibility in their workloads? How do they do it? One of the basic answers is that they are very creative in how they deploy their resources. They move funds among various expenditure categories as resource providers shift: they alter their production functions. For example, they differentiate the course loads of their faculty, increasing the loads of some, substituting teaching assistant, part-time lecturer, clinical faculty, and technician labor for the labor of others, often while increasing instructional outputs. At what cost are these many adjustments made? Does the increasing utilization of other than regular faculty members affect the departments' quality of instruction, student advising, departmental and university service work? Significantly, what are the effects of the increasing stratification of academic labor? There are many such possible consequences to consider and we have barely scratched the surface.

What of the theme of this book? Do incentives matter? Our conclusion is that some incentive systems initiated at the central university level affect departments importantly, even severely, whereas others do not matter very much in terms of overall university operations. In most cases centrally imposed initiatives do not appear to influence *collectively* faculty entrepreneurial research activity, but there is evidence that institutions use incentives and disincentives effectively to leverage departments in *instructional* areas. We also found some internal university stratification between the professional schools versus the arts and sciences as a result of this leveraging. This is a result that many will not view favorably.

Our evidence on these issues was not always consistent. Department head perceptions were not always born out by the objective data. For example, whereas Forest State University heads reported very little faculty research entrepreneurism within their units, both on unadjusted and adjusted bases Forest State U faculty produced more grant and contract revenues per faculty member than did any of the remaining ten institutions. This was the state where university budget reductions had been most severe. Should we conclude that if one wants to increase nonstate funding, the most effective strategy is to reduce state funding dramatically? Almost certainly, this is a conclusion with which no department head would agree. Clearly there was substantial evidence of *individual* entrepreneurial activity; it was the *corporate* activity that was lacking.

One matter on which there was almost universal department head agreement was that the imposed incentives were burdensome in their requirements. According to heads, the primary effect of most special incentive approaches – whether to "claw back" a portion of resources and reallocate them, develop market niches, or institute some other strategy – was to increase their administrative workloads through writing internal university proposals and maintaining the many required records.

Another set of observations regards differences in how the effects of resource shifts and incentives play out among the five FOS and within individual departments. Among the FOS, only the Life Sciences stand out as different from the other fields. Life Science faculty are more engaged entrepreneurially, are more "academically capitalistic" in grant and contract activity, even as their departments routinely accommodate more students, both in service courses and as majors. One can sense the relative dynamism of Life Science departments simply by spending time in them. Virtually everyone – faculty, department heads, students – exhibit an attitude, an outlook, that is distinctly different from that in other FOS. "Business as usual" is anything but the theme within the Life Sciences. The host of commercial firms engaged in agriculture, in plant and animal science, in seed production, development of fertilizers and animal feed, to name a few, offer many prospects for Life Science faculty and staff.

In fact, it was the Life Sciences that made us aware that it was usually opportunity, not resource deprivation, that drove most entrepreneurial behavior in these 11 universities. We had reasoned from our theory that revenue losses would cause departments and their faculty members to behave entrepreneurially in order to make up for lost funds. Rather, with the exception of one university, we concluded that the revenue shortfalls experienced were insufficient to generate the hypothesized behaviors: for the most part, academic units were not destabilized by revenue losses. Entrepreneurism existed primarily where grant and contract opportunities were greatest.

Of course, there is more than mere opportunity in the Life Sciences. There exists also a *culture*, a tradition of entrepreneurism, for example in agriculture, one that can be traced to the origins of the land-grant movement more than a century ago, to agriculture extension and cooperative research. Many agriculture staff work in programs that are partially or totally funded by the federal and state governments, and often those staff must regularly compete for continued government funding. Equally important for the Life Sciences are the opportunities that abound in the biotechnology area. With the possible exception of information technology, no sector of higher education currently is more dynamic than this area and nowhere are opportunities greater.

Another conclusion that we reached from our site visits, a conclusion most strongly affirmed in the Life Sciences, was that most research entrepreneurism emanated from individual faculty members. We saw very little evidence of entrepreneurism being collectively initiated or strategically guided. Whereas many grants and contracts involved more than one individual, one principal investigator, these collaborations were *ad hoc* rather than planned or organized at the unit level. Most were initiated by a single individual, and most grants and contracts overall were the work of a single individual. This result raises important questions. Can such faculty be guided strategically? Should they be? Should incentives be targeted primarily on individuals, rather than departments?

Outside of the Life Sciences, there exist a scattering of departments whose highly entrepreneurial character appears to result from less systematic factors. Most preponderantly these were units that for various reasons perceived that they were somewhat "at risk." They were units that typically were not at the core of the university mission; they viewed themselves as being somewhat marginal to the mission and thus potentially expendable. In contrast to core departments, such as English, mathematics, physics, which serve many fields, they were often units in areas that prepared relatively small numbers of low-status professionals. Probably the best example was in certain areas of education. Like Forest State U in general, these units perceived that they had little choice but to raise external revenues if they were to survive, if not prosper. Of course, there also existed units that were unusually entrepreneurial for reasons that were largely unsystematic.

Sometimes an unusual leader was in place; more often an individual faculty member was responsible for most entrepreneurial achievements in the unit.

CONCLUSION

It is clear that our study leaves much to be learned about incentive-based funding systems in higher education, in part because most of the institutions we studied were early in the process of implementing financial mechanisms. Theoretically, if the goal is to increase effectiveness and efficiency, the imposition of market mechanisms in various forms promises a good deal, other considerations notwithstanding. Our results suggest, however, that unintegrated incentive strategies may not have much positive effect; in fact, the burdens of such approaches may outweigh the benefits, in particular if the frustrations of department heads and faculty are considered. Further, such simple problems as administrative turnover or poor internal public relations can doom the efforts.

Although we found some evidence of the power of RCM approaches to affect the internal workings of academic departments, the evidence was sporadic and many of the effects were viewed as less than positive. If there are major gains to be realized from RCM, the "costs" are indeed unclear. If we are to accept the perceptions of the department heads of our 11 universities as the final word, the verdict is clearly negative.

Our interest in RCM was rooted in resource dependency theory and in "academic capitalism." We began our research expecting to find that incentive structures were systematically and effectively moving public universities towards the generation of more and more of their own revenues through a conscious, strategic, entrepreneurial effort. What we found instead was a set of incentive structures that often were of little apparent effect, other than to generate a good deal of internal hostility. In the cases where RCM-type initiatives were in evidence, they were not institutionally inspired in response to relative declines in state support; rather, they were primarily instruments used by the state to control certain university behaviors, specifically to increase institutional instructional accountability and productivity. It was as though the state sensed it was losing control of its public universities as it reduced its support share and thus initiated actions to protect its interests.

NOTES

1. NSF Grant Number 9628325. The U.S. government has certain rights in this material. Any opinions, findings, and conclusions or recommendations expressed in this material are those of the authors and do not necessarily reflect the views of the National Science Foundation.

2. The five fields of science, Life Sciences, Physical Sciences, Mathematics, Engineering, and Social Sciences, are based upon National Science Foundation taxonomies.

3. Higher Education General Information Surveys and its sequel, IPEDS.

4. Similarly, Stocum and Rooney (1997) report that even when resource consequences are experienced at the college level, systematic departmental effects do not necessarily follow.

5. Ward utilized the national departmental data base developed by the University of Delaware under a grant from the Fund for the Improvement of Postsecondary Education (U.S. Department of Education), and D'Sylva employed the *Data Exchange* files of the Association of American Universities (AAU).

6. D'Sylva uses the rates of return term loosely. Essentially, he simply related departmental revenue variations to variations in departmental outputs of teaching, research, and service. As we discuss in some detail elsewhere (Leslie, Rhoades, and Oaxaca, 1999), D'Sylva makes the dangerous assumption that all departmental resource allocation decisions are made within the department. This and other of his assumptions suggest the need for caution in interpreting his results. In our discussion of his work herein, we utilize the more general term "return," which may prevent misunderstandings among readers knowledgeable about "rate of return studies."

7. The Association of American Universities, which consists of the leading research universities in the United States.

8. Of the 11, one was selected because it had experienced substantial declines in state support, another because of special financial management strategies it employed, and the remaining 9 for sample balance, especially geography. In general we selected institutions that had reported data to the American Association of Universities Data Exchange most consistently. Within each university, within each of five FOS (Engineering, Physical Sciences, Life Sciences, Mathematics, and Social Sciences) three departments were drawn randomly. Within each department three faculty members were drawn randomly, yielding samples of approximately 165 departments and department heads and 660 faculty members, or 60 interviews per university. Whereas inferences to FOS are generally justified, inferences to individual department types (e.g., chemistry, sociology) are not defensible.

9. Multinomial logit results are reported *relative to* a specified, left-out reference group.

10. In the interviews we used the term substantial to give the interviewees some sense of the magnitude of effects that were of interest to us. In those cases in which we were asked what was meant by the term, we asked the interviewee to utilize his/her own definition.

11. Because we guaranteed anonymity to respondents, in the discussion and tables we use pseudonyms for the 11 universities.

12. Primarily ordinary least squares, fixed effects, multinomial logit, binomial logit, and ordered logit models were used, as appropriate to the conditions of the particular analysis.

13. We use the term "state support" here in the conventional sense that will be familiar to university faculty and staff: in departmental accounts state support almost always is a combination of state-provided and tuition revenues.

14. All of our inferential results meet these conditions.

15. Using an ordered logit model.

16. At the sample mean, a 10 percent increase in the probability that a department selected randomly was in the Engineering cluster increased the probability of lowered undergraduate teaching loads by 0.6 percent, increased the probability of having no change in undergraduate teaching loads by 2.5 percent, and lowered the probability of increased undergraduate teaching loads by 3.2 percent.

17. In TBA the respondent reports chronologically on their experiences of the previous day. Because respondents are not aware of the research purposes and because interviewees who misrepresent their activities soon find themselves in a web of inconsistencies, with careful interviewer questioning valid data are obtained. Additional information about TBA is contained in Leslie, Oaxaca, and Rhoades (1999).

18. For example, faculty members often meet with their graduate students to talk over funded research. In this case the faculty member is involved both in performing research and in teaching graduate students.

19. The only two statistically significant time-use variables were the interactions of research time with published articles and with chapters in books. Both of these effects were positive, indicating that an additional article or chapter published increased the positive effect of research time on the professor's salary. Interestingly, incremental time spent on instruction had a negative (though not statistically significant) effect on salary.

20. All analyses reported in this chapter controlled for several explanatory variables. The faculty analyses controlled for personal, disciplinary, and institutional characteristics: departmental field, faculty rank, perceived importance of student teaching evaluations, incorporation of one's research into teaching, external grant and contract funding, planned retirement within five years, interviews covering weekend academic activity, and institutional affiliation.

21. All analyses also control for quality of outputs.

22. Additional, less relevant findings are that assistant professors teach more than full professors and that planning to retire within five years has a strong negative effect on time devoted to research.

23. Institutional effects were assessed using a fixed-effects model although we estimated binary logit models with indicator variables for institutions because of some well-known econometric problems with the consistency of maximum likelihood estimation of fixed-effects logit models. (Consistent estimation of such models can be quite complicated.) As an alternative, we estimated linear probability models with heteroscedastic consistent variance/covariance matrices, which yielded results that were very similar to those obtained from conventional maximum likelihood estimation of the binary logit models. For ease of presentation, here we discuss only the results from the conventionally estimated logit models. In some instances, the marginal effects associated with the institutional indicators could not be reliably estimated. In these cases we report the results based on the estimated logit model without institutional controls.

24. A 10 percent increase in the probability of randomly selecting a department from a university with increased power residing in the central administration was estimated to decrease the probability of experiencing a reduction in overall teaching load by 0.4 percent and to increase the probability of an increase in such teaching loads by 1.7 percent.

25. Sample size was 11 institutions. When particular institutional policies were considered as the "treatment" variable, the sample size was even less, sometimes only one, and we certainly could not claim to have conducted the kind of case studies that might support generalizations.

26. Sometimes referred to as RCB (responsibility center budgeting). In actual practice, there are very few if any total RCB/RCM programs in existence; most only partially permit the keeping of revenues and only partially require units to meet all of their own costs.

27. For explanation of how the expected values were calculated, see the first note in Table 4.4.

28. The lack of significance for faculty rank is probably explained by the fact that many beginning assistant professors receive small, college- and university-level

internal grants. When *amounts* of grants are considered, the rank variable becomes significant.

29. When it is recalled that university by FOS samples are at most three faculty members and at least one, this value becomes plausible.

REFERENCES

D'Sylva, Ashley P. 1998. *Examining resource allocation within U.S. public research I universities: An income production function approach.* Ph.D. Dissertation. Tucson: University of Arizona.

Hasbrouck, Norma S. 1997. *Implications of the changing funding base of public universities.* Ph.D. Dissertation. Tucson: University of Arizona.

Leslie, Larry L., Gary Rhoades, and Ronald L. Oaxaca. 1999. *Effects of changing revenue patterns on public research universities.* University of Houston Law Center, the Institute for Higher Education Law & Governance, IHELG Monograph: 99-100.

Pfeffer, Jeffrey, and Gerald R. Salancik. 1978. *The external control of organizations: A resource dependence perspective.* New York: Harper and Row.

Slaughter, Sheila, and Larry L. Leslie. 1997. *Academic capitalism: Politics, policies, and the entrepreneurial university.* Baltimore: Johns Hopkins University Press.

Stocum, David, and Patrick Rooney. 1997. Responding to resource constraints: A departmentally based system of responsibility center management. *Change* 29 (5): 51-57.

Ward, Gary T. 1997. *The effects of separately budgeted research expenditures on faculty instructional productivity in undergraduate education.* Ph.D. Dissertation. Tucson: University of Arizona.

CHAPTER **5**

RESPONSIBILITY CENTER BUDGETING AND MANAGEMENT AT INDIANA UNIVERSITY

Kenneth R. R. Gros Louis

Maynard Thompson

The Bloomington campus of Indiana University, after three years of planning, initiated i ts v ersion o f r esponsibility-centered m anagement (RCM) i n 1 990, t he second[1] public institution of higher education to adopt this budgeting mechanism, although as most know, it was in use for years at a few private institutions. Our plan is to sketch the history of RCM in Bloomington from its inception through two reviews in 1995-1996 and 1999-2000. Thus, we will describe:

- its positive features as these were perceived initially;
- the major elements of RCM in Bloomington, recognizing that there are other ways to implement this budgeting approach;
- the chief beneficiaries of RCM;
- the potential problems inherent in the mechanism and how these might be countered;
- and finally, the findings of two five-year reviews and their recommendations.

The reviews of RCM (Ruesink and Thompson, 1996; Theobald and Thompson, 2000) illustrate an important aspect of the implementation at Indiana University Bloomington: the involvement of faculty in the design, review, and revision of the system. It has been customary for Bloomington faculty to play an important role in determining the policies and administrative structures within which the campus, the College of Arts and Sciences (the largest unit on campus), and the schools function. The creation of an RCM system was no exception, and faculty played significant roles in the design of the original system through membership on the committees charged with developing the basic policies. According to the timeline developed in 1987-1988, the Bloomington campus was scheduled to implement its version of RCM in July 1989. However, in late 1988 the campus administration decided to defer implementation a year to better understand the implications of various alternatives and to solidify support in the faculty and among the deans. To help in this task, during the 1989-1990 year, the administration established three committees consisting primarily of faculty and chaired by faculty, to review areas that seemed especially complex and make recommendations for handling them. By focusing on a single set of issues in a period of a few months, each committee prepared a helpful report and recommendations, and, in each case, the recommendations were incorporated in the final design. Faculty participation has continued, and the fact that the review committees consisted primarily of faculty has helped give the reviews high credibility among individual faculty members and other faculty groups, including College and school policy and advisory committees, and the Bloomington Faculty Council.

ATTRIBUTES OF RCM

RCM, like all budgeting mechanisms, does not by itself create resources – that's obvious enough. It does, however, create an environment that stimulates resource growth and in which efficient resource use is rewarded. The attributes of this environment, that is, the positive features of RCM, include the following:

1. It offers incentives for schools and departments to strive for excellence in teaching, research, and service.
2. It provides information and incentives that can lead to significant efficiencies and streamlinings, even major restructuring.
3. It decentralizes responsibility and involves more faculty in budget and planning decisions.
4. It makes clear and open which schools are subsidized and to what extent (clearly, this information can cut two ways).
5. It encourages multi-year planning more fully than other budget mechanisms.

There is no one model for how to introduce or implement RCM – the key is giving greater responsibility at the local, that is, the school, and even the department, level. Bloomington chose three key elements:

1. All income generated is retained by the instructional units to meet expenses: all tuition income, indirect cost income, fees collected for services, executive and continuing education, and so on. This was *our* choice – the campus could have retained a portion of fee income, for example.
2. The noninstructional units are supported by assessments charged to the instructional units according to various algorithms, differing for each noninstructional unit. Examples: if a school has 10 percent of the graduate

students on campus, it is assessed 10 percent of the costs of operating the Graduate School; if a school generates 20 percent of the grants and contracts, it is assessed 20 percent of the costs of the research office.

3. A percentage of the incremental state appropriation is retained by the campus to support "common good" needs and to encourage campus-level projects and priorities. Again, this was *our* choice – other institutions implementing a version of RCM might decide differently. (Unfortunately, from 1990 to 1994, Indiana received *no* incremental state appropriation! This led to one of the major recommendations in the 1995-1996 review.)

BENEFICIARIES OF RCM

Who seemed to be the major beneficiaries of RCM in Bloomington? In several ways, the students were. Some observations:

The problem of course unavailability almost disappeared because units had incentives to add additional sections when courses filled, or to close sections with low enrollment and move resources to areas of greater need. Significant curricular innovations occurred. The School of Music, for example, indicated for years that it could not meet the demands of its majors and also offer general education courses in music appreciation. That attitude changed and the school began to offer a number of high quality courses for students across the campus. Such points are supported by resource allocations. In 1990-1991, as a percentage of the operating budget, instruction in Bloomington was 53 percent; in 1994-1995, in a time of alleged "administrative bloat," the percentage rose to 56.5 percent. Students benefited further because there were incentives for deans or unit heads to put the very best teachers into lower level courses to attract not only numbers of majors, but also the very best students as majors. Students also benefited because student services improved. Why? Units providing the services were monitored by the academic deans who paid their bills and who expected their students to be well served. An internal accountability emerged that existed previously only between the service units and the campus administration; under RCM, the relationship also involved the deans of all the degree-granting schools and their elected faculty policy committees. Senior satisfaction surveys revealed dramatic results: students evaluating services at the Student Health Center as "excellent" or "good" increased from 64 percent to 83 percent; for the Office of Student Financial Assistance from 51 percent to 70 percent. Such improvements, of course, may have taken place without RCM, but RCM surely was a contributing factor.

Faculty had much greater participation in budgetary and planning decisions. Prior to RCM, a campus-wide budgetary affairs committee made budget recommendations on distribution of funds to the campus administration. Under RCM, each school had its own budgetary advisory committee that made recommendations on the use of income to each of the deans. The campus might not have lived through the four years of decreased or steady state appropriations without RCM. Under the previous budgetary mechanism, the burden of making ends meet would have fallen solely on the campus administration, which held *all* the tuition income and *all* the state appropriation. Between 1990 and 1994, however, the need to balance the budget became the obligation of each responsibility center and, in fact, some schools were better off in 1994 than they were in 1990. The active participation of school deans and their policy/advisory committees in the fundamental resource allocation decisions of the College and schools clearly enabled the campus to cope better with these financial constraints. Faculty also benefited because unit heads had incentives to employ faculty expertise as needed and over the course of an individual's career. Thus, faculty who excelled at service roles or in teaching large freshman-level courses became very valuable to a unit and their efforts were rewarded to a greater extent than under more traditional budgeting systems.

Staff benefited because even though greater accountability meant more monitoring or reviewing by the academic deans and their advisory committees, there were also greater rewards possible for units that performed well – rewards in the form of resources (through higher assessments), which led to increased staffing and/or new programs. Deans understood the value of centralized student services and were willing to pay more if those services improved.

The state benefited because students benefited; because research dollars increased dramatically, thus creating jobs, enhancing the reputation of the campus, and supporting more faculty and students. The state also benefited because of increased services – whether they were charged for or not. If charged, then the incentive was there to make the service as good as possible; if not charged, the incentive remained to generate goodwill, which could later be translated into greater results in fundraising and/or legislative appropriations. Finally, the state benefited because of the increased efficiency and productivity that resulted from RCM – each school really had incentives to be as efficient and productive as possible, in all areas of its activities.

POTENTIAL PROBLEMS OF RCM

From its inception, we were aware of the potential problems of RCM, either because we sensed them elsewhere, or because they were identified during our three years of planning. Our view is that the greatest risks of RCM might occur when all of the administrators in office at IU Bloomington in 1990 have been replaced and the older values, which governed campus decisionmaking so well for many years, are forgotten, and only the need to generate revenue dominates the discussions of school policy committees and the planning of academic deans. Thus, for example, over time the campus could become a federation of schools that happen to share the same geographic location. Consider the impact on interdisciplinary programs, students changing majors, joint appointments as they affect institutes and centers, etc.

Some are concerned about curricular duplication and overlap, as schools introduce courses that generate additional income. But there have always been grey areas in the curriculum: who should offer statistics? economics? basic computing? composition?

There could be a decline in the view of the "common good" – take, for example, the Library, which schools are assessed to help maintain. Increasingly, schools may become more parochial in their views of what the common good is. The same may occur as faculty committees and/or deans look to common good items and suggest that they be moved to fee for service categories.

Is there a risk of too much decentralization? Schools might pressure the campuses to distribute to the schools all fellowship and equipment monies, all funds for faculty development, all summer fellowships, and so on. The risk, if it is one, is that there will no longer be any monitoring of the quality of what is done with these resources as the financial bottom line dominates. Similarly, too much decentralization may limit the campus' role as disciplines evolve in different schools. What is optimum for one school may not lead to the best outcome for the campus as a whole.

Faculty and deans may link their assessments too specifically to the services received (like school taxes/property taxes). The Law School, for example, when assessed some percentage for the Office of Student Financial Assistance, might contend that its financial assistance is given primarily by the school itself and therefore it should not be charged for the existence of the campus-level service.

There could be constant bickering over the appropriate level of state appropriation or, in another form of RCM, over the distribution of resident vs. nonresident fee income. Obviously, few deans will argue that their appropriation is too large and most will contend that it is too small. These views will get translated to faculty advisory committees and in turn to the campus-wide budgetary affairs committee.

Some fear the loss of campus-wide potential for innovative new programs, even the development of new schools and departments. If the system gets to the point where too few resources are available at the campus level, then clearly the opportunities for new initiatives seen from a perspective that is broader than the school level will decline.

An odd concern, perhaps: would deans hoard funds to guard against drops in enrollment or indirect cost income? Reserves are necessary up to a point, of course, but it is not good for a public institution of higher education to keep funds out of circulation. After all, current accounts are intended for current students and related university services.

In short, these major potential problems of RCM could lead to a significant loss in the collegiality of the campus. Some might argue – indeed some have argued – that such collegiality long ago disappeared at all large institutions and that faculty are as linked, if not more linked, to their national disciplinary communities than they are to the local community. Still, this seems a legitimate issue of concern over time.

AVERTING THE POTENTIAL PROBLEMS

There are means to counter the potential problems of RCM. A strong campus-wide curriculum committee is necessary – not a regulatory body and not a group that looks at new courses or course changes, but one that establishes basic principles to guide curriculum development across the campus and then monitors to ensure that those principles are being met.

Campus leadership must make the case for interdisciplinary programs, for collegiality, for the importance of the common good; argue against fees for services where these are inappropriate; and consider carefully the dangers of too much decentralization. This may be a new role for academic affairs officers, not entirely different, but certainly not where the focus is under other budgeting systems. The challenge is to achieve the proper balance between what schools do on their own (while encouraging their entrepreneurial spirit), and what the campus, as a whole, must oversee.

Campus leadership must also make sure that a strong rationale (not a formula but a set of principles) exists for the distribution and redistribution of the state appropriation (or, in another form of RCM, tuition income). There needs to be an agreed upon means that remains standard over time by which the state appropriation to schools (or tuition income to schools) can be increased and/or decreased. This must involve the budgetary advisory committees of the schools, the deans' advisory group that advises the campus administration on new expenditures, and the campus-level budgetary affairs committee that reviews the plans of schools and makes recommendations on requests for new funds from the noninstructional units.

The campus administration must have sufficient resources of its own – again balancing between enough but not so much that decentralized incentives are diminished.

Campus leadership must stress what a university is, ensuring that faculty and student exchanges between and among schools continue, that the various missions of the campus remain at the forefront of school planning and budgetary decisions, that the relationship between those missions and individual school plans are uppermost in the minds of members of the campus community.

1995-1996 REVIEW OF RCM

After five years of RCM, a task force reviewed the pros and cons of the budgetary mechanism, evaluated strengths and weaknesses, and was asked to make recommendations, including, if desirable, the dropping of RCM by the campus. A major challenge for the committee was sorting out what was *caused* by RCM and what resulted from other factors, such as growing criticisms of higher education, stable or decreased state appropriations, more hands-on actions or interventions by Trustees, and so on. The review committee consulted widely and gathered the positive and negative perceptions of RCM. It may be instructive to list both, noting that they were perceptions.

First, the positive perceptions, most of which are obvious, and not a matter of dispute.

Perceptions of RCM: Positive

• Provides all instructional units with strong incentives to generate income
• Places accountability with the least-centralized decisionmaker(s)
• Increases unit responsibilities, but gives them the opportunity to generate resources to meet those responsibilities
• Accommodates change because budgets can be readily modified at the local (RC) level
• Allows schools considerable flexibility and independence
• Places focus on serving people, i.e., students/customers
• Provides incentive for instructional units to improve quality of instruction and thus attract more students
• Increases responsiveness to students' interests and concerns
• Encourages units to make long-range plans with greater confidence that they will have funds to implement plans
• Encourages bottom-up, rather than top-down, decisionmaking and planning
• Allowed the campus to weather successfully the financial difficulties of the early 1990s
• Encourages units supported by assessments to be more accountable to units paying the assessments

Many of these positive perceptions were either outcomes envisioned during the three years of planning prior to 1990, or experienced during the years after implementation. Perhaps most striking are the favorable perceptions of the effects of decentralizing the budgeting process – opportunities were created, change could easily be accommodated, schools enjoyed the flexibility and independence afforded by RCM, long-range planning became possible, incentives enabled chairs and deans to make use of faculty talents where they were most needed. The last bullet under positive perceptions may seem a negative if one is directing a nonacademic unit, but actually, RCM creates stronger ties between academic and nonacademic units, a relationship that the heads of nonacademic units, on the whole, enjoy. It became clear that the deans would increase their assessments to pay for new services if retention of students, for example, could be improved, or nonresident enrollment increased, or financial aid advice was expanded and improved.

The most troubling issue faced by the 1995-1996 review committee was the effect (or lack of it) of RCM on quality. A positive perception was that units had an incentive to improve the quality of instruction, but some wondered whether quality or quantity was the driving force. The list of negative perceptions gathered by the review committee underscores the debate.

Perceptions of RCM: Negative

- Reduces collegiality by de-emphasizing cooperation and collaboration among schools
- Pressures schools to offer more courses, including those outside the school's areas of expertise, and to lower standards to attract more students
- Fails to respond to the quality of particular programs in any direct way
- Reduces quality because incentives emphasize other factors
- Units don't understand why and how changes in assessments occur
- Fails to provide a ready method for controlling costs
- Provides incentive to accomplish teaching with temporary or part-time faculty
- Instructional units pay costs of noninstructional units but do not have enough control over their management
- Noninstructional units have little means of income generation and are at the mercy of campus administration for resources
- Campus administration has less discretionary funding to help meet "common good" needs
- Noninstructional units have lost access to pool of reverted year-end funds
- Tends to cause proliferation of additional fees
- Encourages grade inflation

Data collected by the committee did not support the negative perceptions. Collaboration among schools in the form of new degrees, for example, was greater during 1990-1995 than it was in the five years preceding the introduction of RCM. Only one curricular conflict arose between 1990 and 1995 and that was satisfactorily resolved by the Campus Curriculum Committee. The data showed no increase in part-time faculty, between 1990 and 1995; no new fees were introduced during the period (in fact, some were dropped); grade inflation continued to inch higher, but at the same relative pace as between 1985 and 1990, and 1980 and 1985.

The vexing issue of quality remained at the heart of the committee's deliberations. Opponents of RCM argued that academic units added sections of popular courses, or created new and appealing ones, to increase credit-hour production and thus revenues. Counters exist to such arguments, but they are not conclusive. Additional revenues, for example, are not pure profit. With more students, instructional costs increase and assessments based on percentage of undergraduate credit hours and/or majors increase. National studies stress that students choose their majors or schools because of a program's quality. More crucially perhaps, the review committee found great pride in all units about their qualitative aspirations. Our belief is that we must have faith in the integrity of the faculty of each academic unit to offer quality courses that are within their historically established mission areas. But others challenge that belief. The quality vs. quantity issue was not definitively resolved by the 1995-1996 review committee, nor is it ever likely to be resolved to everyone's satisfaction.

What the review committee addressed in its recommendations were primarily those negative perceptions that might be reversed.

Recommendations of 1995-1996 RCM Review Committee

Major recommendations

- Maintain current version of RCM, with some modifications
- Create Chancellor's Discretionary Fund to leverage campus priorities and goals
- Encourage schools to recruit more nonresident students by differentially distributing tuition income (from increases in out-of-state student enrollment) above a set base value
- Implement performance measures for noninstructional units and evaluate progress through a series of unit reviews
- Develop governing principles to be used by deans when making decisions that affect other units
- Implement limited pilot program to identify possible fee-for-service arrangements (rather than assessments) in noninstructional units

Additional recommendations

- Distribute income from undergraduate instructional fees based on credit hours taught over the preceding *two* years
- Extend incentives to noninstructional units by permitting them to retain access to 60 percent of year-end balances for approved expenditures in future years
- More effectively communicate goals and concepts of assessment process
- Change the assessment algorithm for the research office from grant volume to faculty FTE
- Chancellor should adopt a pro-active approach to fostering greater campus collegiality and cooperation

The Chancellor's Discretionary Fund (not *that* discretionary!) of 1 to 1.5 percent of the state appropriation each year was designed to: 1) focus on quality; 2) make investments that increased revenues; and 3) stimulate inter-unit ventures and campus-wide activities. Most of the other recommendations tweaked RCM as it had been practiced from 1990 to 1995, or responded to concerns identified during the review. The committee proposed changes in income distribution and in the assessment algorithm for the research office. Linking this assessment to grant and contract volume, as was done initially, had the consequence of providing disincentives for units to secure outside funding that did not carry indirect costs. Indeed, one school dean strongly argued that if the school were to incur additional assessment costs for the research office as a result of faculty members securing outside funding for a project, that fact might influence the dean's willingness to support the application. Indeed, in cases where the increased research did not provide new discretionary resources to the dean, it would be necessary to reallocate from existing activities to generate the resources needed to pay the higher assessments. In response to these concerns, and recognizing that research activity is an expectation for all faculty, in 1996 the driver in the assessment algorithm for the research office was shifted from the volume of funded research to the number of faculty.

The results of the first review of RCM and even several of the recommendations (especially the last one) suggest a particular kind of campus culture in Bloomington that might not exist elsewhere. Perhaps the 1997 North Central Accrediting Team captured the culture best when it noted that there seemed little distinction (some members thought too little) between "faculty" and "administration." Faculty governance leaders identified administrators as faculty first and administrators second; administrators clearly relied heavily on input from faculty committees. This relationship and the culture it has fostered in Bloomington may explain why RCM has been well received and, at least through 1995-1996, well accepted.

THE 1999-2000 REVIEW

In both reviews, one of the tasks was to revisit the basic premises of the system: incentives for generating income and for efficient operations and distributed authority and responsibility. It was noted earlier that a basic decision of the initial design was to allocate all earned income – instructional fees and indirect cost income – and (nearly) all state appropriation to the College and the schools. In each review this decision was re-examined and re-affirmed.

Findings and recommendations, 1999-2000

> • The Bloomington version of RCM was widely viewed as having a positive effect on the ability of the College, schools, and campus to achieve their respective academic goals.
> • The incentives were viewed as leading, in general, to positive outcomes, and the distributed responsibility and authority was viewed as a preferable alternative to the traditional system of centralized decisionmaking.
> • There were, as one would expect, recommendations for changes intended to improve the system and respond to perceived shortcomings.

The question of allocating state appropriation was especially relevant in the 1999-2000 review because in the late 1990s other public universities had designed RCM-type systems in which certain of the noninstructional units were supported with state appropriation rather than through assessment income. One rationale for this decision, to summarize a very complex situation, is that certain core operations (the libraries, museums, and physical plant) are critical to the mission and stature of the university. It is most appropriate for financial decisions on core operations to be made by the unit directors and the Chancellor with advice from advisory committees and the school deans. These decisions are handled better in a centralized system than in a competitive RCM environment. Another rationale is that this approach greatly simplifies the assessment process by reducing the number of units supported with resources allocated through that process. The assessment process is viewed by many as something of a "black box," and if there are ways to avoid using it while retaining other aspects of RCM, we should do so.

Because some of the universities that were implementing new RCM-type systems – or revising existing systems – chose to adopt this approach and fund certain core operations with state appropriation taken "off the top" rather than funds generated through the assessment process, this alternative was discussed in depth by the 1999-2000 review committee. Ultimately, the committee was persuaded that the scrutiny and review of operations by the school deans, which is inherent in the assessment process, was valuable and should be preserved.

At the same time, there is a widely shared view that the assessment process is excessively complex and should be simplified. In addition, better means are needed to communicate about the assessment processes and the levels of assessments. The version of assessments initially used attempted to link the level of assessments with the use of services. For example, at the implementation of RCM in Bloomington, detailed data on the use of various computer resources formed the basis for allocating the costs of the computer services unit. After implementation it became clear that the detailed data were difficult and time consuming to maintain and explain. As time passed, confidence in these detailed cost allocation algorithms diminished, and the various advisory groups recommended moving to cost allocations based on less detailed but more readily understood information. The link between specific services provided and the cost of assessments for several of the noninstructional units have been weakened and a few easily understood "drivers" are now used to determine most assessments.

It is appropriate to review the committee conclusions on assessment methods in more detail. Originally, the goal was to view the assessment process as one of matching the costs to the use of services. A school's charge for the support of a specific noninstructional unit was related in some fairly direct way to the extent to which the school (or its faculty, staff, or students) used the services of that noninstructional unit. In practice, this approach sometimes failed to produce the intended consequences and sometimes led to technical complexity that was not matched by useful outcomes. The example of assessing the costs of the research office was described earlier. Another example is that of the costs of space. As originally designed, the algorithm for assessing the costs of space was designed with twelve rates reflecting the characteristics and the quality of the space. This complexity was based on the belief that if the cost of space were connected in a reasonably specific way to the characteristics and quality of that space, an active secondary market would develop. However, on the Bloomington campus space is such a scarce commodity that deans chose to retain space, even when it was clearly underutilized, in the belief that there would soon be a need for it, and if it were relinquished, it could not be replaced when needed. Thus, the complex assessment algorithm was serving no useful purpose, and it was simplified. This change is one of several that illustrate the dynamic nature of our version of RCM, and the willingness to make changes in response to concerns as they are recognized.

The 1999-2000 review reaffirmed the willingness of academic deans to provide resources to noninstructional units when the activity supported is viewed as one providing value to the academic units. There have been multiple occasions when the deans agreed to provide additional resources to a noninstructional unit, resources which the deans understood came directly from their budgets, for high priority activities that are better located in a noninstructional unit than in a school. Examples of such decisions include funds for recruiting students, retention initiatives, and monitoring compliance for grants and contracts. In some cases the school deans considered transferring activities from noninstructional units to the schools and in some cases chose to do so – an example is financial aid counseling for professional students – and in some cases chose to keep the service in a noninstructional unit – an example is research compliance. ·The explicit comparison of where resources can be used most productively – in a school or in a noninstructional unit – is one of the valuable aspects of an RCM system. This discussion is natural under RCM; it is much less likely to occur under more centralized systems.

It is also the case that modifications of the system are required as the need for new incentives arises. For instance, in the mid 1990s, after a period of flat or declining state appropriation, it became clear that instructional fees would, at least in the near term, play a major role in generating new resources. Nonresident students pay instructional fees at significantly higher rates, at rates intended to cover the full cost of instruction, and consequently, it was decided that the system of allocating instructional fees should be modified to include incentives for the College and schools to attract nonresident students. It was recommended that if incremental revenue was available from a change in the residency mix of undergraduates, then those units that were teaching additional nonresident students should benefit from that income in proportion to the amount of such instruction provided. Appropriate changes were designed and implemented. The 1999-2000 review recognized the value of having courses begin at times other than the beginning of a semester available to students who did not, for various reasons, register for them during the usual registration period. Under the existing income distribution algorithm, the College and schools did not receive instructional fee income for teaching these courses. The committee recommended that the income distribution algorithm be changed to provide incentives for teaching such courses, and the changes are being implemented.

Over time, it may be that the relation between certain expenses and income will change. For instance, an important campus initiative launched in the mid-1990s has led to a change in the way financial aid expenses are viewed. In 1994-1995, the campus began using the concept of financial aid leveraging. The idea is to review carefully the enrollment of various target populations of potential undergraduates, and use financial aid as a recruitment incentive. In this setting, financial aid is no longer purely an expense, but also a means of generating revenue. Indeed, we are moving toward a view of financial aid used in this way as a discount to revenue, and the concept of net tuition revenue is now a regular part of the discussion.

It is tempting for those not directly involved with delivering instruction to think of new instructional fees as resources that are available for enhancing quality and meeting other current program needs. If the instruction needed by the new students generating the incremental revenue can be provided without increasing instructional costs – for instance, if there is unused capacity in the advising system and space in existing sections – then much of that revenue may be available for enhancing quality. However, once unused capacity is exhausted, then costs may increase significantly. The task of estimating the costs of adding students once one moves beyond this margin is a complex one, and the way a school responds may influence the nature of the unit in basic ways. The response is likely to be different when the increase is viewed as long term rather than short term. For example, until an increase in the number of students appears likely to last, a school will probably choose to provide instruction with visiting or part-time faculty, overloads for current faculty, or similar short-term solutions, and to provide support services with temporary staff. If the increase appears permanent, then the school is likely to choose to increase its regular faculty and hire permanent staff. This is a situation where long-range planning is crucial.

A common feature of the discussions about revisions in RCM systems, both at Indiana University and elsewhere, is a reconsideration of the amount of resources allocated to the Chancellor (or the equivalent office) to maintain and enhance quality, to sustain common good activities, to support interdisciplinary initiatives, and to leverage other resources. The 1995-1996 review recommended the establishment of a Chancellor's Discretionary Fund for this purpose, and the 1999-2000 review recommended enlarging that fund substantially, from 1.5 percent of state appropriation each year to 2.5 percent. Much of the faculty support for the increase was a belief that this provided an opportunity to respond to the concern that RCM systems may make it difficult for College and school deans to maintain and enhance quality.

Although one of the frequent concerns raised in discussions with faculty about RCM relates to interdisciplinary activity, the deans have a somewhat different view. In fact, in the 1999-2000 review, several deans commented that they find it easier to support inter-school initiatives under RCM than under the traditional system. There is evidence of successful efforts, including the first inter-school bachelors degree at Bloomington. To some extent, the views of the deans may be a consequence of increased recognition of the values of such activity. It may also be a result of deans being more knowledgeable of the costs of such activities and more familiar with cost/benefit discussions.

A perplexing issue regarding faculty perceptions of RCM arose in both the 1995-1996 and 1999-2000 reviews. Because the system is a significant departure from the traditional system, it is, perhaps, to be expected that many faculty would have misunderstandings of RCM only a few years after it was introduced. It is less understandable why the lack of accurate information persisted long enough to be significant ten years after the system was introduced. Perhaps the traditional lack of faculty interest in administrative detail may be a contributing factor.

During both reviews, committee members were struck by the widespread misinformation about the concepts, goals, and attributes of our system of RCM. In open forums held as part of each review and in communications sent to the committees, it was very common to have strong objections based on either incomplete information or misinformation. An example – noted several times in the comments to the 1999-2000 review committee – is the belief that there have been multiple instances where one school has introduced courses traditionally taught by another school purely to generate income. Most people who raised the issue could give no specific examples, and following up on the situations that were cited to support the statement yielded only one or two instances where there was basis for that conclusion, and even in these cases the situation was more complex than simply income generation. Another example was the belief expressed in the 1995-1996 review that grade inflation had accelerated as schools made courses easier to attract and retain students, but no confirming evidence was presented. These examples illustrate the range of undesirable effects that have been attributed to RCM. This is perhaps understandable in the 1995-1996 review, but the need for better communication is made clear by the persistence of this problem to the 1999-2000 review.

Most of the concerns raised in the 1999-2000 review were those associated with the level of resources rather than the resource management structure associated with RCM. Although state appropriations were flat or declining in the early 1990s, there was a significant shift of resources from noninstructional units to instructional units (by reducing assessments as a percent of total expenditure budgets for the instructional units) and relatively large increases in instructional fee rates. In the late 1990s, there were no corresponding transfers of resources from the noninstructional units and increases in instructional fee rates were more modest. Increases in enrollments moved beyond marginal increases, and real instructional cost increases were associated with volume-based increases in instructional fee income. The results of these forces were significant constraints on the ability of deans to maintain and enhance quality in the College and the schools. The committee specifically noted the challenges posed by raising faculty salaries and providing funds for increases in fringe-benefit costs in an era when state appropriations are a declining fraction of total resources. The basic question in this discussion, to which the Review Committee supplied an affirmative answer, is whether the campus would function better under (a version of) RCM than under an alternative system.

A consequence of the extremely constrained resources is diminished flexibility of school deans, and the potentially severe consequences of errors in financial planning. It has become clear that those involved with campus financial planning must be alert to early signs of deterioration in the financial status of the schools and willing to take quick action. In an effort to stress the responsibility of the schools for their own financial results, the Campus Budget Office has focused on providing information, advice, and suggestions and has been reluctant to take prompt independent action. The 1999-2000 review committee recommended that the Campus Budget Office should be proactive and intervene quickly when problems are identified. It is recognized that in extreme cases this will involve constraints on the ability of the school to make financial decisions.

CONCLUSION

As of this writing for the Bloomington campus, the case study for RCM is positive. Campus administrators plan to continue periodic reviews, fully recognizing that available resources, changes in the campus culture, and new approaches to budgeting, may lead to alterations in a budgeting mechanism, including our version of RCM.

NOTES

1. The IUPUI campus was the first in 1988-1989 to implement RCM.

REFERENCES

Ruesink, Albert, and Maynard Thompson. 1996. *Responsibility-centered management at Indiana University Bloomington: 1990-1995.* Final report of the 1995-96 Responsibility-Centered Management Review Committee submitted to the Chancellor, Indiana University Bloomington.

Theobald, Neil, and Maynard Thompson. 2000. *Responsibility-centered management at Indiana University Bloomington: 1990-2000.* Final report of the 1999-2000 Responsibility-Centered Management Review Committee submitted to the Chancellor, Indiana University Bloomington.

CHAPTER 6

RESPONSIBILITY CENTER BUDGETING AT THE UNIVERSITY OF TORONTO

Daniel W. Lang

Beginning in the mid-1980s the University of Toronto introduced a series of changes in its policies and procedures for planning and budgeting. Initially, none of these changes was aimed expressly at responsibility center budgeting (RCB) and responsibility center management (RCM), but the new policies and procedures had many of the generic characteristics of what the university later recognized as RCB/RCM. Since then RCB/RCM has been formally installed on one of the university's three campuses and in one of its largest faculties, as well as in all of its continuing studies programs, and in many of its student services. The University of Toronto thus has had about 15 years of experience with RCB/RCM and many years longer than that with variants of it. In some aspects that experience has been relatively unique in the sense that the university's approach towards the deployment of RCB/RCM was defined by local factors – for example, a provincial funding formula – that did not obtain elsewhere in North America. But in other respects the University of Toronto's experience was typical and therefore illustrative of many of the issues and problems that arise in the deployment of RCB/RCM. The University of Toronto's experience has been mixed. In some situations RCB/RCM has been successful. In others, its deployment has been at best problematic.

BACKGROUND OF RCB/RCM AT THE UNIVERSITY OF TORONTO

Founded in 1827, the University of Toronto is the largest university in Canada and the fifth largest in North America. The university, by most comparative measures, is also one of the best in North America.

Because one of the attractions of responsibility center budgeting and responsibility center management is the capability to improve decisionmaking in large, highly complex institutions, there are certain vital statistics that should be cited here. The University of Toronto has, in round numbers, 52,000 students, 3,100 faculty, and 3,600 staff on three campuses. The university has 21 faculties, 39 libraries, three federated colleges, four constituent colleges, 80 graduate programs, and is affiliated with 11 teaching hospitals, one of which it owns. The university's annual operating budget is Canadian (as are all $ figures in Chapter) $930 million, plus $290 million for sponsored research. The university manages its own pension fund (currently at $2 billion) and has an endowment of $1 billion. Thus the university is indeed large and complex.

University policy and finance in Canada is also complex. Constitutionally, higher education is a provincial responsibility. Several Canadian universities, however, were founded before the formation of Canada as a nation in 1867. Those universities, like the University of Toronto, are essentially the creations of British colonial administration, and thus share an historical status with many American colleges and universities that were founded prior to 1787, and which were as much public as they were private (Herbst, 1981). Unlike those institutions, most of which are now regarded as private, the University of Toronto has continued to occupy a curious middle ground between public and private. About 45 percent of the university revenue comes from the provincial government, 26 percent from student fees (most of which are regulated to some degree by the provincial government), 17 percent from the sale of services, and 12 percent from gifts and endowments. The majority of funding for research comes from the federal government. So the center of financial gravity at the University of Toronto is slightly more public than private, but it is a very close call.

However, in the absence of the influence and leverage that arises from funding, neither the federal government nor the provincial government has formal control of the University of Toronto. The university owns its buildings and property outright. It directly employs the faculty and staff, determines their rates of pay and terms of employment, and manages their pension fund. Although the provincial government can refuse to fund academic programs proposed by the university, it cannot bar the University from offering them on a self-funded basis. In summary, the university is accountable more to its board of governors than to the government, and therefore refers to itself as a "publicly funded" institution instead of a "public" institution. Thus, to the extent that the utility of RCB/RCM depends on institutional autonomy, the University of Toronto, like many other Canadian universities (Fisher and Rubenson, 1998) has a high degree of autonomy.

The public dimension of the University of Toronto's status does, however, result in some significant limitations on its capability to deploy RCB/RCM successfully and fully. Since 1967, the Province of Ontario has used an enrollment-driven funding formula to allocate funding to universities. For a period of time, the formula was also used to determine the amount of funding that should be made available to the province's postsecondary sector at large.

The Ontario funding formula is weighted to reflect the costs of different programs. The weights range from 1.0 (for first-year undergraduate programs in Arts) to 6.0 (for doctoral programs). The weighting scheme allows individual institutions to optimize revenue and expense by carefully matching enrollments to programs. This means that the focus of planning for enrollment is on individual campuses and faculties more than it is on the institution as a whole. These are factors that tend to favor RCB/RCM and variants of it.

The funding formula's weights, however, sometimes do not correspond to the actual costs of program delivery (Lang, et al., 1989). This disparity can have consequences that are in practical effect different from the province's intended policy of funding universities in a fashion that reflects each university's mix of enrollment and programs. Most universities in Ontario recognize this limitation and do not internalize the funding formula into their budget allocation processes. The government recognizes the limitations too; it uses the formula only to determine block grants or global allocations to each institution. Once these funds reach the institutions, they are free to allocate them as they choose.

At the time when the University of Toronto began to deploy RCB/RCM, and until recently, the provincial government also regulated tuition fees through the funding formula. Instead of the range from 1.0 to 6.0 that applies to the program weights for determining operating grants, the range for tuition fees was only about one to three. This meant that proportionally higher weight programs tended to rely more on grants than fees.

In terms that are important to the effective deployment of RCB/RCM, the University of Toronto's range of autonomy and local discretion depends on a series of somewhat contradictory factors. The university may allocate its revenue as it chooses, but its actual costs may be different from those assumed by the operating grant formula under which it is funded. In terms of price and volume, the university has considerable but not total discretion over tuition fees, and complete discretion over enrollment. In terms of product, the university may make its own judgments about the quality of academic programs, the demand for them, and the optimal mode of delivery. These judgments, however, are mitigated by the government's discretion to fund or not fund new programs.

The funding of university research in Canada poses a special case for deployment of RCB/RCM. By far, the majority of funding for research in Canada comes from the federal government through a series of research councils that make awards competitively on the basis of peer-adjudication. This funding covers only the direct costs of research. The indirect and overhead costs of research are assumed by the federal government to be met by the provincial governments. But, in Ontario at least, the provincial government allocates almost all (about 95 percent) of its funding on the basis of its funding formula that is sensitive solely to enrollment. There is a small, separate fund for "research overhead and infrastructure" that is allocated on the basis of a three-year average of aggregate funding from the federal research councils. To put the scale of this fund in perspective, for the University of Toronto it produces funding for the indirect and overhead costs of research at an effective rate of about 10 percent. In terms of a strict fund accounting for research, the University of Toronto loses about 35 cents on every dollar that it receives to conduct research (University of Toronto, 1996).

The relevance of this discussion to the deployment of RCB/RCM at the University of Toronto is not the adequacy or inadequacy of funding for research. It is about the form that the bulk of the funding takes. American universities, because their funding for research infrastructure is a direct function of the value of each research grant, have as a matter of practical necessity a keen awareness of the relationship between the direct and indirect costs of research. Although Canadian universities are fully aware that this relationship exists, most of them do not have either the algorithms for accurately determining the indirect costs of research or the budget processes by which these costs can be charged to research grants. Moreover, those same algorithms and budget processes would, if they existed, apply to the allocation of indirect costs and overheads to auxiliary services (usually called "ancillary" services in Canada), contracts, and various other nominally self-funded programs and services.

LAYING A FOUNDATION FOR RCB/RCM

The University of Toronto began to prepare a foundation for RCB/RCM before there were any actual plans to introduce RCB/RCM. In the mid-1980s a number of factors converged to cause the university to re-examine and eventually completely overhaul its planning and budgeting processes. One of those factors was unfortunately common to many colleges and universities at that time: government funding began to decline sharply. Moreover, in Ontario, the reductions were problematic in the sense that government fiscal policy was unclear and, in turn, unpredictable. Although still the source of most of the university's funding, the government was becoming an unreliable partner in the public enterprise of higher education.

A number of things became apparent to the University of Toronto's senior administration. It would have to begin to diversify its sources of revenue. It would have to begin to extend conventional year-by-year budgeting into the multi-year realm of planning. It would have to convince its governors, and to some degree the government, that deficits and surpluses were necessary to sound fiscal management as opposed to being harbingers of mismanagement. And it would have to begin to regard programs as cost centers against which revenue could be contrasted. These all would be major changes, not only in the practice of planning and budgeting but also in institutional outlook. The implication and profound conundrum was that the university might not be able to afford all of its programs if it were at the same time to maintain its standards of quality.

The first foundation step, in order to make the budget process as stable and predictable as possible, was to codify the process and make it transparent. By the end of the 1980s the university had a formal document called *General Budget Policies and Procedures* that was formally approved, published annually, and made publicly available. Among these policies and procedures were, for example, a policy on self-funded programs and a methodology for determining indirect and overhead costs. Both would prove to be essential to the university's later application of RCB/RCM.

The second step was the development of a formal budget model by a newly formed Budget Planning Secretariat. The model, which was completed in 1989, was essentially a large algorithm that comprised about 80 separate factors. Some factors were obvious, like price inflation. Others were less obvious and highly complex, like a series of factors aimed at forecasting the expense of library acquisitions purchased outside Canada.

The budget model was constructed to take into account systematically all sources of income and the categories of expense to which those sources could be applied. A central item in the budgeting and planning process thus became a "sources and applications" table, which in concept is a fundamental idiom of RCB/RCM although it was not regarded as such at the time. The purpose of the budget model was twofold. On the one and more obvious hand, the model projected with, it later proved, considerable accuracy the operating income that the university could expect to receive and the claims that would be routinely made against that income by institutional obligations and policies, in both the short and long term. Those obligations and policies were laid down in *General Budget Policies and Procedures*.

On the other hand, the purpose of the budget model was to guide budget planning and development towards those areas where truly strategic decisions were possible and necessary. The scale and complexity of the university's budget were such that it could not be successfully attacked by an advance on all fronts. It made the university's leadership victim to what James March would call "limited rationality" (March, 1994) and Burton Clark would call "demand overload" (Clark, 1998). The whole budget was beyond comprehension, and the putative claims on it more numerous than competent and responsible managers could deal with at any one time, or indeed in any single budget cycle. Recognition of these limitations prompted the university's senior administrators – particularly the Provost, the Vice-President for Administration, and the Vice-Provost for Planning and Budget – to begin to explore the possibilities of RCB/RCM.

BACKING INTO RCB/RCM

By the end of the 1990s, the University of Toronto had formally deployed RCB/RCM on one of its three campuses, and had introduced the *de facto* equivalent in one of its largest faculties – Education – which had been formed through merger with a previously independent institution. *De facto* RCB/RCM was also in place in the university's School of Continuing Studies, in its ancillary operations, and in a series of "self-funded" programs and services. In monetary terms, approximately one-quarter of the university's academic budget and almost all of its student service budget were being planned and managed under some form of RCB/RCM, but the literal term "RCB/RCM" was applied in only one case.

Self-funded Programs

The University of Toronto, by 2000, offered several programs that, without public funding, generated enough income, mainly from tuition fees, to cover their direct, indirect, and overhead costs. The first of these was an Executive MBA program. That program was followed by a Doctor of Pharmacy program, a Diploma in Social Work Research program, a Master of Management in Professional Accounting program, and a Master of Financial Mathematics program. The university also operates an elementary school and a high school on this basis.

The motivation to offer and operate these programs on a self-funded basis was mainly in reaction to government policy. More exactly, the motivation was to escape the limitations and inadequacies of government policies. In some cases, the weights that would have been assigned to the new programs would not have generated sufficient income to fund them fully. In other cases, government policy would have limited tuition fees to levels that were insufficient to provide necessary funding or were below levels that the market for programs would have made possible. Each year, when tuition fees for these programs are brought forward for approval, the proposals are accompanied by budgets that show the full expenses of the programs and the sources of income that will cover those expenses.

All of these programs have been financially (and academically) successful. Some of them have required complex financial arrangements under their own versions of RCB/RCM. When the university constructed a new building for its Faculty of Management, most of the costs were met by grants from the provincial government and from a major benefactor. But because the Executive MBA program was not eligible for government funding, the government's capital grant was proportionally discounted to exclude the program. Self-funding therefore applied to capital as well as operating costs. The Executive MBA program is in practical effect financing its space in the new building under a 25-year mortgage, including interest as well as principal.

In the end, however, this application of RCB/RCM at the University of Toronto is a somewhat artificial example of the concept. The main purpose of RCB/RCM in this case was to execute an end run around government policies that were limiting the scope of the university's planning and budgetary strategies. It is in this sense that RCB/RCM succeeded. Absent the government's policies, the university's interest in RCB/RCM probably would have been minor.

Summer Sessions

Only a very few of the University of Toronto's faculties and colleges themselves offer regular programs during the summer session. Instead, there is a single omnibus summer session that is organized to offer a wide array of courses to students from various programs within the University of Toronto and to students from other universities. The summer session in consequence is very large, usually on the order of 14,000 students.

Because the summer session must be scheduled in the middle of the prior budget cycle, there was always a problem in setting a budget for the session through the normal budget process. Also, because the summer session is not really based on programs, each course is offered in terms of the demand for it individually. Class sizes therefore should be neither too small nor too large.

To solve these problems the university decided to operate the summer session on a cost-recovery basis, including attribution of overhead but excluding the indirect costs of space. An "upset" or default class size is determined annually. Classes with pre-registrations above the upset size go ahead; those with pre-registrations below that size are cancelled. All revenue generated by student enrollments is attributed to the program, as are all costs, including instruction which is funded on a stipendiary basis. If demand for courses exceeds planned levels, the administrators in charge of the session have an RCB/RCM-like pre-authorization to expand enrollment and course offerings, and – most importantly – to make spending commitments above budgeted levels. The consequent overspending is offset at the end of the fiscal year by the additional (but also unbudgeted) revenue.

Merger

Education, as a field of study at the University of Toronto, has an unusual history. Until 1972 the university had no faculty of education. Teachers were trained by a provincial college of education that had branches throughout the province, one of which was adjacent to the University of Toronto. In 1972, the province dissolved the college of education and transferred its several branches to universities. Thus the University of Toronto acquired its Faculty of Education.

This arrangement, however, was lopsided. The Faculty of Education was exclusively undergraduate, offering only a Bachelor of Education and a few professional certificates and diplomas. As a matter of policy and strategic mission, the University of Toronto sought to offer graduate programs in all of its faculties. There was an explanation for this anomaly.

In 1967 the government had established a small, highly specialized institution called the Ontario Institute for Studies in Education (OISE) that concentrated on research and graduate instruction. OISE was affiliated with the University of Toronto but independent of it. Over the years the arrangement was less than optimal. The Faculty of Education lacked a solid foundation in current research and theory, and OISE lacked a connection to practical experience in schools. Moreover, OISE was on the one hand in chronic financial difficulty and, on the other hand, jealous of its independent status.

Despite the obvious advantages of a merger between the Faculty of Education and OISE within the University of Toronto, it was not until 1995 that a satisfactory agreement could be reached. To that point all discussions of merger had foundered, mainly because agreement could not be reached on finance. OISE was concerned in particular that, under merger, its previously independent sources of revenue could be directed towards programs outside Education. There was a further concern that spending patterns believed to be unique to Education would be abrogated in favor either of university-wide benchmarks or of across-the-board expense reductions assigned prior to merger as part of the university's multi-year budgetary process. Although the University of Toronto was more confident about merger, its senior leadership was aware of the fact that the university had no prior experience in managing large-scale mergers and in planning and budgeting for what would become a very large comprehensive faculty of education (Eastman and Lang, 2001).

To resolve these problems and to reassure OISE, the university constructed a highly detailed "integration agreement" that for an initial 10-year term could be renewed and would place the new faculty on terms that otherwise would be described as RCB/RCM. All of the revenue previously generated by OISE as an independent institution and by the Faculty of Education (although it was not independent prior to merger) would be earmarked to flow through to the newly merged faculty. With this revenue the new faculty – called OISE/UT – would have to cover all of its costs, including future university-wide increases in wages and benefits. At its option, OISE/UT could either continue to operate certain academic services (for example, a library) or it could transfer funds to (again, for example) the University of Toronto Library and in effect purchase the services. OISE/UT could set its own enrollment targets, and, within government regulations, its own tuition fees.

In terms of RCB/RCM, a particularly interesting option available to OISE/UT was about the budgetary status of its building, which was very large and had been custom-built by the government. On one hand, the building produced revenue, not only from obvious sources like parking, food services, and room rentals, but also from a number of long-term leases to educational agencies. On the other hand, the building was expensive to operate and had a backlog of deferred maintenance. In the end the option that was elected had the university take full responsibility for operating and maintaining the building in return for the revenue that it generated. This decision was very much along the lines of RCB/RCM and reflected a posture that the University of Toronto had previously adopted towards the management of space.

School of Continuing Studies

The University of Toronto has a separate academic organization through which it offers a wide variety of noncredit programs and courses. This unit – called the School of Continuing Studies – has an annual expense budget of just over $7 million all of which is offset by revenue that the school generates itself, mainly from student fees. In the case of the School of Continuing Studies, being self-funded means covering all direct costs and indirect costs that include building operation, maintenance, and rent.

In academic terms, the School of Continuing Studies has been successful. In terms of RCB/RCM, expressed as self-funding, the school's track record is checkered. A chronic problem – and one which poses a fundamental conundrum for RCB/RCM – is that the School of Continuing Studies operates in a market that is in certain aspects different from that of other faculties and colleges at the University of Toronto. Its fees, although totally unregulated, are lower than those elsewhere in the university. Its faculty, virtually all of whom are engaged on short-term contracts, are paid on a stipendiary basis, course-by-course. The school's permanent staff are appointed and paid according to labor agreements that are negotiated university-wide.

These arrangements seem straightforward and entirely consistent with the basic precepts of RCB/RCM. They are, however, more complex than they seem. If the school seeks to raise its fees too far it may place its programs in jeopardy of competition from some of the university's degree programs, particularly diploma and certificate programs aimed mainly at part-time students. A greater problem has to do with compensation for faculty. The School of Continuing Studies conducts no research, offers no courses or programs for credit, and, other than its courses or programs, performs no public service. From the point of view of expenses, then, one would reasonably expect the school's cost structures to be far below those of other faculties and colleges. The school's cost structures are lower, but not as low as they probably would be if they were not attached to the University of Toronto or were attached to a university with a greater orientation towards undergraduate programs in arts and science. Although not all faculty who teach in the school are employed elsewhere by the university, many of them are. To compete successfully for those faculty, the school must raise course stipends to levels that otherwise would be regarded as artificially high. In other words, although the School of Continuing Studies appears to be operating in a market separate from the University of Toronto, that separateness pertains mainly to its course offerings. In terms of key elements of revenue and expense, the school cannot escape the larger University of Toronto market even if it is not really offering an academic product in that market. This makes self-funding more difficult to attain than it otherwise might be for other programs and in other universities.

This situation causes another difficulty. Normally a program like the School of Continuing Studies would internalize RCB or self-funding. Each course or program would be on its own financial bottom, with full costs attributed to it. Fees would be set differentially to reflect different levels of cost. Courses or programs that could not cover their costs would be discontinued as a matter of planning and budget routine. Because of the School of Continuing Studies inclusion, albeit partial, in the larger University of Toronto market, there are some courses and programs that cannot function literally on their own bottoms. This has made it necessary for the school to cross-subsidize its courses and programs, and to set fees at school-wide averages. In other words, like water finding its own

level, the school has had to find that point between centralization and decentralization where RCB/RCM works optimally.

This is an important observation for the theory of RCB/RCM. One could think of RCB/RCM as one of two polar opposites: centralization versus decentralization, with RCB/RCM representing the latter. A more accurate and realistic perception, however, is to think of a continuum along which RCB/RCM optimally locates decisionmaking, sometimes nearer the center and sometimes further away from it depending on the nature of the decision that is required.

At various points in its history as a self-funding unit, the School of Continuing Studies has made what proved to be bad business decisions and incurred large debts, at one time amounting to over $2 million, an amount equivalent at the time to more than one-third of its annual revenue. Under the university's policies for self-funded programs, the school was held responsible for its debt, which was amortized over several years with interest being charged at internal rates of return. The university's Faculty of Medicine, which runs a professional development continuing studies program for physicians, once found itself in a similar position: a bad business decision resulted in a loss of about $2 million. The same university policies applied; the Faculty had to repay the debt with interest.

Summary

Whalen (1991), in his book *Responsibility Center Budgeting*, implicitly created a small taxonomy for the disposition of various types of revenue under RCB at Indiana University. The following table (Table 6.1) applies that taxonomy to the University of Toronto prior to its deployment of RCB/RCM and demonstrates the extent to which the University of Toronto was already following *de facto* RCB/RCM before it formally introduced it.

RCB/RCM AT UT-SCARBOROUGH

UT-Scarborough is one of the University of Toronto's three campuses. It offers undergraduate programs in Arts, Science, and Management to about 6,000 students. Several free-standing universities in Ontario are smaller than UT-Scarborough. RCB/RCM, in full form, was introduced at UT-Scarborough in 1997. The campus is entirely "on its own bottom" under an elaborate system of protocols that were developed over about 18 months prior to the introduction of RCB/RCM.

RCB/RCM at UT-Scarborough goes beyond the self-funded status that applies to other faculties and programs in the University of Toronto. For example, the RCB/RCM protocols for UT-Scarborough attribute a share of the university's endowment to the Scarborough campus. If the university were to sell land or liquidate other assets, one of the protocols would indicate the share of the

Table 6.1: Disposition of Revenue

Sources of revenue	RCB	U of T
Tuition fees	allocated to faculties	allocated centrally
Other earned income		
- ancillary fees	allocated to faculties	allocated to faculties
- unrestricted investment	allocated centrally	allocated centrally
Indirect cost recoveries	100 percent to faculties	55 percent to faculties
Continuing education income	allocated to faculties	allocated to faculties
Restricted fund income	allocated according to bequest	allocated according to bequest
Auxiliaries and services	allocated to faculties if generated by faculties	allocated to faculties if generated by faculties
Public grants	allocated by budget process	allocated by budget process
Carry-forwards	100 percent retained by faculties	100 percent retained by faculties

proceeds that would go to the campus. The campus is completely responsible for the operation, upkeep, and depreciation of its physical plant. It may operate various services entirely on its own or contract with other campuses for them. For example, UT-Scarborough operates its own information and educational technology center but contracts book cataloguing to the library on the University's St. George Campus. The campus runs its own police service, development office, finance department, and registrar's office. The campus' principal may bring proposals (for example, for new programs) directly to the university's Governing Council; other faculties and colleges would first have to bring such proposals to the university's provost, who in turn would bring them to the Governing Council. The *General Policies and Procedures* require the annual submission of budget guidelines followed by a detailed budget.   Under RCB/RCM, UT-Scarborough must make the same submissions as are made for the university at large.

In early 1993 the Vice President and Provost and the Principal of Scarborough College (as UT-Scarborough was then called) agreed to undertake a pilot project in RCB/RCM. This agreement had an unusually long history, and explains why the Scarborough campus instead of the university's other campuses moved to RCB/RCM. When the Scarborough campus was planned in the late 1960s there was a deliberate expectation that it would not be a clone of the University of Toronto's other programs in arts and science. For example, the campus was built to make extensive use of televised instruction. Twenty-five years later the expectation of a differentiated campus was largely unfulfilled but still desired by the university's senior administration and by the campus' leadership. RCB/RCM seemed to be a means of differentiating the campus from the rest of the university.

The first necessary phase of the pilot project was the full attribution of revenue generated by the campus, and a full attribution of direct and indirect expenditures to the academic divisions in the campus. The methodology of the pilot project comprised several components.

Assignment of the Campus Budget into Cost Centers

The first stage of the analysis involved the realignment of the college's then existing budget into cost centers that would be more appropriate to the project objectives: the college budget was then constructed more along organizational than functional lines, as is still the case with most divisions in the university. By way of example, the Registrar's Office as a budgetary and organizational unit had functional responsibility, among other things, for admissions, classroom scheduling, College Council secretariat functions, and student records. Only certain of these functions were registrarial *per se.* Conversely, such functions as student counseling and high school liaison reported to the Associate Dean (Academic), but might properly have been regarded as registrarial in a functional sense.

Student services and ancillary enterprises were excluded from the analysis, as was the annual revenue/expense transfer for the college's summer session because they were already operating on a self-funded basis. The budget was then realigned into a series of cost centers:

> *Academic Administration,* including the Principal's Office, College Secretariat costs, Co-op program administration, classroom scheduling, and the Associate Dean (Academic).
> *Academic Support Services,* including the library, writing center, academic workshops, computing, audiovisual services, and graphics.
> *General Administration,* including human resources, financial services, purchasing, and the Office of the Director of Administration.
> *Campus Services,* including building maintenance and utilities, protective services, post office, and printing.
> *Registrarial Services,* including Student Aid, counseling, high school liaison, admissions, and student records.
> *Academic Divisions*: Management and Economics, Humanities, Social Sciences, Life Sciences, Physical Sciences.

Assignment of Central Overhead to the College Budget

The next stage of the analysis involved the assignment of central overhead costs to the cost centers identified in the college budget. The university had employed an overhead cost attribution model for these purposes in its *General Budget Policies and Procedures* for nearly a decade, and the methodology was both stable and generally accepted. It did, however, produce a wide variation in overhead cost rates for different academic program areas because it allocated costs differentially based on a variety of measures. Considerable effort had to be devoted to examining and refining the cost allocation to the college budget, taking account of the fact that certain services (for example, purchasing, human resources, and physical plant) were already provided locally within the college budget and therefore had to be excluded from a central overhead cost allocation.

The central overhead costs attributed to the college budget were organized into the following categories:

Institutional Management included the Office of the President, the Governing Council Secretariat, legal fees, the Office of the Assistant Vice-President (Planning), and similar services.

Financial Management included the Office of the Comptroller, the Assistant Vice-President (Finance), the Vice-President (Business Affairs), the cost of financial computing systems, and the Treasury function.

Human Resources Management included the cost of labor relations and negotiations, the cost of HR computing systems, and the cost of centrally budgeted employee benefits plans.

Academic Administration included the Office of the Vice-President and Provost, registrar and student records costs, the School of Graduate Studies, and registrar computing costs.

Student Aid was allocated partially on a direct basis; actual undergraduate student aid costs for the most recent fiscal year were assigned to the college.

Student Services included only the Office of the Assistant Vice-President (Student Affairs) and the Special Services Office.

Development and University Relations included the cost of fundraising, public affairs, communications (the *U of T Magazine* and *Bulletin*), alumni affairs, and community relations.

Library costs were assigned differentially to undergraduate students, doctoral stream graduate students, and faculty members.

The total central cost allocation to the college thus amounted to $5.5 million (or 17 percent) of the campus' direct costs.

Assignment of Nonacademic Costs to Academic Divisions

The next stage of the analysis involved the assignment of all nonacademic costs to the college's five academic divisions. A specific and separate formula was developed for each of these costs. The costs were then "stepped down" to each academic division in the following order:

1. *Occupancy Costs and Campus Services* costs were assigned to all academic and nonacademic divisions.
2. *General Administrative* costs were assigned to all remaining nonacademic and academic divisions.
3. *Academic Administrative overhead, Academic Support Services, Public Affairs, Registrarial Services, and the College Library* costs were assigned to the academic divisions.

Attribution of Revenue to the Academic Divisions

The next logical phase of the analysis was the calculation of revenue attributable to the college. Specifically, the revenue calculations fall into the following categories:

Calculation of government operating grants allocated by the provincial funding formula and tuition fees regulated by the formula. The provincial government's weighted, enrollment-driven funding formula converts enrollment into basic income units (BIUs) in order to recognize cost differences among programs. Significantly, the provincial funding was and is blind to RCB/RCM. It funds institutions, not parts of institutions, and recognizes net enrollment fluctuations only. This aspect of the province's funding formula is in the first instance technical, but it made a very significant difference to the installation of RCB/RCM at UT-Scarborough, and later was a key factor in some of the problems that the campus encountered in using RCB/RCM.

The attribution of revenue to UT-Scarborough therefore had to begin with the creation of a college-specific undifferentiated BIU weight for its programs. These were the weights in the funding formula: First-year enrollment, Arts and Science, 1.0 BIU; Upper-years honors Arts, 1.5 BIU; Upper-years honors Science, 2.0 BIU; Upper-years general Arts, and Science, 1.0 BIU; Commerce, all years of study, 1.5 BIU. These weights were applied to produce a blended or average weight unique to the Scarborough campus. For Scarborough students registered in graduate programs of study, the institutional average BIU weights of 2.879 for Master's students and 4.089 for doctoral students were applied to Scarborough graduate enrollment.

After the BIU weights for the college were established, the next step in the calculation was the establishment of an enrollment count adjusted to take account of undergraduate service teaching provided to the college by other divisions of the university, and to account for graduate instruction provided by the college. Because the provincial funding formula operates on a moving three-year average these calculations had to be repeated for each respective year.

Calculation of other government operating grants. In addition to the formula grants, there were several nonformula grants for which an attribution had to be made to the College:

> • Special Accessibility Grants were distributed to institutions on the basis of slip-year BIU counts, but not averaged.
> • International Student Fee Waivers are grant allocations to institutions based on unweighted graduate enrollment counts.
> • Research Infrastructure Funds were distributed to institutions on the basis of actual research grants received from the three federal granting councils. An allocation had to be made to the college on the basis of actual grants, received by its faculty members, provided that the research was conducted on the Scarborough campus.

Attribution of endowment and other income. The final element of the revenue attribution had to do with the allocation of general university income from a quasi-endowment, from unrestricted endowments, and from short-term cash investments. There was no pre-existing method by which this could be done, but the revenue stream was sufficiently large as to warrant an attempt at allocation.

The quasi-endowment was at the time providing general operating revenue of just over $7 million to the university at large. The capital of the endowment arose from pension contribution savings. Because 4.8 percent of the total employer benefits cost was attributable to the college, that percentage was used to allocate a share of the endowment to the Scarborough campus.

Most endowments at the University of Toronto are restricted by their donors, but some are unrestricted quasi-endowments that arise from underspending in previous fiscal years. It was possible to trace and attribute the underspending that was carried-forward to create the endowments or other cash reserves that could be invested. That percentage was 4 percent and was initially applied to an annual income base of about $9.2 million.

Within the context of RCB/RCM it is important to note that the disposition of investment income was in this case more RCB than RCM. All of the investment income that was attributed to the Scarborough campus was available to be deployed at the college's discretion, but the management of the principal was not. The principal remained fungible within the university's several investment pools, and was under the authority of the university's investment managers.

Installing RCB/RCM at UT-Scarborough

In the end the protocols that were developed to implement RCB/RCM at the University of Toronto's Scarborough campus numbered over one hundred. The time and effort that were invested in the development of the protocols were deliberately intended to serve two purposes. First, the objective was to install RCB/RCM totally. Unlike other universities that have moderated RCB/RCM by holding back some funding (Whalen, 1991) or by taxing some faculty revenue in order to create central funds to protect quality or support innovation (Whitaker, 1995), the University of Toronto sought to allocate literally all revenue and all expense to its Scarborough campus. Second, having studied the deployment of RCB/RCM at other universities, the University of Toronto wanted to obviate situations in which decisionmaking appeared to be devolved but in practice was not because campus and faculty managers had to return frequently to the central administration for various clarifications and interpretations of the RCB/RCM process.

The University of Toronto's application of RCB/RCM also made an unusually careful distinction between indirect costs and overhead costs. Indirect costs were understood to be costs that, prior to the introduction of RCB/RCM, were either known or knowable but were not attributed to faculty budgets. So, for example, space was a free good even though the costs of operating and maintaining it were calculable, faculty by faculty and building by building. Overhead costs, on the other hand, were understood to be costs that were knowable only by imputation of university-wide averages that could be attributed to faculties but which faculties through their own actions could not change. Indirect costs could be changed by faculties, for example, by occupying less space. In experimenting with RCB/RCM the university was as interested in its potential to reduce costs as in its potential to generate additional revenue. To do that, it was critical to ensure that UT-Scarborough would have real discretion over its indirect costs, and that those costs were not understated.

Some changes in governance also were necessary. In terms of accountability and authority under RCB/RCM, the Principal and Dean of UT-Scarborough would occupy a position comparable to that of several different officers of the university, particularly those with *ex officio* responsibility for academic programs, planning, budgeting, and finance. The terms of reference of several committees of the university's Governing Council were modified to re-delegate authority or, more exactly, to allow existing authority to be shared.

The university knew that certain significant impediments stood in the way of the successful implementation of total RCB/RCM on one of its campuses:

• Salaries and some terms of employment were negotiated centrally, thus fixing certain cost structures.
• Government funding was becoming erratic. Before going ahead with RCB/RCM, the university was able to model its effects on the Scarborough campus. The modeling indicated that UT-Scarborough could at least break even under RCB/RCM if assumptions about government funding held true.
• No principal or dean in the university had ever before assumed the management burden imposed by RCB/RCM.
• The direction that government policies on tuition fees might take was highly problematic.
• Some of the costs exposed by the introduction of RCB/RCM could be politically sensitive. Most professors at the University of Toronto had no accurate knowledge of the net costs of their research or of some of their programs that were nominally self-funded.
• At the time RCB/RCM would be being installed the university would also be installing an entirely new financial information system that would require extensive re-training of staff.

Outcome of RCB/RCM at UT-Scarborough

RCB/RCM at UT-Scarborough was regarded as an experiment that might either succeed or fail. Success would be measured in UT-Scarborough's ability to continue to break even and to generate additional net revenue, either by reducing costs or by increasing income. Another measurement, albeit less quantifiable, was the extent to which the Scarborough campus differentiated itself from the other University of Toronto campuses, especially in programs and program delivery. Judged by these criteria, the experiment has not been successful and probably will not be renewed. There has been little differentiation beyond that which was already in place. For example, UT-Scarborough was already the location of the university's co-operative education programs and its undergraduate Management program. Under RCB/RCM these programs were expanded, but more for their revenue potential than for differentiation. The programs weren't changed.

UT-Scarborough entered discussions with a nearby college of applied arts and technology about joint programming and shared facilities. The outcome was an agreement to share building sites. The agreement was financially advantageous to UT-Scarborough. In experimenting with RCB/RCM the university had hoped that the Scarborough campus would explore opportunities that might arise from surplus lands that were located there. A number of possibilities had been considered in the past but Scarborough had been unable or unwilling to act decisively about them. Under RCB/RCM the campus was decisive.

The main test – breaking even and generating additional revenue – was not successful. UT-Scarborough began in a slightly favorable net financial position but rather quickly moved to an unfavorable position. By the end of the 1999-2000 budget year, UTSC had accumulated a $5.5 million debt. It is difficult to put a finger on any one cause. One was the form that certain increases in government funding took. In global terms the increases were what the university and, in turn, the UTSC budget modeling had projected, but as those increases were applied to the particular mix of enrollment, programs and research grants at UT-Scarborough, that campus received less than the university-wide average.

Another funding problem was that the government earmarked funding for the expansion of enrollment in certain programs, some of which were offered at UT-Scarborough. Those programs, however, were among the more expensive offered by Scarborough and were also among those for which the province's funding formula assigned weights that tended to underestimate actual costs. Taking a short-term view UT-Scarborough chose to maximize income by expanding some of these programs. In the long term, however, the campus may end up losing, instead of gaining, net revenue by expanding those programs at costs beyond what government funding ultimately will cover. In other words, UT-Scarborough may have confused *maximizing income* with *optimizing net revenue*. In contrast, it is worth noting that a decade earlier the government launched a similar financial inducement to expand enrollment. At that time, while not operating under a revenue-driven scheme like RCB/RCM, the Scarborough campus declined to participate. This demonstrates two points: RCB/RCM does indeed stimulate greater interest at the faculty and campus level in the generation of income, and it is easy under RCB/RCM to confuse revenue optimization with revenue maximization.

Although the university had understood that attempting to introduce a new financial information system and RCB/RCM at the same time might be risky, the risks were underestimated. A related underestimation of risk had to do with the ability of campus administrators to manage RCB/RCM. Instead of helping them, the new financial information system caused some confusion as the new system produced financial reports that were unlike the reports to which the administrators were accustomed. A particular area of financial uncertainty was the status of funds that were carried forward from one budget year to the next. The allowance of 100 percent carry-forwards is a fundamental part of RCB/RCM, and had been the practice at the University of Toronto for several years prior to the RCB/RCM experiment at UT-Scarborough. Carried-forward funds can be either positive or negative. In the case of Scarborough, some funds were carried forward as favorable variances that were really negative in the sense that they were already committed when they were carried forward from one budget to the next. In other words, what seemed like $800,000 in additional funding that could be applied to reduce the UTSC debt was really the deferral of spending brought forward as an encumbrance from the previous year. This produced a double loss: not only were the additional funds not truly additive, they represented expense commitments that had to be covered.

THE RESULTS OF TRIAL AND ERROR

Lang (1999) examined the deployment of RCB/RCM at several American and Canadian universities and identified a series of advantages and disadvantages in which RCB/RCM resulted. That study provided a framework by which the University of Toronto's experience with RCB/RCM could be further assessed and contrasted with that of other universities.

RCB/RCM emphasizes and exposes costs that are often known but not recognized, or are deliberately not known because of their strategic implications. The experience of the University of Toronto in each of its applications of RCB/RCM, explicit or implicit, confirms that RCB/RCM has this effect. This occurred in several instances. It was particularly applicable in the decisions that UT-Scarborough made in regard to adjusting its enrollments in order to maximize the campus' net revenue. In the past, and in the absence of RCB/RCM, such decisions would have been made globally (that is, without much reference to individual programs) and in terms of gross revenue. In the School of Continuing Studies and the Faculty of Medicine, RCB/RCM could not have prevented the bad business decisions that were made, but it could and did expose those decisions as resulting in large net losses.

RCB/RCM motivates entrepreneurial behavior and the generation of revenue. In most other institutional planning and budget regimes, the generation of revenue is regarded mainly as the responsibility of the university's administration. Although various forms of performance budgeting or benchmarking may come into play in setting college, faculty, and departmental budgets (Garner, 1991), those budgets are predominantly expense budgets, and are planned and controlled as such. Revenue is collected centrally and allocated in the form of expense budgets, usually with no direct correlation to sources of revenue. To academic divisions, most services – for example, libraries, media centers, or campus security – are free goods. That was the situation for most colleges and faculties at the University of Toronto.

Because income as well as cost is attributed to colleges, faculties, or departments under RCB/RCM, the effect on principals, deans, or chairs is virtually immediate: the generation of revenue counts. Mistaken decisions or even wishful thinking about costs *versus* benefits makes real differences close to home. So RCB/RCM clearly captured the attention of those faculties at the University of Toronto that were placed on an RCB/RCM regimen.

Capturing and focusing attention on various means of generating revenue did not, however, in the case of the University of Toronto necessarily mean that there were viable opportunities for generating revenue or that those opportunities, when they existed, could be effectively pursued by management. At UT-Scarborough the campus became responsible for its own fund-raising, but few persons at the college had experience in development, and the college found it difficult to recruit and retain experienced professional fund-raisers. In terms of budget modeling, the college found it difficult to forecast accurately the probable results of some of its initiatives

Entrepreneurial behavior is by nature competitive and sometimes quite aggressively so. An important lesson that was learned from the University of Toronto's experience with RCB/RCM is that it is difficult to steer entrepreneurial behavior. It goes wherever it goes, and in the case of the University of Toronto that sometimes meant that the university was competing with itself for students.

For OISE/UT, its *de facto* variant of RCB/RCM stimulated different thinking about program delivery and about the forms that its master's degree programs for teachers might take. In these terms, OISE/UT made greater use of RCB/RCM than UT-Scarborough, which deployed RCB/RCM mainly to recalibrate the scale and mix of its previously existing array of programs.

RCB/RCM locates decisions about the allocation of resources where there is the most knowledge to make them intelligently. In a large, complex institutions like the University of Toronto, the president and his administration had the authority to make specific decisions about the allocation of resources to colleges and faculties but sometimes did not have the requisite sapience (March, 1994) or proximity (Whalen, 1991) to do so because crucial decisions about plans and budgets were often divorced from the reality of scholarship and program delivery. The senior administration understood that RCB/RCM presumes that the capability to make some decisions would be greater lower in the organizational structure, and that those are often decisions about the allocation of resources and about the tradeoffs between income and expense.

So, in deploying RCB/RCM at the University of Toronto, all parties intended from the start that there would be an extensive devolution of authority. Although the intention was unanimous, there were some doubts about it. Those doubts, which were held mainly by the University's provost, were not so much that the intentions were undesirable as they were that they might not work. Like many large and highly heterogeneous institutions, the central administration, particularly its academic administration, often had to rely on budgetary patronage to enforce its authority. RCB/RCM at the University of Toronto would soon prove that proposition to be true. Not only was budgetary authority devolved, as was intended, but other authority went with it.

RCB/RCM reduces the scale of planning and decisionmaking in large, complex institutions. RCB/RCM is to large scale institutional master planning as distributed computing is to mainframe computing. RCB/RCM redistributes responsibility for planning and budgeting. In this context, redistribute does not simply mean relocate the planning process intact. The central process is disassembled and redistributed. Some of it remains central or top-down but other parts are moved to new and varied points on the top- down/bottom-up continuum. The result is a series of plans and budgets that when taken together look like an anthology and form an institutional plan that is of value to governors and government. But each college or faculty need understand only its own plan and budget. Moreover, unlike other budget plans that are developed bottom-up, the RCB/RCM plan does not make any given local plan contingent on other local plans, which is often the case in large-scale planning exercises, and which often is an obstacle to the successful linking of plans and budgets (Schmidtlein, 1989; Griffin and Day, 1997).

This is much the way that RCB/RCM functioned at the University of Toronto. In fact the university was a particularly significant test of the proposition. Not only did each faculty and college have its own plan, because only some of them were operating under RCB/RCM their plans looked and functioned differently. Although awkward at first, this came to be understood. The estate for which it was most difficult to grasp was the university's governors, some of whom took the view that a plan that did not look like other plans must in some way be deficient.

One of the concerns that OISE had prior to its merger with the University of Toronto was that it might become lost within an institution as large as the University of Toronto and that its plans and needs might not be understood within the university's budget and planning processes. It is indeed often true that large, complex institutions gravitate towards a "one size fits all" mentality. The deployment of a variant of RCB/RCM as part of the formal integration agreement proved to be wise, and addressed effectively the concerns of the smaller partner to the merger.

RCB/RCM encourages the creation of markets as well as stimulating responses to markets. In time the experience of RCB/RCM at UT-Scarborough might confirm this proposition, as planning for joint programs and a joint campus with a nearby college progress, but the evidence so far seems to be that UT-Scarborough under RCB/RCM tended towards "more of the same" expansion. Where this proposition has proven most true at the University of Toronto is in the School of Continuing Studies and to a smaller degree in OISE/UT.

RCB/RCM may assume more knowledge of costs than an institution might actually have. If the implementation of RCB/RCM at the University of Toronto were to reveal only one thing it would be that the accurate determination and attribution of indirect costs and overhead was absolutely essential and very demanding. The problem has several dimensions.

First, there must be a standard methodology for determining overhead costs. There proved to be two important reasons for using a standard methodology. Deans of faculties affected by RCB/RCM, at least initially, questioned the rates as being too high. Providers of services to those faculties thought the rates were too low. It was important that these administrators be made confident that the rates were determined consistently across the university.

Second, the methodology had to be accurate and inclusive as well as comprehensible – characteristics that often worked against one another. Predictability, although apparently a mundane technicality, proved to be essential. A fundamental hope for RCB/RCM as deployed by the University of Toronto was that once cost structures were known, income and expense attributed, and authority delegated, the heads of academic programs and administrative services would seek to minimize costs and maximize revenue. So, for example, the Dean of OISE/UT needed to understand the overhead methodology well enough to know how the overhead rate of his faculty might change if it were to occupy less space, reduce its academic complement, or add students. If the methodology could not pass these tests, RCB/RCM would be little more than an elaborate and expensive accounting exercise.

Third, the methodology had to be replicable. If managers indeed tried to reduce overhead and indirect costs by various means, the RCB/RCM methodology had to be sufficiently reliable and robust to allow manipulation and periodic recalculation.

RCB/RCM at the University of Toronto met these tests. Meeting the tests, however, was not easy. The effort took several months. Knowledge of the costs of space was especially valuable and was often used.

RCB/RCM requires high level supporting financial information systems. The capability to allow manipulation and recalculation of RCB/RCM overhead and indirect costs rates depends as much on the availability of reliable and accurate data as on the methodology. Although RCB/RCM inherently involves extensive delegation of authority, and that delegation is essential to the full realization of the advantages of RCB/RCM, it does not relieve the senior administration and the board of governors of their fiduciary responsibilities. As well, good faculty managers must be protected from incompetent ones, or, more exactly, from the financial consequences of their incompetence. The implication of all of this is that the financial information system must have a strong and reliable audit capability to give early warnings of poor management at the faculty level. RCB/RCM inherently increases business risk.

These are some of the reasons that the University of Toronto began to develop new financial information systems before beginning its major experiments with RCB/RCM. Two of the university's large self-funded programs had previously incurred large losses of which the university had little advance warning. Without its new financial information system, the University of Toronto almost certainly would have been wary about deploying RCB/RCM. But timing was a problem. It would have been better if the introduction of RCB/RCM at UT-

Scarborough had been delayed long enough for the campus administration to become more familiar with the new system.

But the experience of the University of Toronto also indicates that some of the business risks inherent in RCB/RCM are beyond mitigation by virtually any financial information system. At UT-Scarborough, for example, the local administration for all practical purposes created and used a shadow budget that in the end could not be reconciled with the university's year-end statements. The shadow budget, whether used for the purpose or not, had the effect of obfuscating a series of major liabilities that seriously compromised the entire experiment with RCB/RCM on that campus.

RCB/RCM may demand more local managerial skills and appetites than may actually exist. Based on the University of Toronto's experience, this proposition is absolutely true. RCB/RCM is as much a managerial system as it is a planning and budgeting system. This is why the architecture and methodology of RCB/RCM at Toronto had to be comprehensible and robust. The tradition of leadership in university faculties and departments depends primarily on scholarly reputation and only coincidentally on administrative skill (Keller, 1983). That was the tradition at the University of Toronto.

Conventional budget planning and management systems are largely centralized and supported by professional financial managers. The demands that those systems make on the heads of faculties and colleges are not frivolous, unusual, onerous, or difficult to comprehend. But RCB/RCM in practical effect invests college principals and faculty deans with the responsibilities of CEOs, which for many academic administrators is a new concept. Most of them are not prepared for such responsibilities. Many do not want to assume them. Virtually none of them was selected and appointed on the assumption that he or she would have to carry out such responsibilities (Blau, 1994). This, too, was the tradition at the University of Toronto.

These problems were anticipated by the University of Toronto as it laid the groundwork for RCB/RCM. OISE/UT added a position for a chief financial officer, and recruited the university's budget director to fill it. UT-Scarborough upgraded its most senior finance and administrative position to the level of Associate Principal. Like OISE/UT, UT-Scarborough recruited a senior administrator from the university's central administration to fill the position, but in the case of Scarborough this occurred after the experiment in RCB/RCM was already underway. OISE/UT had its new CFO in place before the merger actually took place.

For publicly funded institutions there may be an asymmetry between government funding formulas and actual institutional cost structures. In the United States and Canada, many if not most schools, colleges, and universities are funded under allocative formulas. There are different types of formulas, each with its own strengths and weaknesses. But despite these differences, funding formulas have one thing in common: in one way or another they all make assumptions about institutional cost structures.

The validity of those assumptions is often debated, but valid or not they are inherent to funding formulas and can have a complicating effect on the deployment of RCB/RCM, as indeed was the case at the University of Toronto, where it proved to be a very serious and virtually debilitating problem. Under RCB/RCM all revenue and all costs are attributed to each faculty or college. Each unit must then adjust its spending patterns to coincide with its revenue patterns. That is the basic idea of "each tub on its own bottom."

The idea is simple enough until one considers the possibility that large components of revenue may be based on assumptions about costs that are either erroneous to begin with or so generalized that they cannot be validly applied to specific programs in specific institutions, which is exactly what the University of Toronto tried to do. Funding formulas have a powerful homogenizing effect; they are based on averages that treat all programs within certain categories as the same. Therefore, for any given program in any given institution under RCB/RCM, the attribution of income may be accurate but may also be unrealistic.

Some universities that have introduced RCB/RCM correct for this by not attributing all income to colleges and faculties. Some is held back and allocated by other means, often and ironically by the same means that preceded the introduction of RCB/RCM. Others correct for the artificial effects of funding formulas by inserting a local formula between the system formula and the RCB/RCM attribution process. In hindsight the University of Toronto might have done well to introduce one or both correctional devices, especially for RCB/RCM at UT-Scarborough. The failure to do so seriously undermined RCB/RCM's potential for success on that campus.

The basic cost structures at the Scarborough campus were more or less similar to those on the university's other campuses. One significant exception was the age/salary profile of UT-Scarborough's academic staff. The Scarborough faculty was relatively younger than the faculties on the other campuses. In budgetary terms this meant that the savings that normally accrue when higher paid faculty exit by retirement and are replaced by lower paid junior faculty were relatively low.

Although the Scarborough campus' cost structures were similar to those elsewhere in the University of Toronto, its revenue structures, under the government's funding formula, were not. Most of that campus' programs were at the lower end of the province's weighted enrollment formula. In simple terms, that meant that while UT-Scarborough had average costs, its programs and enrollments generated below average per student revenues. One of the advantages of the University of Toronto's being very large and diverse is that funding anomalies like those at UT-Scarborough could have been offset by other anomalies elsewhere in the University. RCB/RCM largely neutralized that advantage insofar as UT-Scarborough was concerned.

The province's funding formula uses enrollment in advanced doctoral programs as a surrogate for the costs of research infrastructure. Generally, the assumption that infrastructure costs are linked to graduate enrollment is crude but broadly valid. So it was on that basis – graduate students supervised – that the university attributed operating grant revenue and tuition fees to UT-Scarborough.

The catch was that although most faculty at the campus were members of the university's School of Graduate Studies and were active researchers, most of the university's graduate students were resident at the university's main campus. Thus, whereas the infrastructure costs were more or less the same across all three of the University of Toronto's campuses, the attribution of revenue to the Scarborough campus was based on an input measure that did not fully recognize those costs. The university might have been wiser to have overridden that aspect of the province's funding formula in favor of a revenue allocation scheme that was based on the number of graduate faculty members instead of the number of graduate students.

Service teaching and RCB/RCM are not always compatible. This was a proposition of which the University of Toronto was keenly aware from the start of its planning for RCB/RCM. The university saw the issue from two fundamentally opposing directions. On one hand, the conventional approach to the question about the proper attribution of the income and expense that service teaching generates is to assign the costs of service teaching to the faculty that provides it, in other words, to the cost center. That makes senses from an accounting point of view. It then follows that income ought to be as closely aligned with expense as possible. So the revenue that enrollment in service courses generates is attributed to the faculty that provides the service teaching.

On the other hand, an ultimate objective of RCB/RCM is to generate revenue, encourage market-like behavior, and improve the fit between educational supply and demand. In that case, the attribution of revenue ought to be to the faculty that decides on critical balances between enrollment, programs, and resources, and then recruits and registers students, notwithstanding the possibility that some of those students might take some courses in other faculties. The cost of service teaching then would appear as a charge by the faculty that provides the service teaching against the expense budget of the faculty that registers the students and is credited fully for the revenue that they generate.

The University of Toronto understood that RCB/RCM can work against collegiate tradition as individual programs and departments compete with other programs and departments for students, mainly because they do not want to share the revenue that the enrollments generate. In the protocols for the deployment of RCB/RCM at UT-Scarborough the university opted to attribute the revenue generated by service teaching directly to the faculties that provided it to the Scarborough campus. This was not an insignificant number; it amounted to about 5,000 course enrollments annually. Basically, the revenue that these enrollments generated was never attributed to UT-Scarborough.

If all the university's faculties and campuses were operating under RCB/RCM this might have proven to be the better choice. But because they were not, the choice proved to be unfortunate. UT-Scarborough had little leverage with other faculties because it did not appear to be a "purchaser" of service teaching. To the providers of service teaching, the attribution of income seemed to be no more than arcane bookkeeping.

LESSONS LEARNED FROM THE DEPLOYMENT OF RCB/RCM

Do not expect RCB/RCM to be useful and effective in all circumstances. Its application should be specific instead of broad. RCB/RCM appears to be a creature of circumstance. It has so far been an effective means of addressing a number of specific contemporary problems and issues. At the University of Toronto RCB/RCM provided the assurances, stability, and local decisionmaking expertise that were necessary to a successful merger. As funding shrinks, RCB/RCM can help improve the quality of decisions about the optimal allocations of resources and balances between income and expense. That seems to have been the experience at UT-Scarborough but only up to a point. Decisions that were made were made well, but RCB/RCM, because of its allowance of 100 percent carry-forward of deficits (as well as surpluses), seems to have engendered the deferral of some important decisions.

Do not expect RCB/RCM to be a "quick fix" or inexpensive solution. It takes time and effort to install. Sometimes it requires expensive investments in management infrastructure. The University of Toronto needed new financial information systems, and would have installed them whether or not RCB/RCM was introduced. Nevertheless, the university's experience has demonstrated the necessity of those systems to the successful implementation of RCB/RCM. In each of the faculties into which RCB/RCM was introduced, it was necessary to supplement divisional management with senior staff experienced in financial and budget management.

Do take the ways in which public funding is allocated to universities into account in implementing RCB/RCM. The success or failure of RCB/RCM can depend on the form that the public allocation takes. Some funding formulas distort the connection between revenue and cost. This was certainly true in the case of the University of Toronto. It had a seriously debilitating effect on RCB/RCM at UT-Scarborough, and would have had a similar effect on OISE/UT had the merger agreement not expressly addressed the problem. The fundamental lesson is that if a funding formula does not at least approximately reflect an institution's cost structures, that institution should be very wary of RCB/RCM.

Do not generalize the effects that RCB/RCM may have on collegiality and cooperation. It may be beneficial in some cases and detrimental in others. This is one of the most important and most surprising lessons learned from the experience of the University of Toronto with RCB/RCM. On the one hand, RCB/RCM promoted collegiality by expanding the degree of participation in making decisions about plans and budgets which otherwise would be made centrally. By exposing and attributing all costs and revenue, RCB/RCM allowed a far more extensive understanding of the overall financial condition of the faculties in which it was deployed. On the other hand, RCB/RCM in some circumstances engendered internal competition that discouraged collegiality and cooperation. In the spatial terms of an organization chart, then, one might characterize RCB/RCM as promoting vertical collegiality but discouraging horizontal collegiality. As vertical collegiality grew, the central administration, especially the academic administration, necessarily lost some control, particularly because it had previously relied on patronage in resource allocation as a means of exerting control. As RCB/RCM shifted the center of gravity of decisionmaking towards the college and faculties, the idiom of collegial discourse between, for example, the Dean of OISE/UT and the Provost, also shifted in the direction of academic plans, standards, and performance measures, and away from budgets and resources. But in the case of UT-Scarborough this seemed, unfortunately, to discourage all discourse between the two levels of administration.

Do expect some special problems if RCB/RCM is not deployed in all faculties. Although the deployment of RCB/RCM at the University of Toronto was extensive, it was not a majority practice. This resulted in at least two particular areas of difficulty. It was very difficult to implement RCB/RCM in conjunction with a unitary school of graduate studies. Likewise, it was very difficult to manage relations between RCB/RCM and non-RCB/RCM faculties in regard to service teaching.

Do expect a steep learning curve for divisional administrators who have little experience in making the sorts of decisions for which RCB/RCM calls. Do not expect automated financial information systems to flatten that learning curve. In the case of RCB/RCM at UT-Scarborough the learning curve was too steep, and the university's new financial information system – or, more exactly, the approximately simultaneous introduction of that system – tended to make the curve steeper. The learning curve at UT-Scarborough was finally flattened by the arrival of two senior administrators with extensive planning and budgeting experience.

Do expect RCB/RCM to generate interest in raising income, but do not expect the difference between maximizing income and optimizing net revenue to be recognized automatically by faculty and campus managers. Because RCB/RCM is often deployed in response to budgetary shortfalls that have already occurred, there is a tendency to favor the maximization of gross income over the optimization of net revenue. RCB/RCM is most effectively deployed in conjunction with multi-year planning and budgeting that can project the steady state effects of budget strategies.

Do invest however much time and effort are needed to develop clear and complete protocols for the deployment of RCB/RCM. A principal objective of RCB/RCM is to decentralize decisionmaking. In the absence of clear and complete protocols and processes, decentralization may be an illusion if faculty and campus administrators have to return frequently to the central administration to negotiate interpretations and clarifications of the rules.

REFERENCES

Blau, Peter M. 1994. *The organization of academic work,* 2nd ed. New Brunswick, NJ: Transaction.

Clark, Burton R. 1998. *Creating entrepreneurial universities.* Oxford: Pergamon.

Eastman, Julia, and Daniel Lang. 2001. *Mergers in higher education: Lessons from theory and experience.* Toronto: University of Toronto Press.

Fisher, Donald, and Kjell Rubenson. 1998. The changing political economy: The private and public lives of Canadian universities. In J. Currie and J. Newson, eds., *Universities and globalization: Critical perspectives.* London: Sage: 77-98.

Garner, C. William. 1991. *Accounting and budgeting in public and nonprofit organizations.* San Francisco: Jossey-Bass.

Griffin, Susan, and Susan Day. 1997. Progress made on a plan to integrate planning, budgeting, assessment and quality principles to achieve institutional improvement. *AIR Professional File,* No. 66.

Herbst, Jurgen. 1981. Church, state, and higher education. *History of Higher Education Annual* 1:42-54.

Keller, George. 1983. *Academic strategy.* Baltimore: Johns Hopkins University Press.

Lang, Daniel W. 1999. A primer on responsibility centre budgeting and responsibility centre management. Canadian Society for the Study of Higher Education. *CSSHE Professional File,* No. 17.

Lang, Daniel, with A. L. Darling, M. D. England, R. Lopers-Sweetman. 1989. Autonomy and control: A university funding formula as an instrument of public policy. *Higher Education* 18 (5): 559-584.

March, James G. 1994. *A primer on decision making.* New York: The Free Press.

Schmidtlein, F. A. 1989. Center findings reveal planning problems. *News From SCUP,* 19 (4): 2-11.

University of Toronto. 1996. Final brief to the advisory panel on future directions for post-secondary education, Appendix VII. Toronto: Office of the Vice-Provost and Assistant Vice-President, Planning and Budget, University of Toronto.

Whalen, Edward L. 1991. *Responsibility center budgeting.* Bloomington: Indiana University Press.

Whitaker, Gilbert R. 1995. Value centered management: The Michigan approach to responsibility center management. *University Record,* January 9.

CHAPTER 7

ACTIVITY-BASED BUDGETING AT THE UNIVERSITY OF MICHIGAN

Paul N. Courant

Marilyn Knepp

We begin this discussion on the budget system at the University of Michigan with a history of the events that brought us to adopt activity-based budgeting. We begin by describing a series of management incentives initiated through the 1980s and 1990s that culminated in the 1997 implementation of value-centered management (VCM), the university's version of a responsibility center budgeting system (RCB). Next, we discuss why VCM was short-lived and how it changed into our current system, university budgeting (known as university budget, UB), which we describe as an activity-based or a modified responsibility center management approach to budgeting. The rationale for the change is an important part of the story, and we will spend a little time on it before turning to a richer description and evaluation of the system as it works now.

EVOLUTION OF ACTVITY-BASED BUDGETING AT MICHIGAN

Decentralized Management at the University of Michigan

Michigan has a long history of decentralized management. Following a series of actions, moving to an activity-based system of budgeting was a logical next step (albeit a large one).

The university's circumstances, in a variety of ways, foster both decentralized management and the ability to change budgeting systems. Although we are a state-supported institution, we have a high degree of autonomy guaranteed in the state constitution and affirmed over time through court rulings. We are governed by an elected Board of Regents, which has ultimate authority for all matters of policy and operations. Thus, we (the Regents) set our own tuition, make all decisions regarding academic programs and offerings, and have full financial authority and autonomy. The revenues we earn flow directly to us and, in every respect, are under our control. Although these factors may not be necessary for a public institution that wants to move to responsibility center budgeting, their presence makes such a decision vastly easier to implement than in institutions without such independence from state authority or governance.

Other attributes of Michigan contribute to our ability to successfully implement an activity-based budgeting system. The Provost is the chief budget officer as well as the chief academic officer. This combination provides more certainty that budget decisions will support academic priorities and that the design of an activity-based system will be tailored to support the academic mission. Our schools and colleges have strong deans and substantial unit autonomy. The deans are accustomed to engaging in entrepreneurial activities that enhance the flow of resources to their own units and are accustomed to the management responsibility that accompanies such activities. In areas other than the General Fund, revenues flow directly to units rather than into central coffers for allocation. All revenues that support the direct expenditures on sponsored grants, revenues from nondegree educational offerings or from conferences and publications, and almost all gifts for operating or endowment purposes, are entirely under the control of the dean rather than any central administrator. In general, the deans are expected to be academic leaders, savvy financial managers, and responsible stewards of the unit's and the university's resources.

Our management practices encourage responsible oversight by unit managers. For nearly two decades, our units have had the ability to carry forward unspent balances, and have had the obligation to cover any overspending that may occur. We have a diversified and strong portfolio of revenue sources and the flexibility to exploit opportunities as they arise. All of our schools and colleges, and many other units as well, derive substantial revenue from gifts, from external grants and contracts, and from the provision of services (and sometimes goods) to entities both internal and external to the university. Our managers are accustomed to taking an all-funds approach to budgeting, as is the Provost's office.

In the context of this culture and these circumstances it was quite natural for us to take a number of actions during the 1980s and 1990s that further decentralized management responsibility. Year after year saw the implementation of a number of "management incentives." In each case, prior to the incentive, the central administration had been paying for activities for which the locus of decision was at the unit level. In implementing a management incentive, we would distribute the central pool of funds into unit budgets and make the units responsible for covering the costs (and enjoying the savings) and any subsequent changes. Thus we would align responsibility and costs.

The list of items handled in this manner included the tuition grants that are paid for graduate student assistants, staff benefits for all regular and temporary faculty and staff, obligations for a furlough year prior to retirement for faculty hired prior to 1984, and a pool of funding that represented the derived share of some basic infrastructure items (phones, networks, equipment) that could be attributed to the volume of sponsored research activity.

We also had a number of management initiatives that returned revenues to units when their actions created an increased flow to the university. We initiated several programs that distributed a portion of indirect cost recovery to units as research incentives. Tuition returns were made to units for differential tuition rate increases, for special purpose fee assessments, or for special programs boosting overall enrollments. Similarly, units that chose to implement differentially lower tuition increases or planned enrollment decreases had to adjust to budget reductions resulting from these actions. In sum, many elements of RCB were already in place by the early 1990s.

The Implementation of VCM

Robert S. Holbrook, professor of economics, served as Associate Provost from 1980 until his retirement from active service during the 1998 fiscal year. Holbrook's leadership and vision, working with five different provosts during this time period, were driving forces behind these changes as he worked to introduce many of the principles of RCB into Michigan's budgeting practices, readying the institution to consider the more radical change of adopting a responsibility center management system.

During the tenure of Provost Gilbert R. Whitaker, Holbrook led a full-scale effort to investigate and define Michigan's version of responsibility center budgeting. This system, known locally as value-centered management or VCM, was implemented for the Fiscal Year 1997 budget, following a study period of about two years (Report, 1995).[1]

VCM put all of the university's units on an activity basis. The schools and colleges and separately budgeted research units received revenue allocations based on earnings formulas for tuition and other student-related fees, indirect cost recovery revenue, and interest. Simultaneously, they were assessed cost attributions for financial aid, space-related charges, the costs of administrative and service units, the costs of the university's academic-related public goods units (libraries, museums, and such); and were taxed a modest amount for what was called "university participation." All other units including administrative, service, and the academic-related public goods units received as revenue the costs that were assessed to others and, in turn, were assessed costs associated with their own use of administrative, service, and public goods units.

Initial implementation. The initial implementation of VCM was done in such a way as to hold all units harmless relative to the change in budgeting system. That is, all units' budgets for FY 1997 were determined under the old incremental budgeting system, at the same time that all of the elements of the value-centered budget, VCM, were computed for each unit. At the very second that the Board of Regents approved the FY 1997 budget that had been developed under the "old" incremental scheme, the computed VCM system was put into place, with each unit receiving a Provost's allocation of precisely the magnitude necessary to ensure that the bottom line, that is the unit's base budget, was unchanged. Thus, all units were funded adequately to do what they had been doing before the implementation of VCM, and the incentive effects of VCM were expected to make themselves manifest going forward. Subsequent budgets were to reflect the discretion of the academic leadership, as well as the workings of the VCM formulas.

Initial reception. The initial reception on campus was mixed at best. A number of faculty expressed concerns about the applicability of the language of business to the purposes of the academy. Many faculty expressed concern that the identification of responsibility centers would weaken the incentives for interdisciplinary work in both teaching and research. Indeed, the Vice-President for Research appointed a committee, chaired by Professor Michael Savageau of the Department of Microbiology and Immunology, to advise the Vice-President on ways to mitigate the untoward effects of VCM on interdisciplinary research. The committee's report was widely circulated and discussed. The Institute for Social Research (ISR), which had operated for nearly five decades on RCM-type principles internally, looked to be unsustainable under the new model. Concerns about ISR's health helped to crystallize skepticism about the new system on the part of social scientists. This, in turn, led to a set of transition rules that were designed to limit the effects of VCM on the ISR. At the same time, many humanists expressed outrage that the model treated the university library as a service unit rather than recognizing its academic mission. Humanists and others were also concerned that units unable to survive on their own revenues would be disadvantaged under VCM. There was also worry that the central administration would lose interest in containing costs, because under the VCM model, administrative costs could simply be passed on to the units.

The new system was not without support, of course, and it particularly enjoyed the support of the President, the Provost, and a substantial majority of deans and academic directors, who appreciated the flexibility and autonomy that they would enjoy under VCM.

Changes in leadership. Provost Whitaker stepped down just as the first VCM budget went into effect. His successor, Bernard Machen, who had been involved in the planning for VCM as Dean of the Dental School, served as Provost for the succeeding two years. One of his last acts as Provost was to develop the FY 1998 budget in the VCM model. As it happened, this was the only budget to be developed in the VCM model.

Early in 1997 a new President, Lee C. Bollinger, took office, and in July, he announced the appointment of Nancy Cantor as Provost effective in September. Bollinger made one important change in VCM affecting the attribution of tuition before the 1998 fiscal year began. Quite soon after her appointment, Cantor, in turn, proposed and implemented a substantial revision of the VCM system overall, which took effect FY 1999. Like VCM, the revised university budget model (UB) also was implemented with the principle that units should initially be held harmless with respect to the change in budgeting systems. This time, however, the changeover to the new model was made as the final action of the 1998 fiscal year and so the FY 1999 budget was developed fully using the UB model. In it, the Provost made a number of substantive policy changes that led to the FY 1999 budgets being noticeably different from those that would have obtained under VCM. Thus, VCM was in full force for only one year, FY 1998, and even then was a lame duck for more than half the year.

The UB system has been used to determine three budgets, and is now being used as the university puts together a budget for FY 2002. It has changed only slightly since it was put in place, and we discuss those changes as we describe the system below.

HOW AND WHY DID MICHIGAN REVISE ITS FIRST RCB SYSTEM?

The UB system was announced (although not yet named) and described in broad outline in a speech to the university's Senate Assembly made by Provost Nancy Cantor in November 1997. The case for revising VCM was made both in Cantor's speech (1997) and in a companion paper written by Cantor and Courant (1997).[2]

Like VCM, the UB system is an "activity-based" budget system, in that increases in certain activities lead to automatic flows of resources and costs to the units that do the work and obtain the revenue. Put simply, revenue follows revenue-generating activity and units that engage in revenue-generating activity are given (at least) the lion's share of those revenues. At the same time, increased activities generally create increased costs, both directly in those units and indirectly in other university administrative areas, and so associated costs generally also rise as revenues increase. The advantage, at the heart of RCB systems and their derivatives, is that the costs and benefits of various activities can be seen most clearly where the activities are undertaken – in the schools, colleges, and research units.

Michigan's change from VCM to UB is one illustration of the fact that most of the potential problems with activity-based budgeting derive directly from its strengths. By providing support for activities that are directly attributable to individual units within the university, there exists the possibility that activities where such attribution is difficult or contested will be under-supported. In addition, many vital parts of the university, including libraries, the campus police, and a number of academic departments, cannot possibly survive based on revenues that they generate directly. For these reasons, many universities that have implemented or contemplated activity-based models have conducted campus-wide debates on the possible negative consequences of the model on collaborative work, on interdisciplinary research and teaching, on activities whose compass is campus-wide, and activities that are academically vital but not especially popular. It was just this set of concerns that led Michigan to adopt UB, an activity-based system that leaves considerably more room for central discretion and for support of campus-wide activities than is the norm for such systems.

The Provost identified five clusters of problems associated with VCM:

1. *The use of attributed costs and the financing of central service units.* Under VCM, service unit costs were attributed to academic units, auxiliary units, and to other service units according to some 24 different attribution formulas. For example, the formulas for attributing the costs of units that provide extensive support for students placed a heavy weight on numbers of students, while the formula for attributing the cost of research support units was based on the volume of research. The attribution formulas led to three sets of problems. First, no matter how detailed the formulas are they never fit perfectly, because the actual cost drivers in higher education are hard to identify and even harder to measure. Thus, there was continuing pressure to change the formulas (the 24 started as four) and continuing complaints by some units that the formulas overcharged them. Second, some cost drivers in higher education are related to things that we want to encourage, rather than discourage. Third, the system had relatively weak incentives to control service costs, because the costs were not under the control of those who would benefit from their reduction. Rather, if a manager or senior administrator reduced costs, the savings would be distributed to the academic and auxiliary units according to the attribution formulas, rather than be available for that administrator to reallocate. Likewise, increased service costs could simply be passed on by the Provost and President to become a problem for a dean to deal with instead of a problem for the central administration. Under UB, cost attribution has been dropped.[3]

2. *Incentives for teaching.* In its original form, tuition attribution in VCM was a mixed model with a portion allocated based on unit of enrollment and a portion allocated to the unit of instruction. The latter basis led to a strong incentive for units to duplicate offerings of popular courses, to regulate their own students' curricula to require them to take courses "at home," and, possibly, to provide courses of dubious academic value that could generate substantial attributed revenue. Under UB (and under the actual implementation of VCM as revised by President Bollinger prior to the 1997-98 Fiscal Year), tuition attribution follows the unit of enrollment. This reverses the set of incentives discussed above, generating problems of its own, while minimizing incentives for duplication of course offerings and for requiring students to take more courses in their home units than warranted by curricular considerations.

3. *Definition of service units.* Under VCM, service units were distinguished from academic units largely as a function of their revenue structure. In particular, libraries and museums were seen as service units (just like the Department of Public Safety or Financial Operations) because their revenues do not come directly from charges levied to external customers. Under UB, units are defined by their function (academic or service) rather than by their sources of support. Thus, libraries and museums are part of a new category of University Academic

Units that directly perform academic missions for the university in general, rather than in a particular school or college.

4. *Language.* From the beginning, many on campus resisted the "business" language in which many of the discussions of VCM took place. In partial reaction to this concern, the name VCM (value-centered management) replaced the original, more general label RCM (responsibility center management) in order to signal strongly that the embodiment of academic values would continue to be the primary purpose of the university budget. This change generated new problems, in that many faculty members were troubled (quite vocally so) by the implicit proposition that the university's values could be embodied in a budget model. In naming the current system simply as the university budget system, known as UB, Provost Cantor meant to emphasize that budgets serve policy, rather than make it.

5. *The problem of penurious units.* Notwithstanding the initial hold-harmless implementation and repeated statements to the contrary, many members of the university's communities were concerned that under VCM, units that could not survive on their "own" resources (principally tuition and indirect cost recovery) would be allowed to disappear, regardless of their academic quality and importance, while units that could charge high tuition or market their research successfully would prosper. This concern was closely tied to the concerns about language, in that one of the values that VCM seemed to be based upon was the value of having a positive financial bottom line. UB addressed this problem by a change of name, a change of leadership, and by increasing the ease with which the Provost can reallocate resources from year-to-year.

BUDGET MODELS AND BUDGET SYSTEMS

Before going any further, it will be useful to distinguish between budget systems and budget models. Both VCM and UB are budget models, which we define as a set of rules for arranging the elements of a budget. For example, under the rules that constitute UB, indirect cost recovery (ICR) is generally allocated as revenue to the unit(s) that generate the direct research associated with the ICR. Units are allowed to keep any balances in operating funds across fiscal years, and units with students in the Rackham Graduate School are assessed for financial aid based on the number of their students who are enrolled in Rackham programs. These are but a few of a long list of rules under which budgets are developed in UB.

The budget system is broader than the budget model. The system includes all of the discretionary elements (including the authority and values of relevant decisionmakers) as well as the budget model that policymakers use to help them with budgeting. The distinction is easily seen with reference to the fifth cluster of concerns about VCM discussed above. The concern that the condition of units could not float on their own bottoms was in jeopardy under VCM was allayed in part by a change in leadership, which was a change in the budget system unaccompanied by any change in the formal budget model.

One could imagine a perfectly mechanical world in which a university budget system was coterminous with a university budget model. In such a world, once the model was written down there would be nothing further for the central leadership to do, at least with regard to resource allocation. Of course, no budget system is that mechanical. Still, one can imagine a continuum anchored by a completely mechanical system at one end and a completely discretionary one at the other. On such a continuum, the budgeting system at the University of Michigan is some distance from either extreme. The UB model has a number of highly consequential rules (rules that could be changed by the leadership, of course) but it is also designed to leave a fair amount of room for judgment by the President and Provost.

Discretion for discretion's sake is not the only reason why budget models and budget systems differ. As a practical matter, no set of rules can encapsulate all possible contingencies and policy responses to those contingencies. Thus, even if the leadership of a university were disposed to prefer that their budget system was based as much as possible on a budget model, there would still be cases where the outcome from such a model would create unintended consequences, requiring leadership intervention.

As a general matter, we believe that budget models should get in the way of good decisionmaking as little as possible, but we recognize that there will always be cases where the model will generate incentives that are not consistent with the best policies and practices. Thus, we take it that any budget system should include the principle that when the model seems to be getting in the way of making sound decisions, units should have an easy route to alert the budget authorities to the problem, and the budget system should have sufficient flexibility to override the budget model. Thus, budgeting models in general do not and should not determine budgets, any more than the specific characteristics of an automobile determine (except in the most general way) where and how fast it is driven.

The budget model itself neither knows nor cares whether its administrators are committed to, for example, building up the arts, or allowing all incremental resources to flow automatically to those units that enroll the most students, or producing across-the-board changes in budgets that leave every unit's share of resources the same as last year, or aggressively courting potential Nobel Prize winners, or any other specific set of policy commitments. All of this is as it should be; the purpose of budgets is to implement policies, not to substitute for policymaking.

We view our budget system, of which the UB model is one part, as a cohesive whole; it is by definition a system. As with any system, it is important to consider the whole as well as the parts because, in general, tinkering with any single aspect will have consequences elsewhere in the system. Individual parts may appear to serve separate and distinct functions but their interrelationships require that one understand the system and its goals in order to understand fully each of its parts. The analogy to automobiles is again instructive; increasing the horsepower without adding to braking capacity and strengthening the suspension is likely to be dangerous. Complicated systems are often criticized piecemeal. Evaluating criticisms intelligently requires that proposed improvements be examined in light of all of their potential consequences.

HOW THE MODEL WORKS

As a technical matter, General Fund revenues all flow to the central administration and it is the Provost's task to determine budget allocations in order to make the most effective use of the resources available to accomplish the university's missions. In explaining the UB model, we refer to "automatic" flows of revenues and costs. It is important to note that in fact, allocation and attribution decisions made in the model and the rules in place today do not create a forever-after entitlement to those particular methods of allocation. Of course, no administration would change these rules lightly, and current university practice is generally undertaken on the assumption that UB will be in force indefinitely.

The Provost uses the UB model as an aid in developing the General Fund budgets of both academic units and service units – that is for units that have significant activity-based revenue, and for units that do not. The Provost budgets to units at a fairly high level – to a school or college, not the departments within it; to an executive officer area, not the separate offices or functions within it. This is seen quite clearly in the level of detail within the UB model. Note that the system, as distinct from the model, represents a rich and detailed sharing of both qualitative and quantitative information among the Provost, the deans, executive officers, and other academic leadership. Throughout the annual budget cycle, the Provost seeks, develops, and is provided with information on faculty quality, salary pressures, national trends in the various fields, legal requirements, etc. She also learns a great deal about individual departments and offices that are within the larger units to which she provides budgetary support. All of this information affects the budget system and the decisionmaking within the system, even when it has no direct impact on the activities to which revenue flows in the UB model.

Types of Units

The way in which units are budgeted depends on their position on each of two dimensions. Units can be classified according to function – direct providers of academic services (teaching departments, research units, libraries) vs. other units, including service units and auxiliary units (financial operations, admissions, campus police, residence halls). Units can also be classified according to whether or not they generate activity-based revenues. The resulting 2 by 2 matrix yields entries in all four cells. Examples are shown in Table 7.1.

Table 7.1: Classification of Academic Units

	Academic (direct providers)	Nonacademic (other units)
Activity-Based	Schools, Research Units	Athletics, Housing
Centrally Budgeted	Libraries, Museums	Police, Admissions, General Counsel's Office

From a budget model perspective, units divide according to whether their budgets are activity-based or not. Activity-based units receive a significant portion of their revenue as a function of what they do – whether it be enrolling students, obtaining NIH grants, or selling football tickets. As a result, the budget *model* treats the university library much as it treats the general counsel's office. Both have their budgets determined centrally, because neither directly generates sufficient revenues to cover an appreciable portion of its operations. But the far more important division is based on whether a unit contributes directly to the university's core missions, and therefore, the budget *system* treats these two units very differently. The library is an academic unit and as such its activities are viewed as valuable in their own right. The general counsel's office is an essential unit, but its value is derived entirely from the support that it provides to the academic missions of the university.

Against this backdrop, we consider first the three types of academic units and then those that are nonacademic, starting with the activity-based units in each category.

Academic Units

1. *Schools and colleges.* These, of course, are the units that enroll students, provide instruction, grant degrees, conduct research, and perform public service and outreach. Their activities are responsible for the university's receipt of revenue from student tuition and fees, recovery of indirect costs of sponsored research, and some interest from the balances they hold in the General Fund. Their activities create direct costs in the school or college itself, but also create costs in the many administrative and service units that support their activities and that provide services to their students.

All the schools and colleges, with the exception of the Rackham School of Graduate Studies, have their budgets developed using an activity-based approach. At the same time, there is no expectation that deans will follow UB model rules or, for that matter, any other set of similar rules when making resource allocation decisions for the separate departments and areas within their schools. Our budget system is very effective in determining the budgets of the schools. It was not, however, developed to provide a standard template to guide budgeting *within* our schools.

2. *Research units.* Organized research units exist to conduct research and to provide centers of collaborations in areas of university emphasis. These

separately budgeted research units generally report to the Vice-President for Research. These units have their budgets developed using an activity-based approach. Although other "research units" exist as areas within schools and colleges, they are not budgeted by the Provost but rather by the dean who is the chief academic and budgetary administrator for a particular school. So, the set of research units within the UB model are only those that exist organizationally outside of the schools and colleges.

3. *University academic units (UAU).* These are primarily the museums and libraries, including the university library, which are not organizationally a part of a school, college, or other unit. The Provost has aptly described these units' missions as the production and enhancement of the university's shared public culture, and has characterized their activities as essential to the accomplishment of the university's academic missions. However, UAU activities are rarely associated with the generation of direct revenue. Therefore, the UAUs (and the Rackham Graduate School, which does not directly generate activity-based revenue) are not budgeted using the activity-based model components, but have their budgets determined centrally.

Nonacademic Units

4. *Auxiliary units.* Auxiliary units are those whose activities are maintained by their own revenues. They are quite disparate, including the hospitals, housing, and the university press among their number. For the most part, their budgets lie outside of the General Fund and are, inherently, activity-based. However, these units impose a set of costs of the university in areas supported primarily by the General Fund and so a component of the university's overall General Fund budget is a recovery of a portion of these costs.

Even prior to the initiation of VCM, we assessed two types of charges to the auxiliaries and the spirit of both lives on in our current system. The first, the business service offices' recharge, was levied to recover the costs of transactions and services that could be measured, costed, and assigned reasonably accurately. For instance, the payroll offices' costs can be allocated based on payroll transactions that can be unambiguously counted and assigned to units. We continue to use this mechanism to recover the costs of a set of offices that includes payroll, purchasing, financial operations, the general counsel, and others.

The second historical assessment was the "administrative recharge" which was assessed to recover some of the costs of a set of administrative offices where one could not easily identify, count, and assign transactions. This recharge used a standard accounting metric, volume of expenditure, to identify the portion of costs of a set of central administrative and service offices such as the President's office, the Provost's office, the CFO's office, the campus security force, and others that would be recovered from auxiliary units. We continue to use this mechanism for a subset of the university's auxiliary units (primarily for our hospitals and our HMO) but have replaced it with transactions within the UB model for all others.

The following description of the UB model incorporates details pertinent to the auxiliary units that are "in the model." Those units also pay the business service office recharge, as noted above. Auxiliaries that are outside the model continue to pay the administrative and business service office recharges, but the description of auxiliaries in the UB model made later in this chapter does not apply to them.

5. *Central administrative and service units.* These include everything else – from the President's office to the Department of Public Safety and the Center for the Education of Women. These units' budgets are not activity-based but rather are set to allow the unit to accomplish the set of activities and tasks that comprise its support of the academic enterprise. The UB system provides an incentive to the Provost to keep these budgets as small as possible, as doing so allows her to allocate more resources to the central academic missions of the university.

COMPONENTS OF ACTIVITY-BASED BUDGETS UNDER UB

An activity-based budget is developed using a set of rules for the attribution of a set of revenues and costs. Although the components are consistently included in all activity-based budgets, those that apply to students have no effect on the budgets of research or auxiliary units.

Revenues

Tuition. Under the UB model, tuition attribution follows the unit of enrollment, rather than the unit of instruction. Thus, the School of Music has attributed to it the tuition paid by students who are registered in the school, regardless of how many courses those students take outside the School of Music or how many students from other units take courses within the School of Music.

As noted before, the reason for this choice was to eliminate the incentives for duplicative course offerings or the possibility of "pandering" that might arise on a credit-hour based system. However, the enrollment-based system gives rise to a *prima facie* incentive to enroll students and then forgo the costs of teaching them. As a result, under UB, the Provost's office takes careful steps to assure that units continue to contribute their share of total teaching in the university. The Provost is also receptive to proposals that increase a unit's base support if that additional support measurably increases the amount of teaching the unit provides to other units' students.

Undergraduate student tuition is attributed such that all undergraduate units get credit for the university-wide average in-state/out-state mix, regardless of the unit's actual distribution of enrollment by residency. The purpose of this attribution formula is to remove any unit's incentive to admit and enroll based on residency, as overall residency limitations are managed centrally. Our tuition rate structure is highly differentiated, so that students enrolled in Engineering, for example, pay a higher rate than students in the College of Literature, Science and the Arts (LSA), who pay a higher rate than those in Art and Design. Undergraduate tuition attribution incorporates the differential tuition rates paid by students across units, but treats each student as having average undergraduate residency characteristics. This means that the average attributed tuition of a full-time student in Engineering is more than that attributed to LSA for one of its full-time students.

Graduate and professional student tuition is attributed such that the unit receives what students are actually charged, incorporating both rate differentials and residency differentials.

There is good reason for handling tuition attribution differently at the graduate and undergraduate levels. The cost to a unit for an enrolled undergraduate is basically the same regardless of whether the student pays resident or nonresident tuition. Attributing average tuition provides consistent revenue for the number of students enrolled, which is the main driver of the unit's costs. In contrast, because units often use their own funds to provide substantial amounts of financial aid to graduate students, the cost of a student to a graduate unit is often directly related to residency status because of the differential tuition charged. The cost of a tuition grant rises with the actual cost of the tuition charged, and in order to provide such grants, a unit requires the revenue in the first place. So, unlike enrollments at the undergraduate level, an important set of costs associated with graduate and professional student enrollments is related to the residency mix in the unit.

All other graduate and undergraduate student-related fees are attributed based on unit of enrollment.

Indirect cost recovery (ICR). Indirect cost recoveries on sponsored research represent a revenue source to the General Fund. If a grant carries such recovery, then this ICR is attributed to the unit where the grant's direct expenditures occur. A system of subaccounts in our financial systems permits both direct costs and ICR to be shared among any number of units.

Interest. Imputed interest to units is calculated and paid based on their monthly General Fund balances. The rate paid is the T-bill rate lagged a quarter and is the same rate paid to our units on their balances in other operating funds accounts. Paying interest on General Fund balances ensures consistency between it and the other operating funds. This means that units have no specific financial incentive to spend from one fund rather than another, as was the case when all balances except those in the General Fund earned interest for the holder.

Costs

Financial aid. The costs of centrally awarded financial aid are attributed to units based on the same distribution as tuition. That is, units are assessed a charge for centrally awarded financial aid on the basis of the number of students whose tuition flows to them. Different offices handle centrally awarded graduate and undergraduate financial aid, but the same principles apply to each. Assessments for financial aid are based on averaged amounts; that is, a unit is assessed a charge for financial aid calculated as if all the unit's students received the average aid package awarded to students of that level. The UB model incorporates this approach rather than one based on the actual aid furnished to a unit's students for two reasons. First, we hold the view that financial aid is a university priority that should be supported across the campus. Second, our aim is to admit students based entirely on relevant academic criteria, independent of the students' financial circumstances.

Space. In the UB model, the direct operating costs of "General Fund space" are assessed directly to the units that occupy the space. There are three components to the space costs we assess: (1) utilities; (2) plant operations, which includes maintenance, custodial, grounds and landscaping, refuse, and recycling; and (3) rental costs. Almost all of our buildings are separately metered for utilities so we can charge the actual costs of electricity, steam, natural gas, water, and sewer for the buildings occupied by a unit. We assess a charge per square foot occupied for the costs of maintenance, custodial, refuse/recycling, and grounds. This charge is building-specific and is based on the historical expenditures for that building. For both of these items, the charges levied on a building that is shared by multiple units are split based on their proportion of occupancy. When a unit occupies nonuniversity rental space, the costs of the rental are charged to the unit.

Although we do not fully cost space in the UB model, even this modest set of charges provides units with an incentive to economize on space, somewhat countering the traditional incentive for units to grab as much space as they can get. In our system, if one unit leaves space and another picks it up, the Provost generally *does not* transfer the funds to cover the operating costs of the additional space. Rather, the first unit gets to keep the savings that arise from occupying less space, and the second unit pays for the increase in costs from its existing resources.

Taxes

Activity-based units pay a set of expenditure taxes. These taxes flow to the Provost and increase the funds that are available each year for flexible allocation. All taxes are levied on an adjusted expenditure base, with a two-year lag. The adjusted base is designed to assure that an expenditure is taxed once and only once, and to exempt from tax activity-based unit expenditures on financial aid, capitalized equipment, construction, subcontracts over $30,000, and general transfers. The formula also subtracts internal rebillings from the taxed expenditure base so that expenditures incurred in one unit on behalf of another are taxed only once and are paid by the ultimate user of the service. The university's standard source/use financial categories are used to construct the tax base.

The two-year lag is used because it makes taxes in the coming fiscal year, the year that units are budgeting for, entirely predictable. By early fall of, say, the year 2000, we knew actual FY 1999-2000 adjusted expenditures exactly, and hence we knew FY 2001-2002 taxes exactly. For most of our units, it is clear that the predictability of their taxes is a net plus, although taxing contemporaneously would have two advantages: 1) The current year's expenditures measure more accurately than lagged expenditure both a unit's fiscal capacity and the costs that a unit imposes on the rest of the university; and 2) Because in general, revenues are growing, lagging the tax base two years makes the tax rates seem higher than they actually are and the size of the tax does occasionally invite complaints.[4]

There are three types of taxes and six different tax rates imposed on different activities and different types of units. There are also a number of special provisions that apply to specific activities in specific schools.

University participation. All of the units that pay taxes, pay a 2 percent tax called university participation (UP) on their full-adjusted expenditure base. UP can be thought of as a payment for the general benefit of being able to use the University of Michigan name and for being affiliated with this remarkable institution and all the benefits it offers.

Research taxes. All externally sponsored research undertaken is taxed at the rate of 9 percent. The base for this tax is constructed using the same categories of included and excluded expenditures noted above, but includes only those expenditures on externally supported grants (research and training) and contracts.

General taxes. A general tax is levied on the adjusted expenditure base other than externally sponsored grants and contracts. The general tax rate varies according to the type of unit. Auxiliary units pay a rate of 2 percent, as do significant auxiliary-like activities undertaken in academic units. Research units pay 19 percent on their expenditures that are not sponsored research. Schools and colleges that have most or all of their students in undergraduate and Rackham programs (and hence make extensive use of centrally provided student academic services) are taxed at 28 percent. The remaining schools and colleges are taxed at 22.5 percent on their general expenditures. In all cases, adjusted general expenditure is the residual after externally sponsored research and auxiliary-like activities are subtracted. (The Medical School, consistent with a seemingly universal principle that medical schools are always different from everyone else, has somewhat different treatment of its auxiliary activities. The purpose of this is to prevent changes in fiscal relationships between the Medical School and the hospitals from having major effects on tax revenue.)[5]

The tax system plays two important roles in the budget system. Because the tax base grows at approximately the same rate as expenditures within the university, growth in tax revenues creates an automatic mechanism for reallocation. That is, the year-to-year increases in tax revenues create an automatic amount of reallocation in activity-based units' budgets and the funds freed up by this mechanism become available to the President and Provost to reallocate beyond within-unit reallocation if appropriate. At the same time, the system provides the potential to redistribute some resources from those units that are gaining wealth, both from general fund sources and from such activities as sponsored research, sale of services, and success in fundraising, to other units that are, for whatever reasons, not as well-situated financially. The Provost and President may choose to make such reallocations or not, but the tax system permits them to make such choices without explicitly cutting budgets in one place and raising them in another.

The General Fund Supplement (GFS)

The last item in this discussion of the components of the activity-based budgets is perhaps the most important of all the components. The general fund supplement (GFS) represents the additional support provided to a unit beyond the net of the revenues and costs mentioned above. The UB model (like VCM) was designed so that every unit would still need supplementation rather than function as "a tub on its own bottom." It is this element that gives the Provost leverage in determining the budget and, therefore, the sets of activities undertaken by units. The GFS represents both the historical measure of a unit's necessary funding and the accretion (or decline) of funds provided through subsequent policy and programmatic decisions.

Recall that when VCM was initiated the GFS (then known as the Provost's allocation) was determined to be the residual needed to create the identical bottom line for a unit once all the revenue and cost items had been calculated. Since that time, the GFS changes have been based on deliberate additions or subtractions. This is where central policy decisions are reflected.

Budgeting, Projections, and End-of-Year Adjustments

The budgets that are activity-based are the algebraic sum of a number of debit and credit items for the year, some of which are known in advance and some of which must be projected. Those that are firmly known are the GFS, the facilities plant operations charge, the general and research taxes, and the university participation tax. The projected items include tuition, application and registration fees, indirect cost recovery, General Fund interest, rental and utility costs. Projected items are adjusted after the close of the fiscal year. For each of these items, the unit projects an amount for the coming year that is incorporated into the budget itself. At the end of the year, we calculate the value of each of those items and then a transfer of funds is made either to or from the unit to correspond to the actual amount.

Clearly, wildly inaccurate projections or circumstances of extreme unpredictability would create situations that put a unit at significant financial risk. In general, this is not a concern here. Our enrollments are highly predictable and stable in aggregate and are managed and measurable at the unit level. The volume of research and ICR moves steadily upward. Spending patterns for operations do not vary much from year-to-year. Utility costs fluctuate as a result of weather and fuel prices but even years with hard weather do not result in swings that create significant overall financial vulnerability. Even so, we are not complacent.

We have three types of safeguards in place to ensure that the inclusion of projections in budget development does not lead to eventual bankruptcy. First, our units are generally well managed and aware of their own circumstances. The academic leaders, assisted by professional budget administrators, have proven to be capable of accurate forecasting. Most of our units have implemented conservative approaches that lead to both budget stability and a flow of year-end money that can be allocated to high priority one-time needs. Second, the central budget office staff pays a great deal of attention to projected figures and creates secondary analyses whenever an item looks questionable. During the year, the central budget office and unit staff monitor the flow of actual income and expenses so that variances are identified early, enabling an immediate response to occur, when appropriate. Third, both units and central administration hold a set of reserves that can be called on to supplement shortfalls in critical areas. The Provost's and deans' interest is to ensure adequate resources to mount the academic programs deemed essential to a unit's mission. If a shortfall occurred that put those programs at risk, we would identify a short-term option to ensure viability while longer-term planning occurs to create a lasting fix for the problem.

Budgeting Units That Are Not Activity-Based

Units whose budgets are not activity-based receive a budget developed through a more traditional style of incremental budgeting. Typically, these units are provided with an annual increase, known as the general operating program (GOP), that is typically an amount that is somewhat less than the rate of wage growth. In addition, the relevant director (for a UAU) or Vice-President submits a budget request, and the Provost and her staff evaluate these requests, weighing them against the requests for support that have been made for the activity-based academic units. The formal system is thus incremental (the GOP) and at the same time augmented by discretion.

Putting the Budget Together – the Provost's Sources and Claims

The Provost has three significant sources of allocable revenue in any given year – the increase in the state appropriation, increases in taxes, and planned reductions in units' General Fund supplements or General Fund budgets (for administrative units). With these sources, she must support the GOP, cover any increases in mandatory charges such as debt service or insurance costs, fund increases in imputed interest, honor any base commitments made in prior years, and provide other base allocations to both academic and nonacademic units. The allocation decisions must incorporate the entire set of university needs and desires and explicitly weigh the tradeoffs between academic and support priorities.

One-Time Funds

All of the discussion so far has taken place in terms of presumptively recurring base budgets. However, at every level of the university, the ability to make budget decisions using flexible one-time or time-limited funds is of great value. These funds are used for everything from upgrading wiring and repairing buildings to seeding new academic initiatives, helping to provide laboratory facilities to a new hire, or helping a unit to weather a temporary fiscal crisis. Having flexible funds also allows the leadership to respond to opportunities that arise unpredictably, that is, outside of the regular budget cycle. Such items can be funded on a contingency basis until they can be incorporated into a unit's base budget.

One-time funds appear in two different ways. Some of them are budgeted directly. Thus, the Provost budgets a line of flexible funds for her use in making one-time allocations, as do many of the deans. In this case, the total amount of these flexible funds is actually a recurring budget item in the existing base budget. It is the specific projects and items that these funds support that change year-to-year. The second source of flexible funds is the year-end adjustment of projected items mentioned above. This is essentially the underbudgeted amount of a recurring revenue source available as a lump sum for one-time items in the year earned and is generally then incorporated at the higher expected level in the following year's base budget.

ASSESSMENT

Overall, we think that the UB system has served the University of Michigan well, striking a reasonable balance between the strengths of activity-based budgeting systems and the difficulties that such systems pose in the University of Michigan's culture. Relative to its immediate predecessors, it has provided the Provost considerably more discretion than did VCM or incremental budgeting, while generating a far greater variation in annual and cumulative percentage changes in unit budgets than did the old incremental system. The system allows the university's leadership to see clearly the fiscal implications of the activities at the school, college, and research unit level, while allowing considerable flexibility to determine how best to adjust to fiscal circumstances in light of the university's missions. The system is well designed for an active provost who is willing to reallocate resources towards the academic mission and among academic units.

In assessing the system, we return to the areas of concern about VCM that led to the change to UB and ask how well UB has done in addressing those concerns, and what further improvements and changes might be warranted?

1. Although the change in language and tone has generally reduced the level of contention about the academic legitimacy of the budget system, there is one set of issues that has not gone away, that still causes difficulty, and that seems to be an inescapable feature of activity-based based systems. The problem is that users of the system often assume that each activity-based revenue stream must be adequate to support the associated activity.

Academic leaders are sometimes prone to strict interpretation of the "rules" as fully embodying institutional values or viewing their budget in discrete components rather than as a whole. These views can lead to their turning back grants or cutting back on curricula because the ICR on the grant or the tuition costs associated with the curriculum will not cover the full costs. This is both detrimental to the accomplishment of mission and is at odds with logic and the intent of the system. The unit engages in a range of activities, some of which may not only cover full costs but may even subsidize others. In order for an activity-based system to work well, there needs to be enough overall revenue in the system to allow academic leadership to choose among activities based on their overall merit, recognizing that the net financial cost or benefit, while often relevant, should never be dispositive. That a grant or a gift comes with strings attached such that it does not cover its cost does not in itself imply that the grant or gift should not be accepted Similarly, a unit should not engage in activity simply because it is profitable when the activity is inconsistent with the accomplishment of the university's missions.

This sort of difficulty seems to be unavoidable, and the Provost and her staff spend a good deal of energy trying to explain that we do not believe that every little tublet is meant to float on its own little bottom.

2. The system of taxes provides an ongoing stream of revenue that allows the Provost and President to support penurious units and to engage in substantial reallocation across academic priorities. At the same time, the tax system (like any tax system) provides disincentives to some activities that could be self-supporting without it, and adds to the complications discussed above that arise when decisionmakers are "too" responsive to the details of the budget model. Moreover, the nonuniformity of the taxes leads to modest incentives to reshuffle the locus of some activities, although we have not detected any significant behavior resulting from these incentives. (We have, however, made a number of adjustments where the incentives were large, as in cases where academic units facing 30 percent tax rates also operate auxiliary activities facing 4 percent tax rates.)

It would be possible to have a model similar in structure to UB with a lower and more uniform set of tax rates. The advantage of lower tax rates would be less distortion of behavior. The disadvantage would be less revenue available to support academic priorities that would not be self-supporting on an activity basis. This is precisely the design conundrum facing public institutions generally, and the right answer depends on the culture and leadership of the relevant institutions. At Michigan, this implies taxes that are surely higher than the 2 percent university participation tax that was part of VCM. That tax generated reallocable revenue of only about 0.1 percent (2 percent of 5 percent) of the budget, if expenditures were growing at 5 percent per year. Whether a set of tax rates ranging from 4 percent to 30 percent is optimal is less clear. Optimal or not, the leadership seems to be quite comfortable with it and the deans generally seem to be able to live with it, as well.

3. A more fundamental issue with respect to the tax system is the expenditure tax base itself. A revenue-based tax would have a number of advantages, not the least of which would be ease of explanation (everyone is familiar with income taxes). Revenues are more easily classified and identified, and it is generally more difficult to use the accounting and financial system to reclassify revenue sources than it is to move expenditures from one category to another, at least in the university context. Revenue taxes also have two perceptual characteristics that might make them operate more smoothly: a) A revenue tax that raised the same revenue as an expenditure tax would have a lower rate – due to the fact that generally there are positive savings; and b) Under a revenue tax, the tax can get taken off the top and the units see only their "take home pay," which they can spend as they choose, whereas with the expenditure tax, the taxpayers see the gross flow of revenue and then see the taxes as deductions, leading, perhaps, to a sense that they don't get to spend all of their revenue. This is one of the few points on which the authors of this chapter disagree. The economist believes that taxes are taxes, and that the taxpayer will care only about the net amount of money he or she has available; the only effect of revenue vs. expenditure taxes would be on the incentives for saving, which are greater under an expenditure tax. The experienced university budgeter and realist believes that there is a psychological advantage to giving a portion of revenue (e.g., 70 percent of tuition and ICR) where there had been none before, and that attributing the full revenue stream and then taking some of it back causes needless resentment. We both agree, of course, that it would be perfectly possible, of course, to exempt certain expenditures (e.g., financial aid) from a revenue tax. These expenditures would simply be deductible from the tax base.

4. Tuition attribution is an area where we believe that the budget model might be revised to do better. In conversations with people at other universities, we have frequently heard that credit hour-based tuition attribution systems tend to result in the most effective teachers being deployed in the largest classes. There is no incentive for this in the UB system. Of course, no formula can capture the perfect balance between incentives to teach well and the elimination of incentives to pander and to duplicate course offerings, but basing tuition attribution 100 percent on unit of enrollment and zero percent on credit hours is surely too extreme. Further, UB is not obviously superior to a credit hour-based system in encouraging interdisciplinary teaching, as the latter could lead to units looking for

and finding productive opportunities for collaboration. Indeed, the academic leadership at Michigan is currently considering moving towards a mixed tuition attribution plan, albeit one that would still give the majority of the attribution to the unit of enrollment, rather than to the unit of instruction. We are also looking at the possibility of implementing a general program, with budgetary consequences but outside the formal budget model, that would make it easier for academic units to support teaching that involved faculty from more than one unit. This is an example of how fiscal flexibility in the budget system permits us to improve on the mechanical workings of the budget model.

5. The set of space costs that are currently in the budget model constitute a bit less than half of true space costs. As the system evolves and measurements improve, we hope that more space costs, including long-term maintenance, implicit rent, or depreciation may also be charged to the units. When new elements of space costs are imposed in this way, funds to pay them will generally be made available to the units that face the new charges. However, the incentive to reduce the use of space will become more powerful, because units that economize on space will be able to keep the new revenue but shed the new, higher cost.

6. In the initial implementation of VCM, we made what we now believe to have been two significant technical errors, the consequences of which were foreseeable but not foreseen. The first had to do with the articulation of the initial year's hold harmless policy with the adjustment of actual activity-based revenues (principally tuition and ICR). Suppose a school or college underpredicted its tuition revenue by $1 million. Under the hold harmless policy, we would give them $1 million more than we should have in their initial General Fund supplement, to keep the budget where it would have been under incremental budgeting. Then, when the actual tuition revenue was calculated, we would have given them an additional $1 million in one-time money at the end of the year, because the actual was $1 million higher than budgeted. What we should have done, but only figured out recently, was to have reduced their GFS for the second year by the amount that actual activity-based revenue exceeded the budgeted amount in the first year. Of course, for units that overpredicted their initial activity-based revenues we should have done just the opposite. At the time, we thought our behavior was holding units harmless, but it was not. We systematically (albeit accidentally) rewarded those who underpredicted their FY 1998 revenues and punished those who overpredicted.

A second implementation error involved what had been a systematic practice of underbudgeting both tuition and ICR. The underbudgeting would generally yield year-end funds that were mostly used to support major maintenance and renewal projects. With the advent of VCM and then UB, even if the units chose to underbudget these revenue streams, the process of adjustment at year-end would provide year-end funds to the units, rather than to the central administration. Had we also decentralized the responsibility for major maintenance and capital renewal to the units, this might have made sense, although even then an argument can be made that the central administration has an interest in the quality of the overall physical plant. But the way in which we did the implementation, significant flow of resources was transferred from central major maintenance to distributed academic priorities without anyone explicitly considering whether that outcome best met the university's priorities. We now find ourselves squeezing annual growth in central budgets to replace the flow of funds that were used for major maintenance.

CONCLUSION

The UB system is a modified form of responsibility center budgeting that has been adapted to the University of Michigan. It has worked well enough to generate three budgets, with a fourth in prospect, that have substantial variation in their impact across units and have met with general approval. The basic structure of the model works well, yielding a combination of predictability and adaptability that make it a useful tool for budgeting and fiscal management. We cannot emphasize enough the importance of adaptability, a property that is at the heart of the distinction between a budget system and a budget model, and that allows for adjustments in the model that meet the goals of the academic leadership. Models must run on what can be straightforwardly measured, which perforce leaves the discretionary parts of the system to do a good deal of heavy lifting that can look informal and ad hoc. In fact, such discretion is an essential part of the system.

NOTES

1. See http://www.umich.edu/~urecord/9495/Mar27_95/20.htm
2. See http://www.umich.edu/~urecord/9798/Nov19_97/speech.htm and http://www.umich.edu/~urecord/9798/Nov26_97/budget.htm
3. Our problems with attributed costs are plainly not universal. We have been interested to learn in discussions with other universities using RCB that where there are fewer schools and colleges (UM has 19), it is often possible to obtain consensus among deans as to appropriate levels of overall expenditure by administrative and service units. Perhaps this would have evolved to become the case at Michigan, but our experience prior to scrapping the attributed cost system was that far more energy was spent arguing about the formulas than examining the costs and benefits of the service units.
4. The two-year lag means that in present value terms, expenditure undertaken today and taxed at rate t faces a present value of taxes of about $.9t$, assuming an interest rate of 5 percent. If taxes were imposed contemporaneously they could all be cut 10 percent without materially affecting either the unit's or the Provost's fiscal position. Yet absolutely no one (with the exception of one of the authors of this chapter) sees, for example, that 22.5 percent tax currently imposed on professional schools and colleges (with a two-year lag) as "really" being a 20.4 percent tax on current expenditures.
5. Total tax revenue under this system is set so that the sum of research and general taxes in FY 1998 is just equal to the total attributed costs for central service units in FY 1998. Neither the Provost nor the academic units made any profit on the switch from VCM to the tax system. Indeed, Provost allocations (later called General Fund

supplements) were revised such that unit by unit, each academic unit had exactly the same General Fund support, net of attributed costs (under VCM) or taxes (under UB) at the end of FY 1998.

REFERENCES

Cantor, Nancy E. 1997. The new budget system will counter barriers to collaboration. *University Record*, November 19.

Cantor, Nancy E., and Paul N. Courant. 1997. Budgets and budgeting at the university of Michigan – A work in progress. *University Record*, November 26.

Report of the Responsibility Center Management Implementation Team. 1995. Value centered management at the university of Michigan. Ann Arbor: University of Michigan.

CHAPTER 8

BUDGET INCENTIVE STRUCTURES AND THE IMPROVEMENT OF COLLEGE TEACHING

Michael B. Paulsen

Edward P. St. John

The research to date on incentive-based budgeting, as summarized in the prior chapters, suggests that the implementation of incentive budgeting can have an indirect effect on improvement in instruction. To the extent that incentive-based budgeting methods allow tuition dollars to follow students to academic units, there is an incentive, at least indirectly, to affect instruction. This incentive is indirect because the rewards are not explicitly tied to improvement in college teaching. Indeed, the decision to focus on instructional improvement remains ancillary to the formal conceptualization of the responsibility center management (RCM) model, or other incentive-based models in the literature.

This chapter focuses on ways of building tighter links between improvements in college teaching and the RCM process. First, we review the RCM model, focusing on why explicit linkages between incentives and instructional improvement do not exist in the first place. Next, we consider the questions of academic freedom that might underlie faculty resistance to including a focus on teaching improvement. Then we explore ways of improving the link between college teaching and the incentive structure for faculty. We conclude by suggesting a few specific strategies for making these connections more explicit.

BEYOND THE LIMITS OF RCM

Before the advent of RCM as a budgeting and management model for public colleges and universities, there was a relatively long history of formal, systematic budgeting and management models in higher education. Some of the early budgeting models, such as PPBS (planning, programming, budgeting systems) and ZBB (zero-based budgeting), were borrowed from government and adapted to higher education. Other models, such as MBO (management by objectives) and TQM (total quality management), were borrowed from private corporations. While RCB (responsibility center budgeting) and RCM (responsibility center management) can be reduced to a set of letters, like many of these earlier budgeting models, it differs from these models in some important ways. First, RCM was developed as a model within private higher education and was not borrowed from other sectors of the economy. This difference is important for research universities and is more than symbolic. The basic assumptions of the model are compatible with academic values. There is a clear incentive in higher education to maximize revenue (Bowen, 1980), an incentive that can be passed down to academic units, which is why RCM has the potential to induce improvement in college teaching.

The notion that internal policy decisions in universities often focus on maximizing revenues is increasingly accepted as an explanation for organizational behavior in higher education. Bowen (1980) argues that universities aim to maximize revenue in pursuit of excellence. In a review of financial trends and research evidence, St. John (1994) found that Bowen's theory did explain university responses to changes in public funding, but that the primary incentive for faculty was research. More recently, Slaughter and Leslie (1997) found the trends in finance also support assumptions in resource dependency theory. They concluded that research universities have found other sources for revenue, including tuition and external research support, to substitute for declines in state support. However, these conceptions of university finance do not provide insight into the ways changes in internal budget incentives might encourage faculty to concentrate more on improvements in college teaching. RCM seems to have this potential, but the linkages are not sufficiently defined. Second, RCM respects the autonomy of faculty as well as of unit administrators. The elite private universities that originally experimented with "each tub on its own bottom" and other predecessors of RCM were highly evolved institutions that "banked on" the quality of their faculty. The quality of their faculty enabled them to attract research dollars and elite college students who understood the value of a research-centered education. Thus, there was an inherent respect for the role of faculty in RCM that was simply not present in any of the prior alphabet models of management and budgeting. This aspect of RCM models is crucial and should not be overlooked.

RCM is a resource allocation model that respects the role of faculty; the model itself is neutral relative to the emphasis placed on college teaching. The large private research universities that originally developed the model are known for their endowments and their ability to attract research funding, but college teaching *per se* has not been the hallmark used to judge these institutions. Furthermore, members of the faculty at private research universities typically receive tenure and promotion based on research rather than on teaching. Thus, RCM does not place an inherent value on teaching *per se*. Presumably there is reason to expect that these institutions have incentives to retain their students, an issue that receives substantial research attention nationally (Braxton, 2000). However, the lack of explicit links between budgeting and incentives to teach has persisted since the development of the original RCM model.

Third, because RCM was adapted from private universities into public universities, it has introduced free market forces into these universities, forces that could continue to value research over teaching. Implementation of RCM has paralleled the privatization of public research universities, as documented by an increased emphasis on tuition revenues and revenues from research in place of state revenues (St. John, 1994; Slaughter and Leslie, 1997). When the model is fully implemented, faculties within responsibility centers have an inherent incentive to focus on generating revenue to replace the loss of state funding. Indeed, public universities with RCM were in a better position to develop shared governance approaches that responded to the new budget predicament facing public colleges and universities in the 1990s (Leslie, Oaxaca, and Rhoades, 2002, in this volume).

However, the links between improvement in teaching and the decentralized budgeting process in RCM were not well specified, nor are they well understood. Certainly the early literature on RCM emphasized adaptability (Whalen, 1991, 1996) and related models (Kidwell and Massy, 1996; Massy, 1996), but this literature essentially ignored the literature on college teaching. Therefore, as we reflect on the first decade of experience with incentive-based budgeting models in higher education, it is important to reconsider whether there should be a more explicit linkage between the budgeting system and efforts to improve the quality of instruction. Of course, the old adage "if isn't broken, don't fix it" still carries weight. But the weight of evidence does suggest that universities should be concerned about teaching (Braxton, 1996; Cross and Steadman, 1996; Fairweather, 1996; Feldman, 1994; Paulsen and Feldman, 1995a).

Therefore, the question of how to build such a linkage does merit consideration. From our perspective, such an inquiry must necessarily start with a closer examination of the role of faculty and their freedom to teach. We think that efforts to build a linkage between instructional improvement and budgeting would be foolish unless they somehow complemented the role of the faculty. We do not reach this conclusion just because we are university faculty members; rather we are concerned both about the quality of undergraduate and graduate teaching, and have an interest in budgeting and finance. This inquiry into the link between budget incentives and instructional improvement starts with an exploration of the faculty role in teaching.

ROLE OF THE FACULTY: ACADEMIC FREEDOM RECONSIDERED

The freedoms to teach and to learn – *lehrfreiheit* and *lernfreiheit*, respectively – were the core aspects of academic freedom adopted from German universities in the late nineteenth century (Metzger, 1955). They not only set boundaries that protect faculty, but also help define the core functions of faculty. During the 20th century, three core functions emerged – teaching, research, and service – which remain integral to the role of faculty. It has also been argued that the service role includes both service to internal and external communities and to the academic profession (Paulsen and Feldman, 1995b). The concept of academic freedom is applicable to all of these core functions. The freedom of faculty to pursue topics of interest to them and society in their teaching, research, and service has been integral to the evolution of the economy and society, as well as to the creation of new knowledge. But how can the concept of academic freedom be reconciled with the need for academic restructuring? And, how can the role of faculty be integrated into restructuring? These questions are crucial to the discourse about restructuring.

First, how can the concept of academic freedom be reconciled with the need to build more explicit linkages between budget incentives and college teaching? The academic freedoms of faculty are not absolute; market forces already impact such academic freedoms. The freedom of faculty to teach is linked to the freedom of students to learn – that is, students' educational choices – which are manifested in their freedom to choose courses of study that are of interest to them (Metzger, 1955; Riesman, 1980). The freedom of faculty to do research is linked to a marketplace of ideas in which faculty work is reviewed and evaluated by peers, and these reviews influence the success of faculty within the academic professions. And the opportunity of faculty to maintain their positions is linked to the financial health of their institutions, and their ability to attract and retain students and obtain funding, through the litigation on financial exigency. Thus, faculty members have many reasons – or incentives – to be responsive to various market forces.

More importantly, inherent in the faculty role is the responsibility for participating in the discourse within the academic community. The notion that faculty members are responsible for the academic side of the higher education enterprise is not only integral to the viability and success of great universities, but also to the maintenance of a massive and diverse higher education system. This responsibility resides in the freedom of faculty to take action on issues they consider important. Moreover, the academic organization may be more capable of adapting and restructuring when it is needed than is any other form of formal organization. In fact, one of the key lessons learned from the wave of corporate restructuring has been that decentralized action is crucial to adapt to new market forces (Gumport, 1993; Whalen, 1996). In other words, the academic side of the university is potentially compatible with the need to restructure, if only we can better integrate the nature of incentives and decisionmaking processes that characterize the financial and academic aspects of the organization.

However, there is a basic incompatibility between the centralized nature of financial decisions in universities and the decentralized nature of academic decisions. Indeed, the centralized nature of financial control separates rather than integrates financial and academic responsibility. Therefore innovations in the financial structure within the academy are needed for reasons other than achieving balance between research and teaching. It is also needed to encourage academic units to adapt to the new budget environment. Incentive-based budgeting models, such as RCM, are decentralized. They are consonant with the decentralized nature of academic governance, which is probably one of the reasons why early efforts to implement these models have had some success.

Second, how can the role of faculty be effectively integrated into an incentive-based budgeting system? While RCM and academic governance are compatible, responsibility centers are left to find their own ways toward improvement in college teaching that will help them attract and retain students. The crucial issue in these models is not how to control or constrain faculty, but rather how to integrate faculty into the central nexus of this model: the intersection of budgeting and governance within responsibility centers.

While the notions of control and constraint are increasingly used in educational public policy in higher education, they represent the antithesis of the faculty role and therefore could seriously inhibit the capacity of universities to generate new knowledge and facilitate social and economic development. The academic inquiry process is at the heart of the faculty role – the discovery of new knowledge (basic research), the communication of knowledge to students (teaching), the development and application of knowledge in the context of professional communities and society in general (service) (Paulsen and Feldman, 1995b). Positivist notions of knowledge production, linked by the scientific method to the pursuit of universal truths, played a crucial role in the secularization of American universities in the late nineteenth century (Marsden, 1994) and in the massive growth in technology and economic productivity throughout the 20th century. Thus, attempts to restructure the core academic functions – that is, building linkages between budgeting and academic improvement – need to address this central role of academic inquiry. Once an inquiry approach is adopted, it is possible to envision a systematic process of academic restructuring that involves faculty in appropriate ways.

COLLEGE TEACHING AND INCENTIVE BUDGETING

The notion that academic inquiry generates a universal body of knowledge began to break down in the late 20th century, while the notion that the generation of actionable knowledge and the use of inquiry to support social and economic change is a perspective that has gained support in professional learning communities (e.g., Argyris, Putnam, and Smith, 1985; Schon, 1987). In addition, action inquiry offers a way to promote organizational learning and restructuring within higher education (Brunner and Hopfenberg, 1996; Levin, 1991; St. John 1994, 1995). In our view, there are three issues relative to the faculty role that are crucial to promoting academic restructuring:

1. Using *action inquiry* as an integral part of the core academic functions across the disciplines.
2. Focusing action inquiry on *linking student choice* to teaching, learning, and curriculum development.
3. Focusing action inquiry on *transformations in professional learning communities* that will facilitate increased congruence between student learning in college and the transition to professional work.

The Action Inquiry Process

Focusing academic inquiry on action situations adds to the complexity of research, which means that it is more difficult, but it does not mean that standards should be reduced. Historically, a distinction was made in academe between basic and applied research, with the former having higher value. Increasingly, however, the problems that challenge inquiry across disciplines have a direct link to action situations. The research methods typically used in education and the social sciences emanate directly from the scientific method and are applied to systematically study problems and test hypotheses about why problems exist.[1] These basic elements are also integral to action inquiry methodologies. Generally, the methods of action inquiry address challenges that emerge in practice, situations that defy routine responsibilities. The typical elements of action inquiry include:

Building an understanding of the challenge. This element includes brainstorming about why the problem exists, generating hypotheses about the causes of the problem, and testing those hypotheses through formal and informal research. These practices can be based on a systematic review of prior research, as well as field research, including surveys, interviews, and observations.

Identifying possible solutions. This element focuses on looking externally to other colleges and universities to find experiments that have been tried, looking internally to see how others have contended with related challenges, and thinking creatively about new possibilities. It is also important to think critically about how potential solutions might address the problem identified.

Synthesizing the solutions into an action plan. This component emphasizes assessing the possible solutions relative to the understanding of the challenges based on the results of hypothesis testing; developing a plan that considers time horizons, resource requirements and acquisitions; and formulating strategies for pilot testing and evaluation.

Pilot-testing solutions (treating new policies and practices as experiments). This step involves the "trying out" of new ideas as action experiments. A fundamental problem with conventional planning and budgeting methods in higher education, including the processes of proposing and implementing plans for the improvement of curricular and instructional effectiveness, is that they too frequently assume that the selected solutions will work as intended. Evidence to the contrary is generally ignored. If new solutions were treated as pilot tests (or experiments) by faculty – that is, by those who make the decisions about curriculum, teaching, and program strategies – then they would have an opportunity to improve their practice (that is, to develop as reflective practitioners).

Evaluating and refining. This last component emphasizes assessing whether or not the solution has actually addressed the challenge, investigating how the new practice can be refined and improved upon, using the results as feedback to enhance understanding (closing the "loop" between planning and action), and making decisions about the continuation and refinement of the new practice. (Adapted from St. John, 1994).

The steps in the action inquiry process have similarities to the scientific method, but are more directly related to the decision processes embedded in professional practice. However, action inquiry differs from conventional scientific methods in a couple of important ways. First, it integrates research and action, indicating a need for collaboration between practitioners engaged in planning and policy development and researchers engaged in inquiry. Second, action inquiry places a priority on formulating and testing solutions in practical situations, rather than in conventional, controlled laboratory settings. These differences lead to a reconcepualization of the roles of practitioners and researchers, in which both become engaged in testing their assumptions about theory, practice, and the interaction between theory and practice. Action inquiry is potentially highly compatible with the core academic functions, especially given the emphasis on the freedom to learn embedded in the inquiry process.

Focusing on Student Choice

Action inquiry is appropriately focused on promoting student choice, including persistence and educational attainment within students' chosen disciplinary or professional fields of study. While there has been extensive research using scientific assumptions that have focused on student choice processes (Pascarella and Terenzini, 1991), there has been substantially less action research addressing challenges facing colleges in their efforts to promote student choice. There are a few notable exceptions. These include experiments with the use of information dissemination to increase the percentage of students choosing to attend college (Hossler and Schmidt, 1995), experiments with pricing strategies to promote access and equitable use of resources (Hamm, 1995; Hearn and Anderson, 1995; Rothman, 1995), and experiments with new approaches to science education for African American students (Allen, Epps, and Haniff, 1991). However, most research still does not involve researchers and practitioners in collaborations aimed at improving learning outcomes.

Faculty in diverse academic fields can use action inquiry methods in their efforts to develop new curricula and more effective strategies for teaching and learning. This is especially important when curriculum development and instructional improvement are aimed at improving enrollment, retention, and educational attainment in a field of study. Too frequently, faculty members debate reforms in curricular and instructional practices based on notions of content that are virtually abstracted from the ways students learn in a field of study (Kolb, 1994; Shulman, 1986). There is also a tendency to ignore the types of professional knowledge and skills that are needed in the professional settings students will encounter when they leave college (Cavanaugh, 1993). By viewing the need for new curricular and teaching strategies as challenges that merit experimentation, program faculties could begin to use inquiry methods to address the learning needs of students (Cross and Steadman, 1996). However, this approach would involve a change in the predisposition of many faculty, from assuming that predefined bodies of knowledge should be the exclusive criterion in designing curriculum and instruction, to viewing the design and development of curriculum and effective teaching and learning activities as action-learning processes, aimed at enhancing students' learning, persistence, and educational attainment in their chosen fields of study.

Research has consistently demonstrated the connections between effective teaching behaviors and students' learning or academic achievement in college coursework (e.g., Cohen, 1981; Feldman, 1994). Empirically derived sets of teaching behaviors that are significantly related to students' learning typically include both task-oriented behaviors (such as preparation, organization, and clarity) and relationships-oriented behaviors (such as encouragement of class discussion, openness to opinions of others, availability and helpfulness to students, and sensitivity to class level and progress). Researchers have also examined the relationships-oriented or social aspects of effective teaching and learning in terms of the characteristics of effective learning environments. For example, findings indicate that students' academic learning and/or intellectual development are enhanced when learning environments:

- promote student-faculty interaction both inside and outside the classroom (Franklin, 1995; Pascarella and Terenzini, 1991);
- encourage student-peer interaction both inside and outside the classroom – for example, in cooperative or other types of collaborative learning groups (Chickering and Gamson, 1987; Cooper and Mueck, 1992; Franklin, 1995; Johnson, Johnson, and Smith, 1991); and
- consist of a shared curriculum (a common set of courses), cooperative or other collaborative learning activities, and a collaborative pedagogy based on team teaching, which, in combination, constitute what is commonly called a "learning community" (Tinto, 1997).

Finally, research has indicated that higher levels of academic achievement, student-faculty interaction, and student-peer interaction are also positively related to students' persistence decisions (Pascarella and Terenzini, 1991). Tinto's (1997) work has indicated that students who participate in learning communities like the one described above are also more likely than students taking more traditional coursework to persist, both from quarter to quarter and from year to year. Furthermore, there are significant differences across disciplines in the frequency with which faculty use various effective teaching behaviors (Murray and Renaud, 1995). There are also differences in the importance faculty attach to various goals for learning outcomes of students in their fields (Smart and Ethington, 1995) and in the social environment of the classroom across fields. These include the differences in nature of student-faculty interaction, student-peer interaction, and the general supportiveness or openness of the classroom environment (Vahala and Winston, 1994).

In combination, these sets of findings about what teaching behaviors and what characteristics of learning environments tend to enhance students' academic learning, intellectual development, and/or persistence decisions, provide a solid foundation and context within which faculty can be directly involved in academic restructuring. Within this context, faculty can engage in action inquiry that results in curricular and instructional changes that promote increased learning and persistence among their students. Improvements in these areas will permit faculty to take charge of the process of improving their educational productivity. Such improvements are capable of influencing student choices and promoting greater student success and educational attainment. "Meaningful productivity gains" are defined as increases or improvements in educational outcomes for a given level of expenditure (St. John, 1994). Increases in learning or improvements in rates of persistence (course completion rates, within-year persistence, or year-to-year persistence) will yield such gains in productivity. Since the mid-1980s, faculty members in colleges and universities have used various inquiry methods in their efforts to improve the effectiveness of their curricular and instructional practices (Paulsen and Feldman, 1995a). However, because of the many differences across disciplines, action experiments might be most productive if undertaken by individuals or groups of faculty members that specialize in similar professional or disciplinary fields.

Action inquiry based on the principles of "classroom research" would be particularly well-suited to meet these requirements (Angelo and Cross, 1993; Cross and Steadman, 1996). Classroom research (CR) is a form of action inquiry that is dedicated to the study of what, how, and why various cognitive, affective, and behavioral outcomes result from learning experiences in a particular classroom context in a particular content field. CR views the college classroom as an ecologically valid laboratory and a natural environmental context for action inquiry. Just as in other forms of action inquiry, problems and challenges related to content (curriculum) or pedagogy (teaching methods) typically emerged from practical situations (the classroom), and hypotheses regarding solutions to such problems are appropriately tested through action experiments. After faculty conduct their experiments or pilot tests, they would evaluate and reflect upon the outcomes, thereby generating feedback to guide subsequent improvements in their practice.

CR uniquely connects the roles of professor as teacher and professor as action researcher. It draws upon professors' expertise in the content of their disciplines, as well as the high value they place on the rigor of quantitative or qualitative approaches to the systematic investigation of phenomena (e.g., students' learning outcomes). As a result, CR links rigor and relevance in action inquiries that produce what Shulman (1986) has called "pedagogical content knowledge," which refers to effective ways (teaching methods) to promote learning that are unique to the content of a particular field. In keeping with our construct of student choice – and the importance students and teachers attribute to the academic freedoms to learn and teach – CR is a learner-centered, teacher-directed form of action inquiry. When conducting action experiments in the CR format, faculty can collect information on any aspect of any process or outcome related to the learning of their students. As Cross and Steadman (1996, p. 2) explain: "through systematic and careful study of learning as it takes place day by day in the classroom, teachers are gaining insight and understanding into how to make their teaching more effective, and students are gaining the lifelong skills of assessing and improving their learning." In CR action experiments, the professor is both researcher and practitioner and students are the clients of teaching and learning services (see Braxton and Berger, 1996) who collaborate with faculty as partners in the analysis and interpretation of information about processes and outcomes of their own learning. In this way, each action experiment can enhance student choice and chances for academic success.

Action inquiry using CR is also highly flexible in the scope of topics for investigation. For example, faculty can:

- survey their students' most preferred learning styles;
- assess the impact on learning outcomes of various cognitive, motivational, or social aspects of the learning environment;
- determine the extent to which students are developing appropriate levels of competence in the professional skills they will need in specialized work settings after graduation; and
- compare the effects of different content or curricula on students' achievement of learning goals.[2]

Because of the discipline-specific nature of CR, as well as the strong desire of faculty to collaborate with one another in their action inquiries, Angelo and Cross (1993) recommend a departmental program in classroom research like that described below:

A natural first step would be the administration of the Teaching Goals Inventory (TGI) to all members of the department...Faculty members will certainly be interested in knowing, for example, whether, as a department, they espouse a fairly narrow range of goals and have relatively high agreement on priorities or whether they show a wide range of goals and priorities. We would expect departments to differ on TGI profiles...Whatever the departmental profile, the next step is for the faculty to discuss whether they like the teaching profile they have generated as a group. If, for example, no one is teaching certain TGI goals that are regarded as important by the department or division, how should that oversight or lack of emphasis be addressed? For example, should new courses be added, or should faculty assume more responsibility for addressing those goals in existing courses?...A next step is to select, adapt, or create [CR experiments] that faculty might use in their classrooms to see how well they are accomplishing their goals. Some faculty members with common goals might wish to form dyads or triads . . .(p. 383).

Finally, one of the most attractive features of using action inquiry and CR for involving faculty members in instructional improvement is that they can study and improve the effectiveness of their teaching and the quality of their students' learning outcomes. They can also submit their research to one of the numerous journals that publish articles on improving college teaching, learning, and curriculum in specific disciplines or professional fields of study (Cashin and Clegg, 1993). Opportunities to publish results of their action inquiries should help faculty members to dedicate more time and effort to improving their own teaching effectiveness. This, in turn, can enhance learning outcomes – including the persistence and academic success of their students – while still responding rationally to the current structure of rewards and incentives, which often favor research and publication over effective teaching at many institutions (Diamond and Adam, 1993).

Focusing on Linkages to Employment

A second challenge involves using action inquiry to promote congruence between higher education and employment. In a liberal arts environment, faculty members often ignore the practical implications of the research in their field, a practice that can lose students when incentive-based budgeting systems are being used. If resources follow students and students follow their interests, then resources do not follow to responsibility centers that ignore student interests. Thus, there is an incentive, at the responsibility center level, if not at the level of individual faculty members, to consider the practical aspect of academic work. We think it is important for faculty to be concerned about the eventual employability of students who choose their programs. Rethinking the link between academic programs and employment may be especially crucial in liberal arts departments in large public universities, where student interests lead them to applied fields. Incentive-based budgeting can create large problems for these departments if they don't develop a strategy for building these linkages. Action inquiry can appropriately be focused on improving the congruence between higher education within specific fields and professional opportunities after college. The lack of congruence between educational processes and employment opportunities after college seems especially problematic in the traditional liberal arts disciplines (Stark and Lattuca, 1997; Stark and Lowther, 1989). One crucial issue is whether the liberal arts disciplines will continue to dwindle as viable major choices for many college students (possibly with the exceptions of those planning for advanced study within increasingly esoteric fields). An alternative is for these fields to develop in dynamic new ways that have more direct linkages to emerging professional and service fields (Armour and Fuhrmann, 1989; Stark and Lowther, 1989). There are a couple of ways this can be achieved: through action inquiry that focuses on building better linkages between traditional academic majors, professional or career-oriented fields, and employment opportunities; and through action inquiry that involves collaboration with professional learning communities.[3]

The challenge of linking or integrating curriculum in liberal arts fields with education for professional or career-oriented fields has been addressed in a variety of ways across a wide range of fields. Stimulated in large part by the efforts of the Professional Preparation Network, a national task force that produced a set of 10 learning outcomes that educators in both liberal and professional programs shared, many successful projects were completed in the 1980s (Stark and Lattuca, 1997). Some of these exemplary efforts have been documented and reported in the literature (Armour and Fuhrmann, 1989). For example, the business program at Skidmore College developed a set of liberal studies core courses that combine case studies of particular businesses with an understanding of the historical, social, political, and economic forces that constitute the broader environment or context within which the businesses operate (Durham, 1989). The University of Tennessee-Knoxville offers summer programs in which groups of practicing school teachers come to campus for liberal learning experiences such as intensive work in creative writing or hands-on work in science labs with university professors (Wisniewski, 1989). At Rensselaer Polytechnic Institute, the humanities and social sciences departments intentionally seek to hire faculty with research interests in science and technology, each faculty member spends a semester or two working with a member of the faculty in the Schools of Engineering or Science, and courses in technical communication are taught in the English department (Sangrey and Phelan, 1989). Journalism students at the University of Kentucky take pairs of courses in journalism and the liberal arts, such as "Law of the Press" taught in the Journalism department, with "Philosophical Foundations of Law" taught in the Philosophy department (Moore, 1989). And other institutions have developed courses that explicitly connect the liberal and professional, such as the University of Illinois course entitled "Images of Pharmacy in the Arts" (Strand and Winston, 1989).

But the possibilities for such connections cover an even broader range than these. For example, in a recent conversation, a music professor at a major university observed that students in music frequently found employment in the computer industry after college. However, as we pondered this issue, we concluded that this represented a form of incongruence between what was learned in college and employment opportunities after college, which could lead to higher loan default and/or decreased public trust in education (St. John, Kline, and Asker, 2001). Upon further reflection we realized that it might be desirable to define this as a challenge and to design experimental courses that would help students make these connections, relating the mental processes they learned in the field of music to work with the new technologies. We concluded that such adaptations would not need to involve all music faculty, but rather might involve a few faculty who themselves wanted to learn more about the relationship between music and the new technology. Indeed, by systematically addressing new challenges of this type, it would be possible to facilitate meaningful transformations in academic structures and practices that promote greater congruence between liberal arts education and professional opportunities after college.

Further, it is possible that collaborative projects between faculty members in liberal arts and sciences and professional groups in related professional fields could generate new knowledge about the linkages between these conventional fields while facilitating the development of new industries in communities across the country. On the national level, the most impressive and potentially important undertaking along these lines was based on major studies funded by the National Center for Education Statistics and implemented by the staff of the National Center for Postsecondary Teaching, Learning and Assessment (Jones, 1996). Jones and colleagues have surveyed employers of college graduates, faculty from diverse fields, policymakers, members of accrediting organizations, boards or trustees, and state coordinating boards. They have compiled inventories of the key skills in the areas of communication, critical thinking, and problem solving that employers, faculty, and policymakers agreed were essential for college graduates to acquire to be successful in their postgraduate employment (Jones, et al., 1994). These inventories could very well constitute productive resources, particularly for four-year colleges and universities that are concerned with increasing the congruence between the skills their graduates acquire and those that their future employers will seek.[4] They may also serve as guidelines and criteria for the initiation and assessment of a range of action experiments conducted by faculty, departments, and colleges to enhance the congruence between their programs and employment opportunities for their graduates.

In the past few decades, collaborations between universities and industry have influenced major new developments in a wide variety of fields, especially in new technical fields. Such collaborations have traditionally been part of the faculty service and research roles in engineering, business, agriculture, and education (e.g., American Association of State Colleges and Universities, 1988). And as these fields have begun to restructure their practices to adapt to the new global economy and the new information technology, faculty members in these fields have been actively involved in collaborations in the field. In response to questions raised by professionals in industry and government about the effectiveness of engineering curriculum and instruction, The National Science foundation (NSF) funded a five-year grant to support the engineering programs in a coalition of seven universities. The project, called ENGINEER, used interactive teaching methods to enhance the retention rates of students, especially those of women and other underrepresented groups (Fairweather, 1996). This venture resulted in substantial improvements in the curricular and instructional practices at the consortium of schools of engineering. However, further improvement was hindered by the reward and incentive structures at the participating institutions. This finding raised questions about whether incentive-based budgeting systems can be adapted to reward and facilitate faculty efforts to improve educational programs.

There are other interesting examples of this, of course, such as the numbers of education faculty who have actually become involved in accelerated schools and other school restructuring methods (Finnan, St. John, McCarthy, and

Slovacek, 1996). However, faculty in many liberal arts, professional, and vocational fields have not made these adaptations and their academic discourses have become more and more distant from the practice issues facing professional communities. The challenge facing these fields is to begin exploring ways of making these linkages through collaborations that help faculty careers, student learning outcomes, and local economic development. Such strategies would help colleges transform adequate programs into locally situated, high-demand programs that provide relevant learning opportunities. For example, one area where much progress is needed in moving toward greater congruence between higher education programs and subsequent employment opportunities of students is in the sub-baccalaureate postsecondary education and job markets. Recent research has shown that, in many cases, both students who choose to complete only some credits, but not a program, as well as those who complete a two-year program, experience substantial and significant increases in their future earnings (Paulsen, 1998). Therefore, increasing linkages between sub-baccalaureate postsecondary courses and programs can make important contributions to enhancing student choice and employment.

Based on a recent study of the links between community and technical college programs and local employers in the sub-baccalaureate labor market in four metropolitan areas – Cincinnati, Sacramento, San Jose, and Fresno – Grubb (1996) offers a set of practical recommendations for promoting strong ties between colleges and employers. These include increasing the congruence between higher education and employment opportunities for students, thereby enhancing student choice. Most, if not all, of the recommendations below would also clearly apply to four-year colleges and universities that serve a relatively well-defined labor market, such as most urban institutions. They represent activities that call for faculty expertise and involvement in important aspects of academic restructuring in the service of student choice and student success.

> • Advisory committees should meet more regularly, and should be occupation-specific, rather than confining themselves to interchanges of uncertain information, they could undertake joint projects – for example, the creation of new programs, the development of locally appropriate skill standards, or the survey of local labor market conditions – that would enhance the familiarity of employers with education providers.
> • Placement offices need to move beyond offering stay-in-school jobs to more institutionalized connections with local employers, potentially with the help of job training programs that have always had a greater commitment to placement.
> • Student follow-up and tracking mechanisms should be improved, particularly based on readily available Unemployment Insurance records, as a way of making institutions more self-conscious about placements and subsequent earnings.
> • Contract education could be structured so that it provides regular information to occupational divisions about the demands of employers, rather than being independent of regular programs as it usually is.
> • Particularly with the interest in school-to-work programs, co-op programs and work-based learning could be expanded not only to establish close relations between employers and educators but also to provide students with the

combination of experience and formal schooling that is so powerful in the sub-baccalaureate labor market (Grubb, 1996, p. 197).

Each and every one of these recommendations could be viewed as a subject of action inquiry for faculty involved in academic restructuring that promotes student choice. Each approach could first be run as a pilot test or action experiment, before a large-scale budget commitment is made to the long-term implementation of any of these approaches.

INTEGRATING ACTION INQUIRY INTO INCENTIVE BUDGETING

With such a wide range of opportunities for faculty to conduct action inquiry, it is possible to propose ways of involving faculty that might become an integral part of the next generation of incentive-based budgeting models. We suggest a systematic approach to promoting faculty inquiry that might be integrated into future efforts to refine these models. We consider three ways of building a better integration of action inquiry aimed at improvements of college teaching into incentive-based models. We consider the roles of the central authority in promoting innovations, responsibility centers, and the incentive structure for faculty.

The Role of the Central Authority

Most incentive-based budgeting models include a process of setting aside some funds for innovations. For example, Indiana University has a "Chancellor's Discretionary Fund" that is intended to link to the strategic aims of the university (Gros Louis and Thompson, 2002). Given the considerations above, it is possible to envision an approach to integrating action inquiry into these basic systematic processes. A systematic process can become the means of enabling greater collaboration between responsibility centers and central administration. First, systematic assessment processes can be developed that identify challenges that can be addressed through action inquiry. The early stages of strategic planning can be adapted to involve faculty members in assessing the challenges they face in their curriculum and teaching relative to facilitating student choice – for example, enhancing learning outcomes and persistence rates – and improving congruence with employment opportunities. When strategic approaches are used, it is possible to identify a vision, then to compare the vision to actual practices and identify challenges. When comprehensive methods are used, then a systematic approach is frequently used to identify specific challenges in both areas. And when adaptive approaches are used, the focus may be on identifying departments facing the greatest challenges and opportunities. Regardless of the method used, it is important that faculty be engaged in processes in which they identify challenges that are related to their own teaching and research interests. If the challenges identified are of interest to faculty, they will be more likely to focus their academic inquiry on these challenges.

Second, the process of planning to address specific challenges requires substantial reconceptualization to promote action inquiry. Almost by definition, planning processes involve identifying new activities to implement. A linear approach tends to ignore the dynamic nature of educational choice. This traditional conception of planning assumes prior knowledge about what will work best for students and employing agencies. Clearly, these time-honored understandings fall out of alignment at times and require a fundamental rethinking. In the action inquiry process, there is an emphasis on trying to discern why the challenge exists in the first place, rather than simply trying to identify new strategies that relate to preconceived notions of the problem. The professional training of faculty embedded in doctoral training in the disciplines is essentially consonant with the action inquiry process; however, using action inquiry requires a different attitude toward the planning process than is usually held by faculty and administrators. As exemplified by our previous explanation of action inquiry as classroom research, the challenge for faculty is to focus their research interests on their own practice, and how their teaching, research, and service activities can enhance the learning, retention, and academic success and educational attainment of the students.

The third stage of a systematic process involves experimentation and piloting new approaches. Indeed, by viewing possible new developments in curriculum as ideas that need to be pilot tested, or even as intentionally designed experiments, faculty can maintain a learning orientation toward developing new programs. As new courses or sequences of courses are developed, they can pilot their ideas; experimental designs can be developed, enabling a systematic testing of the new approaches, comparing the outcomes (for students and employers) for alternative designs to current approaches. When this approach is used, then the renewal process can be built into the curriculum, and a more dynamic approach to education can be developed. Such an approach is used in accelerated schools (Finnan, et al., 1996; Brunner and Hopfenbergn, 1996), but is not as widely used in higher education. However, since an inquiry-based approach is compatible with this type of strategy (see our discussion of the faculty role above), it seems possible to integrate inquiry into the academic restructuring process.

Stark and Lattuca (1997) posit three stages through which reforms in college curricula – particularly those that emanate from external influences – must pass:

> • an awareness or initiation stage, in which there is a recognition of need or opportunity for change;
> • a screening or adaptation stage, in which arguments for and against the change are debated and evaluated and small-scale trials or experiments may be attempted;
> • an adoption or confirmation stage, in which the new curricular reform is adopted and implemented.

These authors apply the model to interpret the current state of congruence (or more accurately, incongruence) between higher education and employment opportunities, classifying it at only the initiation or awareness stage.

> Thus, undergraduate enrollments (and to a lesser extent numbers of faculty) have shifted to professional schools offering career studies; the labor market is now the major determinant of what students study. The number of students majoring in specific liberal arts fields, especially humanities, has dropped compared to those majoring in business and other professional fields. Yet faculty rhetoric in many colleges ignores this shift and lends little legitimacy to the educational pursuits of this growing number of students. The challenge is to recognize this changing purpose of collegiate education and build it into academic planning (Stark and Lattuca, 1997, p. 357).

We think that the systematic use of action inquiry can better enable faculty to pass through to these stages, to build curricular approaches that address problem-solving skills as well as provide the link to employment opportunities. If the central awarding of special funds in an incentive budgeting system required that the elements of action inquiry be used, then a more dynamic process of change would be encouraged.

Integrating Inquiry into Responsibility Centers

If the central budget authority encouraged the use of an action inquiry approach, it might be possible to illuminate this option within a large campus. However, the core issue within universities that use RCM is to integrate inquiry into the annual budgeting process within responsibility centers (RCs). Specifically, RCs should develop their annual planning and budgeting processes that facilitate action inquiry by program faculties.

Ideally, as part of the annual budget process, the academic departments within responsibility centers would be encouraged to focus on improving student outcomes, to consider how well their current programs attract and retain students. In fact, it is within the academic programs that faculty members should be encouraged to work together with students to build better learning communities. We think that academic departments can use the inquiry process to identify areas of challenge, to engage in experiments aimed at addressing those challenges, and to assess the impact of these experiments on student outcomes. In fact, our review above can be appropriately viewed as an outline of the ways academic programs can become more adaptive, more focused on the learning outcomes of students.

For RCs the financial rewards from improving teaching should be nearly immediate, especially with an improved flow of funds associated with an improvement in student outcomes. Several questions remain however. How can departments within RCs benefit from their innovations, from their successful adaptations? More students bring more revenues, but it is not always a simple process. Marginal gains in tuition revenues alone may be not sufficient to support major new programs. Tax rates for central administrative functions may constrain the benefits of expanding enrollment beyond certain thresholds. Clearly there is a need to involve faculty in thinking through issues related to the ways improvement in educational outcomes relate to financial resources for their programs. This will help to tighten the links between improvement in teaching and revenues within RCs. Faculty within basic units can be involved in addressing these financial challenges, much as they can be involved in addressing educational challenges.

The principle challenge, therefore, is for faculty and deans to review their internal budget processes, to design ways that that might achieve a more explicit integration of inquiry into their program improvement processes. This should provide incentives to improve teaching and might include an adaptation of the RCM model, to further delegate aspects of the budget model to academic units within RCs. For example, at Indiana University, there are recent process adaptations within RCs that merit further study. These adaptations include:

- One of the professional schools has decentralized the responsibility center concept to academic departments, a process that has caused more innovations and more discussion of the shared principles in the school.
- Another of the professional schools is considering a modification of its workload policy that provides more flexibility, but requires revenue neutrality.

These experiments and others like them merit study to discern whether there are ways of adapting the incentive structure further. Further, it is important to encourage faculty in programs to think about – and indeed care about – improving the educational outcomes of their students.

Adapting Incentives and Rewards

The consensus of researchers appears to be that research productivity does not stand in conflict with teaching effectiveness – and there is some evidence of a modest complementary relationship between these two aspects of faculty work (Braxton, 1996). However, evidence also indicates that faculty are rewarded – in terms of pay, tenure, and promotion – far more for their productivity as researchers than for their effectiveness in their roles as teachers and providers of service (Diamond, 1993). Moreover, among four-year colleges, regardless of institutional type or sector or program area, faculty members who publish more and spend more of their time engaged in research are paid higher salaries than those who are more teaching-oriented (Fairweather, 1996). Some disciplinary societies and campuses are beginning to respond to broadening conceptions of scholarship, including the scholarship of teaching and service (Boyer, 1990; Paulsen, 2001; Paulsen and Feldman, 1995b), in their development of guidelines to more meaningfully assess faculty work in the nonresearch elements of scholarship (Diamond and Adam, 1993). However, even the latest reports of efforts to evaluate the various dimensions of scholarship recognize the challenges that still lie ahead before some uniform approaches are widely accepted and adopted in practice (Glassick, Huber, and Maeroff, 1997). And few four-year colleges and universities possess, to any effectual extent, all of the most essential characteristics of a supportive teaching culture (Paulsen and Feldman, 1999).

The sort of academic restructuring that we propose – along with faculty involvement in it – will take place only to the extent that faculty are rewarded for efforts at action inquiry that are directed toward the improvement of their effectiveness in their teaching and service. However, the rate of change in, and the impact of, such academic restructuring can be multiplied if it is coupled with dynamic changes in incentive or reward structures and budgeting systems. If basic units of faculty (e.g., academic departments) realize economic benefits from attracting more students to their courses, improving student learning, persistence, and degree completion, and improving employability for graduates, then the incentive structure will also eventually change. Rewarding faculty members for innovations in teaching and service will then have greater financial value for the faculty, which should provide a basis for thinking differently about faculty reviews for tenure, promotion, and merit pay as well. Thus, we recommend adapting incentive-based approaches to university budgeting and public finance to encourage improvement in teaching and student educational attainment.

CONCLUSION

From our cursory review, RCM appears to provide a way of introducing market forces into large university systems, potentially providing an incentive for improving academic productivity. Changing budgeting systems alone can only change higher education at the margin, introducing change in areas that are overtly threatened. However, it is possible that a refined systematic approach to incentive-based budgeting can include incentives that promote using action inquiry to promote improvement in student outcomes. This involves an explicit focus on the incentive structure within responsibility centers. To do this, it is appropriate to focus on incentives within basic educational units (academic departments and educational programs), as well as on the implementation of budgeting systems within universities.

Action inquiry is appropriately integrated into systematic processes within basic academic units, especially if it can be integrated with delegated, market-oriented budgeting. For example, the transformation of small liberal arts colleges in the 1980s involved systematic critical thinking about the fit between existing academic processes and the new markets in which these colleges were situated (St. John, 1992). In these colleges, budgetary changes were linked to new academic processes designed to address the challenges these colleges faced. They restructured their curricula, as a means of adapting to these new challenges. Some developed new professional programs while others adapted liberal arts curricula to make them more relevant to student learning needs and their probable employment opportunities (Paulsen and Pogue, 1988). These types of changes in academic programs are appropriately made in basic academic units of faculty in large research universities. Within these basic faculty units, faculty members can collectively engage in inquiry processes aimed at identifying and addressing challenges related to student learning, persistence, and employment outcomes; that is, promoting student choice.

The incentive structures within basic faculty units can be adapted to promote faculty inquiry. Not only is it possible to reward faculty for their service in these processes through the annual reviews, but faculty can also be encouraged to publish their work. Action inquiry focused on academic innovations has been emerging as an issue of interest across a variety of fields. The more faculty within various disciplines get involved in inquiry projects related to student outcomes and collaborations with professional organizations, the more likely it is that professional journals will adapt to publish the results of this work. This is not to argue that such changes are easy to make, but there is growing evidence that inquiry into academic practices is gaining acceptance and merits reward in the faculty tenure and promotion process.

NOTES

1. Unfortunately, the tendency is to apply the scientific method in the traditional laboratory setting and to reinvent applied research as having lesser value than "scientific research" (Argyris, et al., 1985). When research on education or professional action is limited to traditional laboratory "experiments," it has limited applicability to practice. An alternative is to use a rigorous research method in action situations.

2. See Angelo (1991), Angelo and Cross (1993), and Cross and Steadman (1996) for numerous examples of action inquiry in the form of classroom research.

3. A professional learning community is a group of practitioners in a field who conduct action inquiry studies and share their work through publication and other resources.

4. These inventories of desired communication, critical thinking, and problem solving skills may be obtained at moderate cost from the National Center for Research on Postsecondary Teaching, Learning, and Assessment at the Pennsylvania State University.

REFERENCES

Allen, Walter R., Edgar G. Epps, and Nesha Z. Haniff, eds. 1991. *College in black and white: African American students in predominantly white and historically black public universities*. Albany: State University of New York Press.

American Association of State Colleges and Universities. 1988. *Allies for enterprise: Highlights of the 1987-88 national conferences on higher education and economic development*. Washington, D.C.: AASCU.

Angelo, Thomas A., ed. 1991. *Classroom research: Early lessons from success*. New Directions for Teaching and Learning, No. 46. San Francisco: Jossey-Bass.

Angelo, Thomas A., and K. Patricia Cross. 1993. *Classroom assessment techniques: A handbook for college teachers*. San Francisco: Jossey-Bass.

Argyris, Chris, Robert Putnam, and Diana M. Smith. 1985. *Action science: Concepts, methods, and skills for research and intervention*. San Francisco: Jossey-Bass.

Armour, Robert A., and Barbara S. Fuhrmann. 1989. *Integrating liberal learning and professional education*. New Directions for Teaching and Learning, No. 40. San Francisco: Jossey-Bass.

Bowen, Howard R. 1980. *The cost of higher education*. San Francisco: Jossey-Bass.

Boyer, Ernest L. 1990. *Scholarship reconsidered: Priorities of the professorate*. Princeton, NJ: Carnegie Foundation for the Advancement of Teaching.

Braxton, John M., ed. 1996. *Faculty teaching and research: Is there a conflict?* New Directions for Institutional Research, No. 90. San Francisco: Jossey-Bass.

Braxton, John M., ed. 2000. *Rethinking the departure puzzle*. Nashville, TN: Vanderbilt University Press.

Braxton, John M., and Joseph B. Berger. 1996. Public trust and research activity, and the ideal of service to students as clients of teaching. In John M. Braxton, ed., *Faculty teaching and research: Is there a conflict?* New Directions for Institutional Research, No. 90. San Francisco: Jossey-Bass.

Brunner, Ilse, and Wendy Hopfenberg. 1996. Growth and learning: Big wheels and little wheels interacting. In Christine Finnan, Edward P. St. John, Jane McCarthy, and Simeon Slovacek, eds., Ch. 3, *Accelerated schools in action: Lessons from the field*. Thousand Oaks, CA: Corwin.

Cashin, William E., and Victoria L. Clegg. 1993. *Periodicals related to college teaching*. IDEA Paper no. 28. Manhattan: Center for Faculty Evaluation and Development, Kansas State University.

Cavanaugh, Sally H. 1993. Connecting education and practice. In L. Curry, J. Wergin and Associates, eds., *Educating professionals: Responding to new expectations for competence and accountability*. San Francisco: Jossey-Bass.

Chickering, Arthur W., and Zelda F. Gamson. 1987. Seven principles for good practice in undergraduate education. *AAHE Bulletin* 39 (7): 3-7.

Cohen, Peter. 1991. Student ratings of instruction and student achievement. *Review of Educational Research* 51:281-309.

Cooper, James, and Randall Mueck. 1992. Student involvement in learning: Cooperative learning and college instruction. In Anne S. Goodsell, M. R. Maher, and Vincent Tinto, eds., *Collaborative learning: A sourcebook for higher education*. Syracuse University: National Center on Postsecondary Teaching, Learning, & Assessment.

Cross, K. Patricia, and Mimi Steadman. 1996. *Classroom research: Implementing the scholarship of teaching*. San Francisco: Jossey-Bass.

Diamond, Robert M. 1993. Changing priorities and the faculty reward system. In Robert M. Diamond and Bronwyn E. Adam, eds., *Recognizing faculty work: Reward systems for the year 2000*. New Directions for Higher Education, No. 81. San Francisco: Jossey-Bass.

Diamond, Robert M., and Bronwyn E. Adam, eds. 1993. *Recognizing faculty work: Reward systems for the year 2000*. New Directions for Higher Education, No. 81. San Francisco: Jossey-Bass.

Durham, Taylor R. 1989. Business and the liberal arts: Managing the constructive tensions. In Robert A. Armour and Barbara S. Fuhrmann, eds., *Integrating liberal learning and professional education*. New Directions for Teaching and Learning, No. 40. San Francisco: Jossey-Bass.

Fairweather, James S. 1996. *Faculty work and public trust: Restoring the value of teaching and public service in American academic life*. Boston, MA: Allyn and Bacon.

Feldman, Kenneth A. 1994. The association between student ratings of specific instructional dimensions and student achievement: Refining and extending the synthesis of data from multi-section validity studies. In Kenneth A. Feldman and Michael B. Paulsen, eds., *Teaching and learning in the college classroom*. Needham Heights, MA: Simon and Schuster.

Finnan, Christine, Edward P. St. John, Jane McCarthy, and Simeon Slovacek, eds. 1996. *Accelerated schools in action: Lessons from the field*. Thousand Oaks, CA: Corwin.

Franklin, Maureen. 1995. The effects of differential college environments on academic learning and student perceptions of cognitive development. *Research in Higher Education* 36:127-153.

Glassick, Charles E., Mary T. Huber, and Gene I. Maeroff. 1997. *Scholarship assessed: Evaluation of the professoriate*. San Francisco: Jossey-Bass.

Gros Louis, Kenneth R. R., and Maynard Thompson. 2002. Responsibility center budgeting and management at Indiana University. In Douglas Priest, et al. eds, *Incentive-based budgeting systems in public universities*. Cheltenham, UK: Edward Elgar.

Grubb, W. Norton. 1996. *Working in the middle: Strengthening education and training for the mid-skilled labor force*. San Francisco: Jossey-Bass.

Gumport, Patricia. 1993. The contested terrain of academic program reduction. *Journal of Higher Education* 64 (3): 283-311.

Hamm, William E. 1995. The Waldorf tuition and grant reduction experiment. In Edward P. St. John, ed., *Rethinking tuition and student aid strategies*. New Directions for Higher Education, No. 89. San Francisco: Jossey-Bass.

Hearn, James C. and Melissa S. Anderson. 1995. The Minnesota financing experiment. In Edward P. St. John, ed., *Rethinking tuition and student aid strategies*. New Directions for Higher Education, No. 89. San Francisco: Jossey-Bass.

Hossler, Don and Jack Schmidt. 1995. The Indiana postsecondary encouragement experiment. In Edward P. St. John, ed, *Rethinking tuition and student aid strategies*. New Directions for Higher Education, No. 89. San Francisco: Jossey-Bass.

Johnson, David, Roger Johnson, and Karl Smith. 1991. *Cooperative learning: Increasing college faculty instructional productivity*. ASHE-ERIC Higher Education Report, No. 4. Washington, D.C.: The George Washington University, School of Education and Human Development.

Jones, Elizabeth A. 1996. Editor's notes. In E. A. Jones, ed., *Preparing competent college graduates: Setting new and higher expectations for student learning*. New Directions for Higher Education, No. 96. San Francisco: Jossey-Bass.

Jones, Elizabeth A., Steven Hoffman, Lynn Melander-Moore, Gary Ratcliff, Stacy. Tibbetts, and Benjamin A. L. Click. 1994. *Essential skills in writing, speech and listening and critical thinking for college graduates: Perspectives of faculty, employers, and policymakers*. University Park: National Center on Post-secondary Teaching, Learning, and Assessment, Pennsylvania State University.

Kidwell, Linda J., and William Massy. 1996. Transformation in higher education: Beyond administrative reengineering. In Sandra L. Johnson and Jillinda J. Kidwell, eds., *Reinventing the university: Managing and financing institutions of higher education*. New York: John Wiley and Sons.

Kolb, David A. 1994. Learning styles and disciplinary differences. In Kenneth A. Feldman and Michael B. Paulsen, eds., *Teaching and learning in the college classroom*. ASHE Reader Series. Needham Heights, MA: Simon and Schuster.

Leslie, Larry L., Ronald L. Oaxaca, and Gary Rhoades. 2002. Revenue flux and university behavior. In Douglas Priest, et al., eds. *Incentive-based budgeting systems in public universities*. Cheltenham, UK: Edward Elgar.

Levin, Henry M. 1991. Raising productivity in higher education. *Journal of Higher Education* 62 (3): 241-62.

Marsden, George M. 1994. *The soul of the American university*. New York: Oxford University Press.

Massy, William F. 1996. Value responsibility budgeting. In William F. Massy and collaborators, eds., *Resource allocation in higher education*. Ch. 12. Ann Arbor: University of Michigan Press.

Metzger, Walter P. 1955. *Academic freedom in the age of the university*. New York: Columbia University Press.

Moore, Roy L. 1989. Journalism: Acquiring something to write about. In Robert A. Armour and Barbara S. Fuhrmann, eds., *Integrating liberal learning and professional education*. New Directions for Teaching and Learning, No. 40. San Francisco: Jossey-Bass.

Murray, Harry, and Robert Renaud. 1995. Disciplinary differences in classroom teaching behaviors. In Nira Hativa and Michelle Marincovich, eds., *Disciplinary differences in teaching and learning: Implications for practice*. New Directions for Teaching and Learning, No. 64. San Francisco: Jossey-Bass.

Pascarella, Ernest T., and Patrick T. Terenzini. 1991. *How college affects students*. San Francisco: Jossey-Bass.

Paulsen, Michael B. 1998. Recent research on the economics of attending college: Returns on investment and responsiveness to price. *Research in Higher Education* 39 (4): 471-489.

Paulsen, Michael B. 2001. The relation between research and the scholarship of teaching. In C. Kreber, ed., *Scholarship revisited: Identifying and implementing the scholarship of teaching*. New Directions in Teaching and Learning, No. 86. San Francisco: Jossey-Bass.

Paulsen, Michael B., and Kenneth A. Feldman. 1995a. *Taking teaching seriously: Meeting the challenge of instructional improvement*. ASHE-ERIC Higher Education Report, No. 2. Washington, D.C.: George Washington University Press.

Paulsen, Michael B., and Kenneth A. Feldman. 1995b. Toward a reconceptualization of scholarship: A human action system with functional imperatives. *Journal of Higher Education* 66 (6): 615-640.

Paulsen, Michael B., and Kenneth A. Feldman. 1999. Faculty motivation: The role of a supportive teaching culture. In M. Theall, ed., *Motivation from within: Approaches for encouraging faculty and students to excel*. New Directions for Teaching and Learning, No. 78. San Francisco: Jossey-Bass.

Paulsen, Michael B., and Thomas F. Pogue. 1988. Higher education enrollment: The interaction of labor market conditions, curriculum and selectivity. *Economics of Education Review* 7 (3): 275-290.

Riesman, David. 1980. *On higher education: The academic enterprise in an era of rising student consumerism*. San Francisco: Jossey-Bass.

Rothman, Michael L. 1995. The Mills college tuition freeze experiment. In Edward P. St. John, ed., *Rethinking tuition and student aid strategies*. New Directions Higher Education, No. 89. San Francisco: Jossey-Bass.

St. John, Edward P. 1992. The transformation of private liberal arts colleges. *Review of Higher Education* 15:83-106.

St. John, Edward P. 1994. *Prices, productivity and investment: Assessing financial strategies in higher education*. ASHE/ERIC Higher Education Report, No. 3. Washington, D.C.: George Washington University.

St. John, Edward P. 1995. Rethinking tuition and student aid strategies. In Edward P. St John, ed., *Rethinking tuition and student aid strategies.* New Directions for Higher Education, No. 89. San Francisco: Jossey-Bass.

St. John, Edward P., Kimberly Kline, and Eric H. Asker. 2001. The call for public accountability: Rethinking the linkage to student outcomes. In D. E. Heller, ed., *The states and public higher education policy*: 219-242. Baltimore: Johns Hopkins University Press.

Sangrey, Dwight A., and Thomas Phelan. 1989. Liberal learning and engineering education. In Robert A. Armour and Barbara S. Fuhrmann, eds., *Integrating liberal learning and professional education.* New Directions for Teaching and Learning, No. 40. San Francisco: Jossey-Bass.

Schon, Donald A. 1987. *Educating the reflective practitioner: Toward a new design for teaching and learning in the professions.* San Francisco: Jossey-Bass.

Shulman, Lee. 1986. Those who understand: Knowledge growth in teaching. *Educational Researcher* 15 (2): 4-14.

Slaughter, Sheila, and Larry L. Leslie. 1997. *Academic capitalism: Politics, policies, and the entrepreneurial university.* Baltimore: Johns Hopkins University Press.

Smart, John C., and Corina A. Ethington. 1995. Disciplinary and institutional differences in undergraduate education goals. In Nira Hativa and Michelle Marincovich, eds., *Disciplinary differences in teaching and learning: Implications for practice.* New Directions for Teaching and Learning, No. 64. San Francisco: Jossey-Bass.

Stark, Joan S., and Lisa R. Lattuca. 1997. *Shaping the college curriculum: Academic plans in action.* Boston, MA: Allyn and Bacon.

Stark, Joan S., and Malcolm A. Lowther. 1989. Exploring common ground in liberal and professional education. In Robert A. Armour and Barbara S. Fuhrmann, eds., *Integrating liberal learning and professional education.* New Directions for Teaching and Learning, No. 40. San Francisco: Jossey-Bass.

Strand, Linda M., and J. Mark Winston. 1989. Liberal arts in pharmacy education. In Robert A. Armour and Barbara S. Fuhrmann, eds., *Integrating liberal learning and professional education.* New Directions for Teaching and Learning, No. 40. San Francisco: Jossey-Bass.

Tinto, Vincent. 1997. Classrooms as communities: Exploring the educational character of student persistence. *Journal of Higher Education* 68 (6): 549-623.

Vahala, Mary E., and Roger B. Winston. 1994. College classroom environments: Disciplinary and institutional-type differences and effects on academic achievement in introductory courses. *Innovative Higher Education* 19 (2): 99-121.

Whalen, Edward L. 1991. *Responsibility center budgeting: An approach to decentralized management for institutions of higher education.* Bloomington, IN: Indiana University Press.

Whalen, Edward L. 1996. Responsibility centered management: An approach to decentralized financial operations. In David S. Honeyman, James L. Wattenbarger, and Kathleen C. Westbrook, eds., *A struggle to survive.* Thousand Oaks, CA: Corwin.

Wisniewski, Richard. 1989. Linking teacher education and liberal learning. In Robert A. Armour and Babrara S. Fuhrmann, eds., *Integrating liberal learning and professional education.* New Directions for Teaching and Learning, No. 40. San Francisco: Jossey-Bass.

CHAPTER 9

REWARD STRUCTURES AND FACULTY BEHAVIOR UNDER RESPONSIBILITY CENTER MANAGEMENT

William E. Becker

Neil D. Theobald

The idea that assessing and rewarding faculty members' productivity provides an incentive for them to change their behavior is not new. Unlike the stereotype of a traditional budgeting systems, where "no one could identify many incentives . . . for maximizing performance or reducing costs" (Carnaghi, 1992, p. 65), responsibility center management (RCM) is to provide direct incentives for units to increase their income and reduce their costs. Under RCM schools and departments are expected to update traditional merit systems to offer faculty members added impetus to engage in and excel at revenue-generating and institutional cost-cutting activities. In this chapter we identify models and explore the implications of this type of reward system, which is based on competition among peers, versus a more traditional reward structure that assesses and rewards faculty behavior that complies with or surpasses a competency standard. Consideration is given to the motivational effects of alternative methods for assigning salaries. In closing, algebraic methods are presented for converting merit scores into salaries in either a competitive or competency-based system.

MERIT SCORES

In essence, an assessment system is a quality control device aimed at sorting things into bins or slots according to criteria. In grading inanimate items, like shoes, whether they pass the quality standard and whether there is a fault in the leather or sewing does not feed back to the item itself in a meaningful way. That is not true of faculty members; they likely will not go passively to one bin or the other. If it makes a difference to them, they will try to affect the category to which they are assigned. This may produce the desired outcome of faculty members striving through productive effort to make a higher "bin," or it may result in them striving to sabotage the system.

In most college and university pay systems, individual merit scores are assigned to a faculty member for teaching, research, and service (Q_k, for $k = 1, 2,$ or 3, respectively), with an aggregate merit score q determined by the sum of these three scores where each score receives a weight of a_k:

$$q = \sum_{k=1}^{3} a_k Q_k \tag{9.1}$$

For example, Braskamp and Ory (1994, p. 152) provide a merit scheme for an undergraduate college in which the weights are $a_1 = 70$ for instruction, $a_2 = 10$ for research, and $a_3 = 20$ for service and citizenship. Centra (1993, p. 120) and Root (1987) report on salary committee ratings "within a research university, with research and teaching getting twice the weight of service." Becker (1999) reports on a department of economics where the weights are research 5, teaching 3, and service 2. As Becker (1975, 1979) shows, the setting of these weights can have a direct effect on expected faculty behavior. Here we are interested in what is done with the aggregate merit score q once it has been determined, with particular emphasis on how competition between faculty members in an RCM setting influences how q is used.

Traditionally, the process of categorizing faculty members has been necessarily based on incomplete data. There exists no universally agreed upon measure of a faculty member's quality in teaching, research, or service. The advent of RCM, though, makes appealing the direct observation of each faculty member's relative contribution to increasing school or department income (e.g., student credit hours taught, indirect grant revenue produced) and reducing unit costs (e.g., overloads taught). This "transparency of the budgeting process under RCM" (Theobald and Thompson, 2000, p. 15) means that faculty members' merit scores can be compared on a less arbitrary scale than was possible previously.

The aggregate merit score q in an RCM setting can be thought of as an index for scholarly quality that is also related to the net income-producing activities of the university or unit in which the faculty member resides, μ, and the error in measuring this faculty productivity, ε:

$$q = \mu + \varepsilon \tag{9.2}$$

The faculty member affects μ by investing time and energy, but ε is the random error inherent in a less than perfect assessment routine. Epsilon is beyond the control of the faculty member; and thus, q is only partly determined by a faculty member's actions.

A faculty member's ability and the amount of time and personal effort devoted to generating larger enrollments, acquiring external grants, and the other scholarly activities are all captured in μ. Each faculty member decides how much effort to invest (μ) in the production of the merit score (q). His or her choice must be made before any randomness (ε) in outcome is realized. In what follows we assume that faculty members seek to achieve higher merit scores on average. We also assume that there is a fixed rule for converting q into dollars. Although more will be said on this later in this chapter for the time being we can think of each quality point in q being worth W dollars.

Even if a faculty member is highly able and works hard, an observed merit score could be low because of chance events. The error in measurement ε could be caused by systematic errors in the assessment process (for example, misuse of student evaluations as the measure of teaching). In addition, faculty member-specific errors associated with an unpopular specialty or even illness could negatively impact μ. Thus, for assessment routine t and faculty member i, the error in measurement can be written

$$\varepsilon_{ti} = v_t + u_{ti} \tag{9.3}$$

where v_t is common to all faculty members (a fixed effect) and u_{ti} is a chance factor specific to the ith faculty member (a random effect). In a competitive RCM environment where one faculty member competes with another, the v_t terms cancel out. On the other hand, if a faculty member needs to clear a threshold value or absolute standard to be considered for the higher grade (and salary), there is nothing that ensures or even suggests the removal of this fixed effect.

Although the outcome of a draw on ε is not known until after the fact, we assume that faculty members know the distribution of ε when deciding on the amount of time and effort to invest in academic pursuits. Let ε be distributed as $F(\varepsilon)$, with density $f(\varepsilon)$, and mean of zero and variance σ^2. These assumptions are consistent with ε being normally distributed.

As a faculty member spends more time and effort in the pursuit of institutionally determined merit, less time is available for other things he or she enjoys and values. Those forgone activities might include satisfaction lost from playing tennis or lost earnings from consulting. The cost of time and effort and its disutility is captured in the faculty member's cost function $c(\mu)$. This faculty member's cost is assumed to increase as the time invested in institutionally determined academic activity increases; that is, the marginal cost of time spent in these activities is positive, $c'(\mu) > 0$. Also, as more time is invested in these academic activities, the outcomes increase but at a diminishing rate; that is, the marginal product of time is assumed to diminish with increased investment, $c''(\mu) > 0$. Diminishing returns to time imply that the harder the faculty member works for the university, the more it costs him or her (in lost satisfaction from other pursuits) to work even harder.

External factors can affect a faculty member's costs and a faculty member's costs may differ from that of the institution. For instance, the opinion of colleagues may enter into a faculty member's cost calculations but not the institution's. If colleagues value basic research that does not lend itself to getting outside grants, and if the faculty member values their opinions, the negative collegial environment effectively raises the disutility cost of grantsmanship to the faculty member. Similarly, high-enrollment classes that produce substantial income for the university, with miniscule incremental changes in short-run institutional cost, may elicit negative reaction from colleagues who worry that larger classes may lower the quality of students attracted to the department. This negative reaction from colleagues increases the disutility of large classes, raising their cost to the faculty member and persuading the faculty member to put less effort into increasing enrollments through the teaching of large classes.

COMPETENCY VERSUS COMPETITIVE MERIT SCORING

Lazear and Rosen (1981) introduced tournament-type reward structure to explain executive pay structures in industry, compensation for lawyers in law firms, and the like. They view the reward structure as a game with many competitors seeking a limited number of prizes, where "winners" get paid more than "losers." Becker and Rosen (1992) applied this competitive tournament idea to assigning grades to students. Here we apply the same idea to faculty rewards.

In the case of faculty assessment, assume that a review process gives rise to one of two merit scores: grade 1 is high performance and grade 2 is low performance. Assign reward W_1 to grade 1 and reward W_2 to grade 2 for the returns to scholarly and university income-producing achievement. As discussed later, W_1 might represent the dollar return to the mean quality of those faculty members receiving the higher grade and W_2 might be the return to the mean quality of those receiving the lower grade on some unidimensional or indexed scale that is associated with the desired achievement.

In judging the value that the faculty member places on the differential $W_1 - W_2$, account must be taken of the faculty member's rate of time preference and attitude toward risk. We will not address these factors here. We will assume, however, that these adjustments have been made so that the difference between W_1 and W_2 would be small only if the review process did not accurately separate faculty members by their true performance, or if the institution did not value the true attainment represented by the merit scores. RCM may be viewed as an attempt to minimize the impact of both of these issues. Neither of these alternatives, however, implies that the $W_1 - W_2$ difference can be increased merely by more assessment, regardless of whether the additional assessment uses external competency standards or is based on a competitive process.

Competency Scoring

If the faculty reward system is based on achieving an absolute merit standard then a faculty member must achieve a score q above the known critical value S to earn W_1. If the merit score q is below S the faculty member gets W_2. Conceivably all faculty members could get W_1; there is no need for a faculty member to worry about the performance of colleagues when such an external or exogenous standard is set and used. In point of fact, however, if W_1 is the mean product of all those receiving this amount, then its value and the number who could receive it is limited by the funds available, as discussed later. Furthermore, if all faculty members can achieve the standard, it is doing no screening and is superfluous.

An alternative to an absolute standard is a relative scoring system in which the threshold value separating W_1 and W_2 is not set, but it depends on a comparison of merit scores themselves. A relative method of scoring provides an *ex post* ranking of performance among faculty members. The magnitude of the highest merit score is irrelevant; it earns the holder the top award W_1. Now, because rewards are based on relative position, faculty members within a department may perceive it to be to their individual advantage to collude in fostering reduced effort without sacrificing relative position. If W_1 represents the return to the true average quality of those faculty members receiving this grade, it is to the advantage of those expecting this merit score not to tolerate collusion. The more noise in the system, and the smaller the department, the more likely that collusion will take place. For example, if perceived teaching quality (as opposed to number of students enrolled) is a dominant input to the merit score, and if it is not well measured, then collusion among teachers can be expected. For research, collusion might take the form of the department saying lower grade journals (where the majority publish) have higher quality than higher-grade journals (where only a few or none have published).

A faculty member must commit to an effort level before review and assignment of reward W_1 or W_2 regardless of the system employed. A faculty member can get either score for a given amount of effort and cost no matter the amount of time and effort invested because random chance may intervene. It is the probability of W_1 versus W_2 that is influenced by effort. Faculty members cannot adjust their strategies to maximize a merit score; they can make adjustments only to maximize the probability of receiving a score subject to constraints.

Let P_1 be the probability that a faculty member achieves grade 1; and P_2 be the probability of grade 2. Because this is a binary probability problem, $P_2 = 1 - P_1$. The expected (mean) gross payoff to a faculty member is now given by

$$P_1 W_1 + P_2 W_2 = P_1 W_1 + (1 - P_1) W_2 \qquad (9.4)$$

Subtracting the cost $c(\mu)$ from this expected value and rearranging terms yields the expected net payoff, which faculty members are assumed to maximize.

$$W_2 + P_1(W_1 - W_2) - c(\mu) \tag{9.5}$$

Because this maximization problem is based on expected benefits and deterministic cost, the same cost is incurred regardless of the benefit later realized; that is, effort is chosen before ε is revealed. The faculty member is guaranteed the lowest reward W_2, no matter what the time and effort invested or the random draw from the ε distribution. The incremental term $(W_1 - W_2)$ is the extra reward from getting the higher merit score.

If a faculty member has to beat an external standard S to earn the higher merit score and reward W_1, then P_1 is the probability that $q \geq S$ or the probability that $\mu + \varepsilon \geq S$. If, on the other hand the ith faculty member must beat the jth faculty member to receive the higher merit score and reward W_1, then P_1 is the probability that $q_i \geq q_j$, or the probability that $\mu_i + \varepsilon_i \geq \mu_j + \varepsilon_j$. In either the standard or competitive system, faculty members choose how hard to work (the μ's) knowing that there is a random error determined by the realizations of the ε's. Unlike the incentives to surpass the external standard, relative competition requires faculty members to consider the amount of effort colleagues (competitors) will invest when attempting to maximize the payoff function (9.5). We will consider first the simpler case of the absolute standard and then the case of competition between faculty members.

When a faculty member must reach a fixed and known threshold for a higher merit score, the probability of success is

$$P_1 = \text{Prob } (q \geq S) = \text{Prob } (\varepsilon \geq S - \mu) = 1 - F(S - \mu) \tag{9.6}$$

from which it can be seen that as μ increases so to does P_1. Substituting (9.6) into (9.5) gives the net payoff

$$W_1 - F(S - \mu)(W_1 - W_2) - c(\mu) \tag{9.7}$$

The optimum value of μ to maximize (9.7) is given by the first derivative of (9.7)

$$f(S - \mu)(W_1 - W_2) = c'(\mu) \tag{9.8}$$

where $f(\varepsilon) = \partial F / \partial \varepsilon = F'(\varepsilon)$. With W_1, W_2 and S fixed outside the immediate control of the faculty member, the faculty member chooses μ to equate marginal benefits, on the left-hand side of (9.8), with marginal costs on the right-hand side. That is, to maximize (9.7), the faculty member chooses μ by comparing the marginal cost (which reflects how hard he or she must work to increase the chances of passing the threshold S) and the marginal benefit (which is the probabalistic value of the higher versus lower grade). As the marginal benefits exceed the marginal cost the faculty member continues to increase his or her effort.

The essence of selecting μ can be seen by plotting both sides of equation (9.8) as in Figures 9.1 and 9.2. Marginal cost $c'(\mu)$ increases with increasing μ. The shape of the marginal benefit function comes from the distribution and density functions. Figure 9.1 assumes a normal density for the marginal benefit. Changes in the standard S shift the location of the marginal benefit curve from side-to-side. Changes in relative rewards $W_1 - W_2$ move the marginal benefit curve up or down.

The solution for μ in Figure 9.1 occurs where the marginal benefit curve intersects the marginal cost curve, satisfying equation (9.8). At this point the faculty member is maximizing the benefit of greater effort net of the added cost of the greater effort. If the return to a higher merit score rises, then the bell-shaped marginal benefit curve shifts up in Figure 9.1 and the faculty member invests more effort in generating merit scores. When the difference between $W_1 - W_2$ decreases, μ decreases too. Thus, if the administration wants to increase faculty effort to surpass a standard then it needs to increase the return to obtaining the standard. This can be done with or without an RCM system. That is, it has nothing to do with the type of management system employed.

As an alternative to increasing return to measured productivity q, the administration can simply increase the threshold for W_1. But increasing the standard does not necessarily produce the desired results. Raising the standard S causes the bell-shaped curve to shift to the right, but as seen in Figure 9.2, some additional complications are raised by the fact that there can be multiple intersections between the curves. As the standard is raised slightly in Figure 9.1, the bell-shaped curve shifts rightward and μ unambiguously increases. Faculty members work harder. However, as S is increased further, eventually we obtain the ambiguity of potential multi-equilibra, as depicted in Figure 9.2.

Figure 9.1: Unique Equilibrium Where the Marginal Cost Equals the Marginal Benefit of Effort

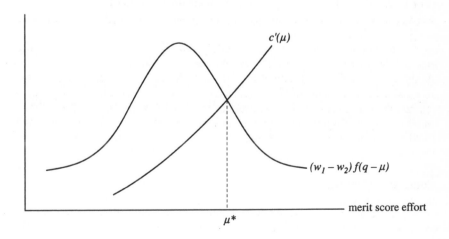

Figure 9.2: Potentially Multiple Equilibria Where Marginal Cost and
Marginal Benefit of Effort Are Equal

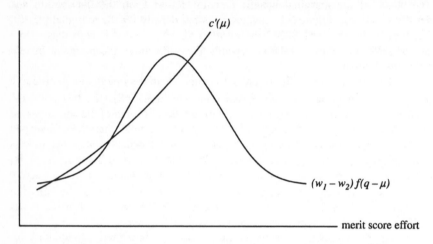

Differentiating equation (9.8) with respect to μ shows that the middle intersection in Figure 9.2 minimizes a faculty member's net return. Thus, it is of no interest for studying actual behavior. The other two intersections are local maxima, but visual inspection of Figure 9.2 reveals that the upper intersection (the one with the higher value of μ) is the global or overall maximum. Moving the marginal benefit curve further to the right as S is increased further would make the lower intersection the global maximum. Thus, if the administration knows that the current standard is low enough, increasing it provides incentives for faculty members to work harder. As the standard is raised further they work harder, but only up to a point. Once the critical point is reached, the situation is reversed and raising the standard further causes faculty members to reduce their efforts. In effect, they give up when the standard is set too high. The cost of meeting it is so high that it doesn't pay to try very hard to get into the higher category (holding the rewards constant).

In summary, standards that are either too high or too low cause faculty members to decrease their effort. A better faculty (defined either in terms of ability or cost) will continue to strive for the higher standards longer than a less able and/or less academically oriented faculty. Whether a standard established by central administrators can be set to produce the desired motivational effects for an entire faculty in a highly heterogenous university is debatable, but a decentralized RCM system does not ensure it either.

Competitive Scoring

In a competitive reward structure, however, an administrator does not have to set standards; only a desired percentile in each classification is needed. By their own behavior, the faculty sets the critical merit score for W_1 versus W_2, conditional on the rewards and the errors in measurement. A faculty member maximizes (9.5) subject to the expected behavior of colleagues who are now rivals.

To illustrate consider a faculty with only two members. As already stated, the probability that i^{th} faculty member is ranked higher than the jth is the probability that $q_i > q_j$:

$$\text{Prob } (q_i > q_j) = \text{Prob } (\mu_i + \varepsilon_i \geq \mu_j + \varepsilon_j) = \tag{9.9}$$
$$\text{Prob } (\varepsilon_i - \varepsilon_j \leq \mu_i - \mu_j) = \text{Prob } (D \leq \mu_i - \mu_j)$$

The probability distribution of each ε determines the probability distribution of D. For instance, if each ε is independently and normally distributed with a mean of zero and variance of σ^2, then D is normally distributed with mean zero and variance of $2\sigma^2$. Defining $G(D)$ to be the distribution of D, equation (9.9) is rewritten

$$\text{Prob } (i \text{ is ranked higher than } j) = \text{Prob } (q_i \geq q_j) = G(\mu_i - \mu_j) \tag{9.10}$$

The net payoff to faculty member i is

$$G(\mu_i - \mu_j)W_1 + [1 - G(\mu_i - \mu_j)]W_2 - c(\mu_i) \tag{9.11}$$

The maximization of this net payoff function is similar to the previous one except now the other faculty member's effort μ_j (instead of S) appears in the probability statement. A faculty member's decision is more complicated because he or she must consider what a colleague/rival might do. Both faculty members i and j must make their decisions about their own effort (μ) conditional on what they expect the other to do.

If the faculty members are of equal inherent ability and face the same costs, they will employ similar strategies. When faculty member i selects μ to maximize the net payoff, he or she must assume that j is making the same calculation. Neither faculty member can get an advantage *ex ante* even though both will try. As long as W_1 and W_2 are fixed, the quest for a higher merit score is a zero sum game. The amount of effort invested by each faculty member depends on the difference in rewards but in equilibrium (i.e., *ex post*) the outcome looks like a coin toss because both work equally hard (*ex ante*) to perform well. If faculty members are of unequal ability, however, the more capable tends to come out ahead. As with a fixed standard that is set too low, the more able faculty member succeeds with smaller effort.

If there are no fixed effects ($v_t = 0$) common to the faculty, then in equation (9.3) $\varepsilon_{ti} = u_{ti}$ and the amount of risk in a competitive RCM type reward scheme is greater than that involved in an absolute standard system – in terms of variances, $2\sigma^2$ versus σ^2. Thus, additional time spent trying to achieve a standard raises the probability of its achievement by more than the same additional time spent trying to beat a rival colleague. Regardless of the reason, when the variability in measuring faculty productivity increases, investment in achieving a standard or beating a competitor falls. If the measurement error is common to all faculty members, however, a competitive RCM system can filter out that fixed component of noise and still provide reliable rankings. When a faculty is highly diverse in ability, extreme errors in measurement can be avoided by using multiple grades. The least appropriate scale is a binary pass-fail competency measure if the faculty is highly heterogenous.

Distributional Effects

As already discussed, faculty members in a competitive pay environment may collude to thwart the system. Whether a faculty member is receptive to a more intensive screening requires consideration of his or her perceived position in the distribution of performance and how that position will be rewarded (Becker, 1979).

We have so far given little attention to the payoff weights (W's) in the merit system other than to state that their values do in some way depend on the mean level of effort and attainment achieved by those so designated. Faculty members in the 85th percentile, for example, might be designated "highly meritorious," and those in the 70th percentile, might be labeled "meritorious," and so on. We need to assume only that those getting the highest meritorious designate receive pecuniary rewards greater than those getting the second-highest meritorious label and those getting the second-highest label receive rewards greater than those getting the third-highest and so on down the merit performance ladder. But, although movement of a faculty member from the 70th up to the 85th percentile implies that a colleague must have moved from the 85th down to the 70th percentile, this apparent offsetting movement does not imply that the faculty members are competing in a zero sum game even though the number of highly meritorious and meritorious grades is unchanged. If the true attainment of the latter faculty member's productivity did not decrease when the former faculty member's true productivity increased, then the mean productivity of all those at and above the 70th percentile must have increased.

In an RCM environment, if the unit becomes more productive then competition between faculty members will increase the revenue the school or department has available. In turn, this should drive up the dollar values of all highly meritorious and meritorious grades even though the percentile thresholds did not change. If this is not the case then the competition is destructive as the game is zero sum. At the university level, RCM must result in more total revenue for the institution or units will simply be competing in a zero sum game for which one unit's gain is another unit's loss and one faculty member's gain is just another faculty member's loss.

A faculty member can attempt to produce a merit score that will likely place him or her in a given percentile of faculty output, but the behavior of colleagues and administrators also comes into play in establishing success. The faculty member in question, colleagues and administrators never know with certainty the true attainment of any other faculty member because μ is not observable and only q is. Assume the density function for true academic productivity in the unit responsible for salary determination is $h(\mu)$. Assume a fairly accurate grading system in which the mean of ε is again zero and variance of ε is small and fixed at σ^2. Also assume that the merit determination process is uniformly accurate across merit scores so the measurement error is independent of merit level. Increases in the accuracy of merit scoring will thus cause the variance of ε to decrease uniformly across the distribution. Again, assuming the density of ε is $f(\varepsilon)$, the probability that a faculty member of true productivity μ is labeled q can be represented by

$$\text{Prob}(q \mid \mu) = f(q - \mu) = f(\varepsilon) \tag{9.12}$$

In accordance with the idea behind RCM, where metaphorically each unit floats on its own bottom, competition implies that each faculty member whose productivity is estimated to be q will receive the value of the mean marginal product of all those who are so labeled. If a merit point is worth m dollars, each faculty member getting a score of q will receive $w(q)$, where

$$w(q) = m \int \mu f(q - \mu) h(\mu) d\mu \, / \int f(q - \mu) h(\mu) d\mu \tag{9.13}$$

Without loss of generality, in discrete measurement the numerator of (9.13) can be viewed as giving the value of the true productivity of all faculty members labeled q and the denominator gives the number so labeled. The mean value of those labeled "somewhat meritorious," for example, is the cumulative value of the product of all those who receive this merit level divided by the number receiving the label. If there are many really highly able faculty members in this meritorious category, then this label will be worth more than if there are few really highly able faculty members so labeled. Within an RCM system this is the way it is supposed to work, but it will work only if: 1) the additional revenue produced by income-producing and cost-reducing activities flows to the units responsible for salary assignment, which in turn flows to the faculty members; and 2) the measurement system is accurate (the mean of ε is zero, with a small and fixed variance of σ^2).

A faculty member investing effort to produce a level of true attainment μ can expect to receive $W(\mu)$, where

$$W(\mu) = \int w(q) f(q - \mu) dq \tag{9.14}$$

A Taylor expansion can be used to approximate the expected return to a true attainment level of μ

$$W(\mu) = m[\mu + h'(\mu)\sigma^2/h(\mu)] \qquad (9.15)$$

For a unimodal distribution of productivity output $h(\mu)$, faculty members below the modal output can expect to receive more than their true product, because $h'(\mu) > 0$, and those above the modal output level can expect to receive less than their true product, because $h'(\mu) < 0$. Intuitively, low achievers [those below the mode for whom $h'(\mu) > 0$] tend to be grouped with more colleagues who are, on average, more able than they, and with few colleagues who are less able than they. The poorest faculty member, for example, cannot be grouped with any who are less able and can only be grouped with those who are more able; thus, his or her expected return to effort is greater than its true value. On the other hand, high producers [those for whom $h'(\mu) < 0$] can always expect to be grouped with more colleagues who are less rather than more able. The most able faculty member, for example, cannot be grouped with anyone who is more able and can only be grouped with those who are less able; thus, the expected return to effort for the best faculty member must be less than its true value. Notice, the truly most productive scholar need not get the highest merit score.

The entire faculty [regardless of individual position in the outcome distribution $h(\mu)$ or the variance in measuring productivity σ^2] is made better off by an increase in m, the value placed on a merit point. Of course, the administration and not the faculty set m. It is constrained by institutional revenue flows. Comparing the difference between expected earnings with perfect merit scores [$W(\mu) = m\mu$] and with less than perfect scoring, as in equation (9.15), shows that on average more productive faculty members [$h'(\mu) > 0$] are made worse off, and less productive faculty members are made better off by errors in measuring outcome.

How faculty members respond to changes in the intensity of the screening of their output depends on their position in the outcome distribution. If the outcome of the majority of faculty members (as given by the median) is above the most frequently occurring outcome (mode), as in a right-skewed unimodal distribution, then the majority of faculty members above the modal outcome should welcome a reduction in the measurement error (ε) [i.e., smaller standard deviation (σ)]. But will they?

All those who perceive that they will be between the mode and the mean might think that they could be made even better off with no informative screening whatsoever, because with no screening they would get the mean, assuming no change in the distribution or value of productivity outcomes. (With no information, each faculty member would receive the mean.) Because the median is below the mean in a right-skewed distribution, the majority of faculty members could perceive benefits of not having a meaningful merit system. This noninformative alternative dominates the perfect screening option for a majority-rule vote because those who think they will end up between the mode and mean are further ahead with no screening than with perfect screening. If the outcome distribution is left-skewed, then the reverse would be true. The egalitarian ethos in one unit on campus and a meritocracy in another may simply reflect the underlying shape of the productivity distribution and not the level of aggregate output.

So what are the policy recommendations for determining faculty salaries? First, from the previous section we know that reward structures can stimulate scholarly and income-producing academic output only if faculty members perceive that they are in a tournament they have a chance to win, with accurate screening processes and worthwhile financial gains for the winners. RCM systems seek to address these latter two issues by first making each faculty member's relative contribution to increasing school or department income (e.g., student credit hours taught, indirect grant revenue produced) and reducing unit costs (e.g., overloads taught) observable, which allows for more accurate screening of productivity. RCM also allocates these additional funds to the units allowing them to financially reward their more productive faculty members.

However, from this section we know that if the majority of faculty perceive that the screening process leaves them worse off than they would be without screening, then they will fight the merit process. In addition, the "new behavior and beliefs required by RCM are often at cross-purposes with the powerful but largely invisible academic culture" (Wilms, Teruya, and Walpole, 1997, p. 46). These conflicts in an RCM system may take the form of "salary equity reviews" in which adjustments are made outside the normal review process to address issues such as "salary inversion" and "salary compression". What remains to be done is to address how merit scores can actually be turned into dollars in a merit system.

TURNING MERIT SCORES INTO SALARIES

When a competency system is used and the amount of money available for raises is fixed, turning merit scores into salaries for those who meet the standard is easy. The total of funds available for each competency level need only be divided by the number achieving it, with the quotient given to each achiever. The algebra for transforming merit score into raises in a competitive system is more difficult, as Becker (1999) demonstrates. In part this is because a single formula for merit pay raises can be based on either a fixed-cash amount or a percentage of base salary, or any combination of the two.

A fixed-dollar reward per merit point leads to salary compression as those who become productive with lower salaries catch up (in relative terms) with those with higher salaries. Salary raises based on percentage increases favor those with the higher salaries. To encourage already high-salaried professors to produce still more, relatively greater dollar increases per merit point may be required. At the low end of the existing salary distribution, a percentage raise based on a relatively low salary may be discouraging as a higher-paid person with a similar merit score pulls further away from the lower-paid person.

As already discussed, competitive pay schemes start with the assigning and ranking of merit scores. Assume that each faculty member has a merit score that is the sum of weighted teaching, research, and service merit scores. For example, in the department of economics at Indiana University the number q_i defines the aggregate merit score (q) of the ith faculty member. Research has a weight of 5, teaching a weight of 3, and service a weight of 2, and each academic outcome is scored 1 to 5:

$$q_i = 5(research_i) + 3(teaching_i) + 2(service_i), \text{ for } 10 \le q_i \le 50 \quad (9.16)$$

How q is determined for each faculty member is irrelevant for the following calculations, but presumably it is done with reference to some explicit criteria with a recognized error as defined in equation (9.2). The only essential item is that each faculty member has a single merit score.

As is typically done in large universities and following the algebra in Becker (1999), assume that a fixed positive amount of money M_t is assigned to the unit for salary raises. For any number of reasons (e.g., responding to an outside offer, providing an equity adjustment) the ith faculty member might get a one-time, fixed-dollar kick in pay of K_{it} in the tth time period, $K_{it} \le M_t$. The amount or pot of money (*POT*) available for merit raises is then given by

$$POT = M_t - \sum_{i=1}^{n} K_{it} \quad (9.17)$$

POT may be divided into ρ proportion for percentage merit raises and $(1 - \rho)$ proportion for absolute dollar merit raises:

$$POT = \rho(POT) + (1 - \rho)POT \quad (9.18)$$

Let y_{jt-1} be the jth faculty member's predetermined salary at time $t-1$, and Y_{jt} be the jth faculty member's yet undetermined salary for time t. Now we have

$$\rho POT = \sum_{j=1}^{n} R_{j\rho} y_{jt-1} \quad (9.19)$$

where $R_{1\rho}$ is the lowest percentage-based raise in the unit and

$$0 < R_{1\rho} \le R_{2\rho} \le \dots R_{n\rho} < 1 \quad (9.20)$$

To maintain the same proportional spread between percentage raises and the merit scores, from the p proportion of the *POT*, the ith person's percentage-based raise is

$$R_{i\rho} = \frac{q_i}{q_1} R_{1\rho} \quad (9.21)$$

and

$$\rho POT = \frac{R_{1\rho}}{q_1} \sum_{j=1}^{n} q_j y_{jt-1} \qquad (9.22)$$

Once *POT* is specified, the lowest raise $R_{1\rho}$ can be determined, which in turn determines all the remaining raises by the proportional spread in merit scores. For the ith person,

$$R_{i\rho} = q_i (\rho POT / \sum_{j=1}^{n} q_j y_{jt-1}) \qquad (9.23)$$

The dollar value of this percentage raise to the ith person is then $R_{i\rho} y_{it-1}$.

The determination of the absolute dollar raise component for the ith person is much easier; it is given by

$$(q_i / \sum_{j=1}^{n} q_j)(1 - \rho)POT \qquad (9.24)$$

The formula for salary determination for the ith person for any $0 \le \rho \le 1$ is thus

$$y_{it} = y_{it-1} + K_{it} + (y_{it-1} q_i \rho POT / \sum_{j=1}^{n} q_j y_{jt-1}) + [q_i(1 - \rho)POT / \sum_{j=1}^{n} q_j] \qquad (9.25)$$

To assess the consequences of changing the proportion of the *POT* allocated to percentage versus absolute-dollar raises, consider three regimes, in which $\rho = 0$, 0.5 or 1.00, and a merit raise pot of $50,000, which is net of an assumed promotion adjustment of $2,000 to faculty member 6 ($K_6 = \$2,000$), and an assumed $3,000 equity adjustment to person 17 ($K_{17} = \$3,000$). That is, from equation (9.17)

$$POT = \$50,000 = M_t - \sum_{i=1}^{n} K_{it} = \$55,000 - \$5,000 \qquad (9.26)$$

The relevant values for the case of $\rho = 0$, where salary raises are determined by an absolute dollar amount only, are shown in Table 9.1. For example, the initial salary of the 4th person is $95,410; this person's merit score of 39.8 yields a raise of $3,460 for a new salary of $98,870. The relevant values for $\rho = 1$ are shown in Table 9.2, where raises are determined by the percentage rule. The 39.8 merit score of the 4th person yields a 4.443 percent salary increase for a new salary of $99,445, which is a $4,239 increase. Notice, however, that the

12th person had a similar merit score (40.03) and 4.469 percent salary increase, but only a $2,632 increase under the percentage merit rule.

For this hypothetical (but realistic) salary distribution for a midrange Carnegie Research I University, the effect of percentage versus absolute pay increases is not trivial. Productive faculty members at the high end of the distribution may be viewed by those at the lower end as benefiting too much from a percentage-based pay scheme. After all, the argument goes, an article in a major journal is an article no matter what the salary of the author; a classroom of 300 students is a classroom of 300 students regardless of the instructor's salary. If one article gets cited more than another or if students benefit more from one instructor than another, then this should be captured in the merit rating. By the same token, the absolute-dollar allocation method leads to a highly compressed salary distribution, which is not conducive to stimulating current higher-paid, older professors or instilling longer term productive behavior in the lower-paid younger assistant professors as they look at a tournament-type promotion method with relatively decreasing rewards for the top rank.

Recognizing the effects of salary compression, in the spring of 1999 the elected salary committee in the department of economics at Indiana University broke with its traditional absolute dollar amount salary merit system and moved to a 50/50 mix. The consequence of this mix can be seen for the hypothetical data in Table 9.3, where $\rho = 0.5$. The salary raises of the 4th and 12th persons are now close ($3,849 and $3,056), but there is still an advantage to having achieved (and an incentive to achieve) a higher salary.

The formula for y_{it} can be used to assess the consequences of different mixes. It enables any department or administrator to pick any combination of per-

Table 9.1: Absolute Dollar Raises

Faculty Member	Base Salary	Adjust-ment	Merit Score	Dollar Raise	New Salary
1	$119,000	$0	45.1000	$3,921	$122,921
2	$112,131	$0	38.7333	$3,368	$115,499
3	$98,502	$0	36.6000	$3,182	$101,684
4	$95,410	$0	39.8000	$3,460	$98,870
5	$91,200	$0	41.4333	$3,602	$94,802
6	$88,888	$2,000	32.3500	$2,813	$93,701
7	$75,432	$0	38.2000	$3,321	$78,753
8	$75,325	$0	35.9733	$3,128	$78,453
9	$74,500	$0	37.4833	$3,259	$77,759
10	$64,589	$0	27.2667	$2,371	$66,960
11	$59,600	$0	24.8767	$2,163	$61,763
12	$58,900	$0	40.0333	$3,481	$62,381
13	$56,789	$0	36.4000	$3,165	$59,954
14	$54,325	$0	27.5000	$2,391	$56,716
15	$52,111	$0	21.6500	$1,882	$53,993
16	$51,000	$0	23.2000	$2,017	$53,017
17	$41,000	$3,000	28.5000	$2,478	$46,478
	$1,268,702	$5,000	575.1000	$50,000	$1,323,702

Table 9.2: Percentage Raises

Faculty Member	Base Salary	Adjust- ment	Merit Score	Percent Raise	New Salary
1	$119,000	$0	45.1000	0.05034	$124,991
2	$112,131	$0	38.7333	0.04324	$116,979
3	$98,502	$0	36.6000	0.04085	$102,526
4	$95,410	$0	39.8000	0.04443	$99,649
5	$91,200	$0	41.4333	0.04625	$95,418
6	$88,888	$2,000	32.3500	0.03611	$94,098
7	$75,432	$0	38.2000	0.04264	$78,648
8	$75,325	$0	35.9733	0.04015	$78,350
9	$74,500	$0	37.4833	0.04184	$77,617
10	$64,589	$0	27.2667	0.03044	$66,555
11	$59,600	$0	24.8767	0.02777	$61,255
12	$58,900	$0	40.0333	0.04469	$61,532
13	$56,789	$0	36.4000	0.04063	$59,096
14	$54,325	$0	27.5000	0.03070	$55,993
15	$52,111	$0	21.6500	0.02417	$53,370
16	$51,000	$0	23.2000	0.02590	$52,321
17	$41,000	$3,000	28.5000	0.03181	$45,304
	$1,268,702	$5,000	575.1000		$1,323,702

centage and absolute salary merit-based allocation method with no hidden manipulation involved. The funds available for raises and the individual merit scores dictate the salary increases, and not some magical box with unknown workings.

POLICY IMPLICATIONS

The implications of our theoretical modeling are fairly straightforward. One of the advantages touted for RCM is that it allows more accurate screening for faculty productivity and rewards the faculty for the desired outcomes. The application of these more accurate screening tools should allow schools and departments to use the reward structure to cause an increase in every faculty member's desire to increase his or her productivity. RCM should have a direct positive effect on the output of high income-generating faculty members. As resources are channeled to these more productive faculty, the improved accuracy in screening, combined with increases in the level of merit pay available (made possible by more efficient allocation of salary resources) should raise the level of output produced, but low producers may not respond in a like manner.

The provision of additional merit pay in this model is crucial, though. The use of competition between faculty members will stimulate academic effort only if faculty members are appropriately rewarded for achieving. Without additional merit pay resources, this becomes a zero sum game and those below the mode can expect to lose income, generating pressure for more parity in the distribution of faculty pay. More homogeneity in pay levels will cause those faculty members

Table 9.3: 50/50 Absolute and Percentage Raises

Faculty Member	Base Salary	Adjust-ment	Merit Score	Dollar Raise	Percent Raise	Percent Dollars	New Salary
1	$119,000	$0	45.1000	$1,961	0.02517	$2,995	$123,956
2	$112,131	$0	38.7333	$1,684	0.02162	$2,424	$116,239
3	$98,502	$0	36.6000	$1,591	0.02043	$2,012	$102,105
4	$95,410	$0	39.8000	$1,730	0.02221	$2,119	$99,259
5	$91,200	$0	41.4333	$1,801	0.02312	$2,109	$95,110
6	$88,888	$2,000	32.3500	$1,406	0.01806	$1,605	$93,899
7	$75,432	$0	38.2000	$1,661	0.02132	$1,608	$78,701
8	$75,325	$0	35.9733	$1,564	0.02008	$1,512	$78,401
9	$74,500	$0	37.4833	$1,629	0.02092	$1,559	$77,688
10	$64,589	$0	27.2667	$1,185	0.01522	$983	$66,757
11	$59,600	$0	24.8767	$1,081	0.01388	$827	$61,509
12	$58,900	$0	40.0333	$1,740	0.02234	$1,316	$61,956
13	$56,789	$0	36.4000	$1,582	0.02032	$1,154	$59,525
14	$54,325	$0	27.5000	$1,195	0.01535	$834	$56,354
15	$52,111	$0	21.6500	$941	0.01208	$630	$53,682
16	$51,000	$0	23.2000	$1,009	0.01295	$660	$52,669
17	$41,000	$3,000	28.5000	$1,239	0.01591	$652	$45,891
	$1,268,702	$5,000	575.1000	$25,000		$25,000	$1,323,702

above the modal output level to reduce their effort because the costs involved in allocating more time to scholarly and income-producing activities will not generate commensurate benefits.

RCM should also put pressure on administrators to operate nonacademic units more efficiently because faculty members will learn to see those units as a cost item. Hansmann (1986) describes a traditional defining characteristic of colleges and universities as a nondistribution constraint. Because universities have no equity owners to whom profit is distributed, Hansmann argues that there has been reduced pressure on administrators to operate efficiently. Under RCM, though, the costs of administrative operations are much more visible because they are directly billed to instructional units. According to Ruesink and Thompson (1996, p. 8), "the negative perceptions of RCM that the 1996 Committee reported receiving most often was 'units paying the bills [instructional units] don't have enough control over the way the non-instructional units are managing their operations.'"

As a result, there have been two university-wide initiatives focused on assessing the costs of administrative and other nonacademic services. The cover letter to the first report (Bepko, Clapacs, and Banta, 1998) stated that "we can be reasonably satisfied that the cost of operations at Indiana University is well within the range of costs that are typical at American Universities." The presence of RCM kept this issue at the forefront, though, and in the 2000 RCM review a dean is quoted as complaining that "non-instructional units are insufficiently accountable for the use for their income – those who are subject to market discipline are not sympathetic to those who are not" (Theobald and Thompson, 2000, p. 9). Just two years after the first review of administrative services, the President launched a second such review and charged the committee to "recommend the means by which these [administrative] services can be provided more cost effectively and without loss of quality – or even better, with increased quality" (Brand, 2001, p. 1).

Concerns have been raised, though, about the "strong incentives for the hiring of lower-paid instructors or bargain-basement graduate students to teach undergraduate courses" (Adams, 1997, p. 61). Yet, this issue has not been raised in either of the two reviews conducted on RCM at Indiana University (Ruesink and Thompson, 1996; Theobald and Thompson, 2000). This suggests that either "the hiring of lower-paid instructors or bargain-basement graduate students to teach undergraduate courses" was well-established before RCM and is therefore not seen as a result of this budgeting system, or the increased savings that are realized from the use of lower-paid teachers is not sufficient to offset lower student demand – and therefore decreased income in an RCM model – for courses taught by lower-paid staff.

In the final analysis, decentralized budgeting systems, such as RCM, may simply be a response to decreasing state financial support for public higher education. At a time when a lump-sum state appropriations provided the bulk of university revenue, the traditional centralized allocation of these funds made perfect sense. As revenues become more dependent on student fees generated by instructional units, however, the role of central administration becomes more subsidiary. According to Whalen (1996, p. 129), "institutionally generated income is very different from revenue obtained from governmental sources. Its generation is dependent on the initiative and effort of operating units and individuals within the organization, not on central direction." If unit administrators or faculty are to take such initiatives in a timely manner, they need financial resources that are readily accessible (Hoenack, 1977). The 2000 RCM review credits RCM with allowing "the campus to better allocate its scarce resources in a time when the state appropriation plays a declining role in the resource base" (Theobald and Thompson, 2000, p. 8).

In such an environment, it is critical that a merit system can identify and reward productive faculty members in line with their contribution to the pool of revenue. The ability of RCM to make the flow of funds visible facilitates the provision of such incentives to faculty members to maximize the effectiveness of their performance.

REFERENCES

Adams, Elie M. 1997. Rationality in the academy: Why responsibility centered budgeting is a wrong step down the wrong road. *Change* 29 (5): 59-61.

Becker, William E. 1999. Turning merit scores into salaries. *Journal of Economic Education* 30 (Fall): 420-426.

Becker, William E. 1979. Professorial behavior given a stochastic reward structure. *American Economic Review* 69 (December): 1010-1017.

Becker, William E. 1975. The university professor as a utility maximizer and producer of learning, research, and income. *Journal of Human Resources* 10 (Winter): 107-115.

Becker, William E., and Sherwin Rosen. 1992. The learning effect of assessment and evaluation in high school. *Economics of Education Review* 11 (June): 107-118.

Bepko, Gerald, Terry Clapacs, and Trudy Banta. 1998. *Task force report on efficiency and cost reduction at Indiana University.* Final report submitted to the President, Indiana Universtiy.

Brand, Myles. 2000. Next steps in the review of nonacademic administrative services. Memorandum to Indiana University faculty and staff. October.

Braskamp, Larry A., and John C. Ory. 1994. *Assessing faculty work: Enhancing individual and institutional performance.* San Francisco: Jossey-Bass.

Carnaghi, Jill E. 1992. Set, go...ready: Planning for responsibility center budgeting. Ph.D. dissertation, Indiana University.

Centra, John A. 1993. *Reflective faculty evaluation: Enhancing teaching and determining faculty effectiveness.* San Francisco: Jossey-Bass.

Hansmann, Henry. 1986. The role of nonprofit enterprise. In S. Rose-Ackerman, ed., *The economics of nonprofit institutions.* New York: Oxford University Press.

Hoenack, Stephen A. 1977. Direct and incentive planning within a university. *Socio-Economic Planning Sciences* 11 (4): 191-204.

Lazear, Edward, and Sherwin Rosen. 1981. Rank-order tournaments as optimum labor contracts. *Journal of Political Economy* 89 (5): 841-864.

Root, Lawrence S. 1987. Faculty evaluation: Reliability of peer assessments of research, teaching, and service. *Research in Higher Education* 26:71-84.

Ruesink, Albert, and Maynard Thompson. 1996. *Responsibility-centered management at Indiana University Bloomington: 1990-1995.* Final report of the 1995-96 Responsibility-Centered Management Review Committee submitted to the Chancellor, Indiana University Bloomington.

Theobald, Neil, and Maynard Thompson. 2000. *Responsibility-centered management at Indiana University Bloomington: 1990-2000.* Final report of the 1999-2000 Responsibility-Centered Management Review Committee submitted to the Chancellor, Indiana University Bloomington.

Whalen, Edward L. 1996. Responsibility-centered management: An approach to decentralized financial operations. In David S. Honeyman, James L. Wattenbarger, and Kathleen C. Westbrook, eds., *A struggle to survive: Funding higher education in the next century.* Thousand Oaks, CA: Corwin.

Wilms, Wellford, Cheryl Teruya, and MaryBeth Walpole. 1997. Fiscal reform at UCLA: The clash of accountability and academic freedom. *Change* 29 (5): 41-49.

CHAPTER 10

USING PERFORMANCE INDICATORS TO EVALUATE DECENTRALIZED BUDGETING SYSTEMS AND INSTITUTIONAL PERFORMANCE

Robert K. Toutkoushian

Cherry Danielson

In this chapter, we take a closer look at performance indicators and the extent to which they can be useful in assessing decentralized budgeting systems and higher education enterprises. We begin with a comparison of for-profit and nonprofit firms, service organizations, and postsecondary institutions, and highlight the implications that their similarities and differences have for identifying a performance indicator system. Although touted as a way of motivating institutions to become more efficient and improve the learning outcomes of students, the differences between the corporate and higher education models introduce several important limitations to indicators used in higher education. We then review some of the most commonly used performance indicators and their limitations within this framework, and look at a case study of how one university is planning to use indicators to assess the success of its decentralized budgeting system.

USING PERFORMANCE INDICATORS

As described in earlier chapters, decentralized budgeting systems have been adopted in recent years by a number of public institutions, including Indiana

University, the University of Minnesota, and the University of New Hampshire. These systems are often referred to as responsibility centered management (RCM) systems, but the label RCM can represent any decentralized budgeting system where revenues are distributed to academic units in proportion to the revenues that they bring into the institution through their research, teaching, and public service functions.[1]

To reiterate briefly, units in an RCM system are responsible for using these revenues to cover their total expenditures. Some institutions have switched to RCM in the hope of improving the management of the institution by providing academic units with monetary incentives. Given that the conversion to an RCM system may involve years of planning, and invoke fears among the faculty of adverse consequences for the institution, there is a great need to measure institutional performance and determine if and how it has changed after moving to RCM. This measurement is increasingly being done through the use of institutional performance indicators.

The concept of performance indicators is not new and, in fact, bears a long and storied history.[2] In the business world, corporate leaders have relied on performance indicators to evaluate their operations for growth and stability, and identify actions that may enhance their performance. Federal and state governments also use indicators such as the Consumer Price Index, the unemployment rate, and Gross Domestic Product to monitor the performance of the economy. More recently, the concept of performance indicators, along with RCM and other common business practices, have been increasingly applied to higher education. Many colleges and universities now find themselves routinely using statistics such as their graduation rate and expenditures per student to evaluate their performance and justify their value to governing boards, state legislatures, parents, students, and other constituents. This global phenomenon promises to continue as institutions of higher education (IHE) seek to inform constituencies of how their contributions are being spent (Cullen, 1987; Dochy, Segers, and Wijnen, 1990; Findlay, 1990; Cave, Hanney, and Kogan, 1991; Gaither, Nedwek, and Neal, 1994). In addition to evaluating the overall performance of the organization itself, institutions that have adopted RCM budgeting systems also look to indicators to provide evidence of whether the new system has achieved its desired goals.

Advocates of performance indicators often ascribe almost mythical powers to their value for evaluating the performance of higher education institutions. This is perhaps best reflected in the subtitle "Vital Benchmarks and Information to Help You Evaluate and Improve Your Institution's Performance" that accompanies the widely-used book on strategic indicators by Taylor and Massy (1996). Taylor and Massy assert that their set of over 100 indicators "...provides a framework for understanding institutional condition and taking steps to improve competitive position" (p. xv). Performance indicators in higher education have been described by others as "...empirical data...which describe the functioning of an institution, [and] the way the institution pursues its goals" (Dochy, Segers, and Wijnen, 1990, p. 72), "...specific quantifiable measures that tell stakeholders, managers, and other staff whether the college or university is accomplishing its goals using an acceptable level of resources" (Dolence and Norris, 1994, p. 64), and "...concrete, substantive, measurable, and easily recognized concepts" that should be a more integral part of a university's strategic planning process than the institution's mission statement (Rowley 1997, p. 30).

Despite the lofty rhetoric surrounding their value in academe, the indicators most frequently identified by colleges and universities to measure institutional goals – such as retention and graduation rates, expenditures per student, and average freshmen SAT scores – fall far short of this ideal. Borden and Bottrill (1994) argue that to be effective, performance indicators need to be tied to an explicit goal or objective for the institution. Ewell and Jones (1994, p. 23) go further and state "To be useful for policy and decision making, indicators should be developed around sound conceptual frameworks and should encompass multiple aspects of institutional or system performance." Some IHE (particularly in the two-year sector) have tried to address this issue by engaging in the assessment of valued student outcomes. Much of the research in this area focuses on the effect of incoming characteristics of students on the overall college experience as well as domain-specific freshmen-to-senior changes (see Pascarella and Terenzini, 1991). However, these measures have not been widely incorporated into performance indicator systems, because of the significant time and monetary costs of collecting such information as well as disagreements among analysts as to how to properly measure such gains.

Many IHE are compelled to target certain indicators because particular stakeholders have pressured them to do so, and these stakeholders may have different political motives and conflicting opinions about the relative importance of different indicators. This is perhaps most evident with the college rankings published annually by *U.S. News and World Report* (*USNWR*). Although many educators question the rankings on the grounds that they are not directly related to institutional goals and quality, they acknowledge that the *USNWR* rankings receive significant publicity and may influence student decisions regarding where to go for their postsecondary education (Patterson, 2000; Thompson, 2000). Accordingly, administrators pay very close attention to their rankings, and may try to identify policies that would result in higher rankings.

In this chapter, we examine the potential use of performance indicators as evaluation tools for responsibility-centered management systems and the extent to which they can function more broadly as valid assessments of institutional performance. We begin by reviewing the historic use of performance indicators in the business and corporate world and comparing the goals and objectives of for-profit firms and nonprofit enterprises with higher education institutions in general. Next, we highlight the implications that their similarities and differences have for identifying performance indicators to assess these goals. We will argue that performance indicator systems are most effective when the goals of the organization are well defined and measurable, and the organization has an understanding of how to use various policy levers at its disposal to reach these goals. While touted as a way of motivating institutions to become more efficient and improve the learning outcomes of students, performance indicator systems have proven to be less effective in a higher education setting for two reasons:

1) There are problems associated with identifying and measuring the ultimate goals/outcomes of colleges and universities because of the multi-product nature of IHE (see Kerr, 1982); and 2) IHE have limited control over the inputs and production processes that might be used to attain these goals. These limitations arise from a failure to take into account how the differences between for-profit firms and colleges/universities might affect the types of indicators that would be appropriate for a higher education setting.

We then review some of the most commonly-used performance indicators and their limitations within this framework, and show that the indicators most often selected by institutions are at best very rough measures of institutional goals, and can in fact be far removed from the actual objectives of the organization. Furthermore, we will discuss the problems associated with setting targets for such indicators and attempting to implement policies to achieve these targets.

Finally, we focus directly on the goals of RCM systems and critique the validity and adaptability of performance indicators as part of the evaluative process of these goals. We will argue that because institutional goals and objectives are extremely difficult to quantify, it cannot be determined through performance indicators whether an RCM system has affected the institution's pursuit of these goals. Institutions with RCM systems often list other goals that are related to their incentive structures, such as to raise enrollment levels, increase sponsored-research dollars received, and limit the growth of per-student expenditures. The fact that these outcomes are affected by a range of other internal and external factors that are also changing over time will make it nearly impossible to attribute any change as a result of RCM. Additionally, the incentives that are typically incorporated into an RCM system may have negative consequences on the institution's ability to meet goals that are not rewarded by the budgeting system. The more process-oriented goals of RCM, such as clarifying the budgeting process, are also difficult to measure with quantitative data or indicators, but can be examined through more qualitative methods such as interviews and surveys of faculty and staff.

ORGANIZATIONAL GOALS, OBJECTIVES, AND PERFORMANCE

Over time, for-profit firms, nonprofit entities, and for-profit service organizations have looked to indicators as a way of assessing the relative performance of their operations. In a different context, indicators have been used by economists and policy analysts to evaluate the health and performance of the economy. The potential contributions that performance indicators can make in each context, however, are centrally related to the goals and objectives of the organization/entity to which the indicators are applied. It is useful to begin by reviewing the traditional "production function" model as it is used in the corporate for-profit world and then see how this model can be applied to IHE[3] (see Winston, 1997).

The production function can be thought of as consisting of four separate components: inputs, production process, outputs, and goals. This is similar to the "Input-Process-Output" model (Cave, Hanney, and Kogan, 1991; Borden and Bottrill, 1994) and the "Input-Environment-Outcomes" model by Astin (1993) that have been used to describe higher education. We add goals as a separate category at the end of the process to highlight the fact that *outputs*, such as the number of students taught and the number of publications produced, can be quite different from the *outcomes* of education (e.g., knowledge production, cognitive gains of students). In its simplest form, these models describe how an organization can use its production processes to convert inputs into outputs for the purpose of meeting specific goals. The inputs for firms consist of the raw materials ultimately converted into outputs and the factors of production such as land, labor, and capital (e.g., machinery or technology) used for the conversion. The ways in which the levels of land, labor, and capital are combined to produce outputs from inputs constitute the production process. Output for the firm consists of the levels of goods and services produced. Despite the obvious oversimplification of the input-production-output model, it is useful for understanding the operations of most any type of organization (Middaugh, 1990; Cave, Hanney, and Kogan, 1991).

Goals of For-Profit Entities

As their name implies, the goal of for-profit firms is to maximize profits. The traditional textbook treatment of the firm posits that firms choose the level of output at which profits are maximized. Note that the firm is not attempting to maximize the level of output produced, but rather output is a means for achieving the goal of higher profits. In the corporate world, indicators of cost efficiency are very important, and follow from the relationship between the firm's goals of controlling costs and maximizing profits. In this model, the firm's success in reaching its goal is measured by the level of profits, and these four components – inputs, production process, outputs, and goals – are fairly well-defined and are measurable, making it possible for management to examine how changes in the production process affect the firm's success in attaining its desired goal of the organization, and to implement changes in the inputs and production process to increase profits.

Goals of Nonprofit and For-Profit Service Entities

In contrast, the goals and objectives of nonprofit (e.g., churches, philanthropic organizations) and service organizations (e.g., hospitals) are often more difficult to define and measure. Churches may be more interested in increasing the spiritual development of their congregations than maximizing profits, and because this objective is difficult to define and measure, churches cannot easily determine how effective they are at meeting this goal. Although some service organizations may share the profit maximization goal with their corporate counterparts, they may also have other objectives that are difficult to quantify. For example, it can be argued that medical professionals share the profit-maximizing goal with other for-profit entities, however they also seek to raise the overall health level of the patients they treat.

Even though the goals for these entities are not always well-defined, the organizations can still be described as having a parallel to the manufacturing model in that they use inputs and a production process to help attain their goals. In these instances, it is difficult for the organization to quantify the true benefits that can be attributed to specific changes in the production function. The lack of quantifiable information about organizational goals makes it very difficult to evaluate whether specific changes could be implemented to better attain the goals.

HIGHER EDUCATION GOALS, OBJECTIVES, AND INDICATORS

When the above framework is applied to colleges and universities to determine whether performance indicators can be used to understand and improve their operations, how do IHE compare to for-profit and nonprofit entities? Given that they are primarily engaged in providing services and most are nonprofit in nature, IHE share many of the characteristics of nonprofit and service entities. Nonetheless, there are also some similarities between IHE and for-profit firms that have in part led the initiative to apply business practices to academe. Colleges and universities can be described in terms of an educational production function with its four categories. The primary raw materials/inputs for higher education institutions are its students and faculty, and institutions employ faculty and other staff, machinery, technology, and land to produce outputs in the areas of teaching, research, and public service.[4] The production process for higher education describes how campuses (land), students, faculty, and staff (labor), teaching materials and technology (capital) are combined and distributed to produce educational outputs. Having access to more financial resources should enable institutions to purchase more and better factors of production and/or improve their production processes, and as a result produce more and better output from their available raw materials/inputs. Thus, in theory, there should be ways in which IHE can alter both the inputs and production process to better achieve their goals and objectives.

Goals for Institutions of Higher Education

Although the production function analogy can be applied to higher education, the consensus among higher education researchers is that decisions in most colleges and universities are not driven by the goal of profit maximization. Public institutions by definition are nonprofit in nature, and the fact that highly selective private institutions set prices below their market-clearing levels suggests that even private institutions do not behave as profit maximizers.

Whereas the goals for colleges and universities seem to have more parallels with nonprofit and service organizations than with for-profit entities, analysts disagree as to what these goals might be. Bowen (1980), for example, argued that institutions attempt to maximize their prestige rather than their profits, and according to Brinkman (1990), institutions neither attempt to minimize or maximize costs. In contrast, Paulsen (2001) suggests that colleges and universities operate in a monopolistically competitive market and attempt to maximize their discretionary budget (also see Paulsen and Smart, 2001). Many IHE describe their goals and objectives in ambiguous terms such as: "Our institution is committed to excellence in education and to supporting the best in scholarship and research while also contributing to economic opportunity in the state," which offers little guidance to those charged with determining if these goals are being met.

However, academics and analysts alike have not been much more successful in devising meaningful measures of institutional goals and objectives, and the goals that they have offered have changed very little over time. Over a century ago, John Stuart Mill (1895) offered three broad categories of educational outcomes: (a) benefits of higher education students receive while pursuing their education; (b) nonfinancial benefits accrued to students following their graduation; and (c) future financial returns for students from their education. The *California and Western Conference Study* (also known as the "Council of Ten Study") argued that colleges and universities produce educated students, and that the learning environment is not the final product but rather a means to produce educated students (Middlebrook, 1955). Harry Hirschl (1965) viewed the learning environment as the nature of a university, and intellectual growth as the product produced by colleges and universities.[5] Public institutions are also obligated to meet other goals, such as providing access to higher education for traditionally disadvantaged students, and serve the specific needs of their states. Further complicating matters is the interrelationship between these activities and the production function, in that the production of research will affect the quantity and quality of teaching produced and vice-versa.[6] The situation with regard to goals in academia is perhaps best summarized by Cohn, Rhine, and Santos (1989), who argue that higher education institutions seek to achieve a multiplicity of goals simultaneously, and that these goals often conflict and are very difficult to define and measure.

In the broadest sense, the goal of a university is to make contributions to society through research, teaching, and service activities. The mission of each institution describes the relative emphasis given to these three areas. However, problems arise when attempting to go beyond a general statement of goals and specify the precise desired outcomes for an institution. On the research side, for example, how should the contributions to society made through faculty research efforts be evaluated? Output measures such as the number of publications in peer-reviewed journals say little about whether such research necessarily has an impact on the advancement of knowledge. It is equally difficult to define outcomes from teaching and public service activities. The graduation rate of an institution, for example, says little about the quality of education that students receive.

Even when a generally agreed-upon goal for IHE is identified, it often proves difficult to quantify. To illustrate, almost every college and university administrator would say that one of their primary goals is to help students learn. Although there is a growing literature on how students gain from their experiences in higher education (e.g., Astin, 1968; Pascarella, Terenzini, and Hibel, 1978; Banta, Lambert, Pike, Schmidthammer, and Schneider, 1987; Pike, 1992; Kuh, Pace, and Vesper, 1997; Toutkoushian and Smart, 2001), a consensus on how to identify and measure student gains has been elusive. There are a number of ways in which students can benefit from college, including cognitive gains, knowledge and academic skills acquisition, creative development, social/personal development, social awareness/tolerance, job skills competencies, and economic advancement (Lenning, Vanderwell, and Brue, 1975; Terenzini, Theophilides, and Lorang, 1984; Pace, 1990; Pascarella and Terenzini, 1991; Kuh, Pace, and Vesper, 1997). Within each of these areas, there exist multiple measures of the underlying goal. Some analysts advocate using the earnings of graduates as a measure of student gains (Solmon and Wachtel, 1975; Wachtel, 1976; James, Alsalam, Conaty, and To, 1989), but others favor using student test scores and grades (Astin, 1968; Rock, Centra, and Linn, 1970; Rock, Baird, and Linn, 1972; Pascarella and Terenzini, 1978; Pascarella, Terenzini, and Hibel, 1978; Pike, 1992). Finally, a number of researchers have turned to self-reported gains based on student reflection as a means of measuring the benefits from higher education that are more difficult to quantify, such as interpersonal skills and tolerance/awareness (Nichols, 1967; Terenzini, Theophilides, and Lorang, 1984; Kuh, Pace, and Vesper, 1997). These unresolved issues, together with the substantial costs of collecting data on student gains, keep institutions from incorporating them into their performance indicator systems.

Goals for RCM

IHE that adopt RCM use a decentralized approach to budgeting where revenues and expenditures are allocated among units (responsibility centers) using formulas defined by the institution. Whereas the specific formulas vary widely across institutions, revenue allocations are usually heavily influenced by each unit's enrollment level and sponsored research funding received, because these two activities bring revenues into the institution. The switch to an RCM system is not a change in the IHE's production process *per se*, but the manner in which revenues and expenditures are assigned to units may lead to changes in the production process through the incentives that they give to increase revenues and decrease costs. For example, if a unit knows that its revenues are proportional to its enrollments, then it might want to implement changes in how its faculty members teach students in an effort to increase enrollments.

Institutions with some form of RCM system define two sets of goals for the system. The first set of goals relates to the process/functioning of the institution's budgeting process. These goals might include items such as simplifying financial reports, clarifying the budgeting process, and increasing participation by units in the budgeting process. Many of the goals in this area are difficult to quantify through standard metrics, however, because they are based on the perceptions of faculty, staff, and administrators, but could be evaluated through qualitative means. The second set of goals relates to the impacts of RCM on institutional goals. At a minimum, administrators hope that the changes in the budgeting system will not come at the expense of the institution's ability to achieve its overall goals in teaching, research, and public service. Some advocates go further and argue that the incentive structure in RCM can help the institution to better achieve its goals and objectives. Even if the system is successful in helping the institution achieve its goals, however, the problems associated with measuring institutional goals mean that it is difficult to identify indicators that could be used to determine if this is true. IHE that attempt to make this assessment are often forced to rely on the same types of metrics that are typically included in institutional performance indicators (e.g., graduation rates, average SAT scores of students, expenditures per student), and, as such, are subject to the same limitations.

Inputs and Production Processes in IHE

A second distinguishing characteristic of the production function model as applied to IHE is that there is a unique relationship between the inputs and production process. The main inputs in higher education – faculty and students – are also an extensive, interactive segment of the production process. Faculty members use their time and talents to produce outputs in research and public service, and, as labor, are part of the production process used to produce instructional outputs from teaching students. Learning is not a passive or automatic process, therefore students are also factors of production in that their academic effort is required to convert *themselves* into instructional output and outcomes. This "cross functionality," where the input resources also serve as critical factors in production, is an important and relatively unique characteristic of the higher education enterprise. The consumer is both part of the production process and influences the quality of the final product.[7] This means that having a specific mix of inputs and production processes in place will not guarantee that the desired outcomes will be achieved. This is perhaps most true in the area of student learning.

In a related process, colleges and universities do not have complete discretion over what inputs they will use to try and reach their goals. Rather than the firm selecting all raw materials, as in much of the for-profit world, in the higher education setting the raw materials (students) select the firm (college or university)! Although colleges can exercise some choice of which students to enroll through the admission process, the pool of applicants ultimately restricts the final set of student inputs used. Potential students have a demand function describing their willingness and ability to attend a particular institution, with this demand being influenced by factors such as their income level and the expected benefits and costs from attending each institution. In this regard, there are parallels between IHE and service industries, where patients select which doctor or hospital to visit for treatment and they have some influence over the success of any treatment. Colleges and universities are also constrained in their ability to choose other factors used in the production process. On the faculty side, the tenure system reduces an institution's flexibility to readily alter the inputs used in the production process in response to changes in demand or to meet different goals and objectives. Likewise, the decentralization of authority to faculty on decisions of how to teach and conduct research limits the extent to which administrators may implement specific policies to attain their goals when they differ from the goals of the faculty.

These two problems – lack of control over the production function and insufficient measures of goals/outcomes – place important limitations on the success of performance indicator systems in identifying strategies that postsecondary institutions can implement to reach their goals and objectives. A consequence of these problems is that while IHE do have influence over some inputs and aspects of the production process (such as expenditures and acceptance rates of students), without clear measures of institutional goals administrators do not know how to change these "policy levers" to help the institution meet its desired goals. A college or university will likely never be able to reliably estimate the degree to which using better computer technology in the classroom contributes to student learning or their future job prospects. Institutions would like to know, for example, if it is best to put additional money into student services, faculty salaries, campus facilities, athletic programs, or other uses. Without good measures of institutional goals and outcomes, such questions are difficult to answer for those policy levers at their disposal.

The presence of multiple goals also introduces the possibility that changes in inputs and/or the production process may help the institution achieve certain goals and hinder its progress towards other goals. Lowering the acceptance rate (increasing the selectivity) at an institution may improve the academic profile of an entering class of students and hence the reputation of the institution, but it could also mean reduced educational opportunities for disadvantaged students and increasing expenditures per student if enrollments fall as a result. Likewise, policies that would raise the minimum time commitment for faculty in the classroom may lead to gains in student learning, but may also have negative consequences for faculty research and public service contributions. This last example is particularly relevant for institutions with RCM systems because the revenue allocation formulas tend to provide incentives to engage in activities that generate revenues for the institution, most notably teaching and sponsored research. The presence of resource constraints (e.g., time, number of faculty) means that units may choose to divert resources away from activities that do not generate revenues in order to respond to the incentives to increase enrollments and sponsored-research dollars. Therefore, activities such as general public service, nonsponsored research, participation in institutional, collegiate, and departmental committees, and other nonrevenue generating activities might suffer as a result of the RCM incentive structure. Some of these activities, such as nonsponsored research, are highly concentrated in particular academic disciplines. If there are valued institutional outcomes associated with these activities, then it is possible that RCM may ultimately lead to changes in the mission of the institution. This is a plausible example of how goals/values of RCM systems can conflict with and unwittingly take precedence over institutional goals/values. Institutions with RCM budgeting systems need to be aware of these possible adverse effects and have a governance structure in place to ensure that highly valued, but nonrevenue generating, activities are still supported by the institution.

The *Ceteris Paribus* Assumption

Even when goals are measurable and the organization has policy levers at its disposal, it may be difficult to isolate the effects of a single policy on these goals. In many instances, there are multiple factors that are changing at the same time that affect the organization's goals. The temptation among decisionmakers who observe a simultaneous change in an outcome and input is to then attribute the change in the outcome to the input. However, this inference requires the assumption of *ceteris paribus*, (that all else is held constant) and when this is not true, incorrect conclusions can be drawn about the effects of the policy on organizational goals. This most certainly applies to higher education, where demographic, social, political, and economic factors are often changing at the same time, which results in a combined impact on IHE. When goals are measurable and data exist on relevant input and process factors, multivariate statistical techniques can be used to estimate the effects of each factor holding the others constant. Where the outcomes are not clearly defined and measurable, however, statistical methods have limited value for this purpose.

Administrators seeking to evaluate the impact of RCM on an institution need to recognize the limitations that the *ceteris paribus* issue imposes on them when using performance indicators. Advocates for RCM will be tempted to attribute positive changes in indicators to the implementation of RCM, and opponents of RCM will tend to blame the new budgeting system for any negative changes in indicators. For example, if sponsored-research funding were to rise following the adoption of RCM, advocates might argue that the system's incentive structure has led to this outcome. Likewise, if enrollments within a unit were to decline following the implementation of the RCM system, critics might conclude that this is proof that the system is not working. In each instance, it needs to be recognized that the indicators in question are also affected by constantly changing internal and external forces, many of which are beyond the control of the institution.

COMMONLY USED PERFORMANCE INDICATORS

Most analysts accept the production framework for classifying performance indicators, but there is little agreement when it comes to determining what specific measures should be used for assessing IHE. In their review of performance indicator systems, Borden and Bottrill (1994) compiled a list of 268 different indicators that have been used by various colleges and universities. Some recommend that colleges and universities should use long lists of indicators that encompass a range of financial and enrollment data (Middaugh; 1990; Taylor and Massy, 1996), while others argue that to be useful to policymakers, the set of indicators must be relatively small (Ewell, 1994; Gaither, 1997; Layzell, 1999). Most of the indicators in use tend to rely on pre-existing data at the institution rather than require new data collection efforts.

Analysts' opinions differ not only on the size and scope of performance indicator systems, but also with regard to what are the most essential indicators for an institution to monitor. For example, of the "top 10 indicators" that Taylor and Massy (1996) describe as being especially important for institutions, only one of these is also considered to be among the "core indicators" identified in a 10-state project conducted by the Education Commission of the States (Ewell, 1994). In part, these differences reflect the emphases that states and financial administrators give to different educational outcomes, because state legislatures are generally more interested in the number of residents who receive an education from a particular institution, and campus administrators may focus more on the financial health of the institution. Nonetheless, the variations in what experts consider to be the best measures of performance highlight the fact that academe has not agreed on what indicators best reflect performance. Some of the most commonly used performance indicators in higher education and how they might be classified according to the production function model are listed in Table 10.1.

Most of the indicators listed here suffer from the limitations described in the previous section. Beginning with outcomes, measures such as the reputational ranking of the institution, and student satisfaction have not been shown to be measures of, or even correlated with, the true outcomes or goals of the institution. Likewise, output measures such as the number of degrees awarded may or may not be directly related to the ultimate goals of the institution. These lists also rarely include specific measures of student gains. This gap was highlighted in the National Center for Public Policy and Higher Education's (2000) report *Measuring Up 2000*, in which all states were given a grade of "incomplete" in the area of student learning.

The goal of advancement of knowledge through research is especially underrepresented among the sets of indicators that are used in higher education. Faculty publication counts are more correctly viewed as output measures than outcomes, and are difficult to obtain because this information is not often collected centrally at a college or university. Policies aimed at raising faculty publication counts may have adverse effects on the quality of research if these in-

Table 10.1: Commonly Used Performance Indicators in Higher Education

Category	Common Performance Indicators
Input	Student headcounts
	Percentage from underrepresented race/ethnic group
	Average SAT/ACT scores of freshmen
	High school GPA or class rank of freshmen
	Percentage of applicants who are admitted
	Percentage of admitted students who enroll
	Average faculty salaries
Production Process	Expenditures per student
	Student-to-faculty ratio
	Credit hours per faculty member
	Percentage of courses/students taught by tenure-track faculty
	Expenditures per student by major category
	Revenues per student by major category
	Level of deferred maintenance
Output	Number of faculty publications
	Number of degrees awarded
Outcomes	Reputational rankings (e.g., *USNWR*)
	Percentage of alumni who have donated to the institution
	Retention rates (two-, three-, and/or four-year)
	Graduation rates (four-, five-, and/or six-year)
	Average time to degree
	Research grant dollars received
	Student satisfaction (from surveys)

centives lead faculty to choose research projects based more on prospects for publication rather than on their potential for knowledge advancement. The most commonly used research performance indicator is based on dollars of sponsored research at an institution, because this information is readily available to administrators. However, there is no evidence that the level of sponsored-research dollars is correlated with the quality of research produced. More importantly, these measures tend to neglect nonsponsored research, which is central to many disciplines in the social sciences, arts, and humanities.

The lack of institutional outcome measures, and the need in academe to continue to evaluate institutional performance, has led many institutions to monitor available metrics such as graduation/retention rates, expenditures per student, and the average qualifications of incoming students. Even though IHE may target such variables, they are not the true goals of the organization, and it is not known whether or how they are tied to the ultimate (unobservable) goals. For example, if the average SAT scores of incoming freshmen increase at an institution, does this mean that the institution is doing better helping students to learn? Likewise, although time to degree is a commonly used performance indicator in higher education, and there is a sense among decisionmakers that the time to degree should not be "too long," it is not clear how the average time to degree influences an institution's success in reaching its goals and objectives.

The reward structure in an RCM system may, if left unchecked, lead to behaviors that have a detrimental effect on institutional goals. For example, suppose that the RCM system makes each unit responsible for covering its expenditures, and in response, units implement changes to reduce costs per student; the hope is that the system would provide incentives for units to become more efficient, but the cuts may in fact hinder the institution's ability to meet its ultimate goals and objectives depending on how they are made. Personnel costs for instruction are the largest cost component in institutions of higher education, so departments may resort to using more nonregular faculty (e.g., adjunct faculty, lecturers, and graduate students) for instruction. Such a policy could lead to concerns that the quality of educational services provided to students will diminish as a result.[8] Colleges often find themselves in a conundrum of sorts since the college rankings produced by *USNWR* reward colleges and universities for having higher per-student expenditures, on the premise that they can then provide better services to students, while legislators, trustees, and RCM formulas pressure institutions to contain or even reduce costs.

These examples highlight the fact that when indicators are not clearly tied to the true goals and objectives, the institution may implement ineffective policies that can potentially lower effectiveness by suggesting misdirected incentives. Furthermore, the constraints under which the organization operates have to be taken into account when evaluating particular indicators. Performance indicators based on the quality of graduates, for example, would penalize institutions that view providing access to higher education for marginal students as an important institutional goal. This indicator may not capture academic growth and development of such students because it does not take into account their incoming characteristics and potential for gain. Careful thought needs to be given to any incentives that might be created for faculty, departments, and institutions by the use of any set of performance indicators.

PERFORMANCE INDICATORS AND RCM: A CASE STUDY

The above discussion highlights many of the difficulties faced in assessing the success or failure of specific institutional programs such as RCM through the use of performance indicators. When IHE cannot measure the outcomes that they produce from their efforts, they cannot easily determine whether a change in budgeting systems has had an impact on the attainment of these goals. As a result, institutions often point to available metrics such as their graduation rates and average SAT scores of students as measures of their institution's academic quality. Here, however, the *ceteris paribus* problem becomes especially important, because these indicators could be changing or not changing due to many different factors. Other process-related goals associated with RCM cannot be readily measured by performance indicators, and would require qualitative information from faculty, staff, and administrators who have worked with the old and new processes.

The experiences of the University of New Hampshire (UNH) help to illustrate the type of goals and objectives that are often associated with RCM systems, and the challenges involved in defining performance indicators to evaluate the system. The development of the revenue and expense attribution formulas in the RCM system at UNH began in 1997 with the creation of a steering committee.[9] On July 1, 2000, the university officially switched to an RCM budgeting system. The revenue formulas distribute tuition revenues to the responsibility centers in relation to their enrollment/credit hour levels, sponsored-research dollars (indirect cost recovery) are allocated based on the dollars brought into the university by the unit, and state appropriations are distributed on the basis of faculty salary levels and "balancing adjustments" to hold units financially harmless at the point of transition to RCM. Likewise, direct and indirect expenses are assigned to each responsibility center based on their level of employee compensation, space utilization, and revenues.

The Operating Manual prepared by the steering committee for the UNH community describes the following goals of the RCM system: 1) decentralize financial authority and accountability; 2) simplify budget procedures; 3) improve budget forecasting and planning; 4) increase central administration focus on strategic matters; 5) improve institutional flexibility to match resources with program demands; 6) clarify financial reports to the university community; 7) improve management of budget surpluses; and 8) increase incentives for revenue generation. Of these eight goals, all except goals (5) and (8) can be described as process-related because they pertain to operational aspects of budgeting, financial management and reporting. Performance indicators would not be very useful for evaluating these goals that do not readily lend themselves to quantification. The university must rely on interviews with administrators and others in the campus community to help examine these goals.

The fund balances accumulated within responsibility centers can be used as one measure of goal (5), with the presumption that larger fund balances lead to greater flexibility. Growing fund balances, however, do not guarantee greater flexibility at the unit level, which depends on the ease at which the unit was able to secure additional funding from the central administration under the old budgeting system. The goal of increasing the incentives for revenue generating activities (8) was met once the RCM system was fully implemented, and thus no assessment is needed for the goal as written. What is not known is whether these incentives have led to the desired changes in behavior by academic units at UNH. Whereas indicators can be created based on revenues generated by source, these revenues may change within specific units for any of a number of reasons, only one of which may be the switch to an RCM budgeting system.

In addition to the stated goals of the RCM system, UNH also hopes that the new budgeting system will help the university to better meet its overall goals and objectives, or at a minimum, will not have a detrimental effect on these goals. The steering committee's description of the limitations of the old budgeting system it notes that: "The old system did not recognize academic quality since quality was not explicitly measured or rewarded with few exceptions (tenure, merit increases, and promotion)." The steering committee has stipulated that a formal review of the university's RCM system will be conducted after five years. They note: "Criteria used to evaluate RCM will include, but not be limited to, trends in academic quality, student quality, institutional financial health, and faculty and staff morale." Under the Quantitative Academic Quality Review, the steering committee has identified the following indicators:

> Statistical data and other appropriate data will be analyzed to determine what effect the budget system has had on the University's teaching, research, and service missions. Some of the statistical data to be reviewed are class size, grades (grade inflation), tenure track faculty to non-tenure track faculty ratios, admission data (SAT, class rank, etc.), faculty/student ratios, graduation rate, freshman retention, and student satisfaction.

Similarly, the indicators in the area of Research and Scholarly Activity Review are described as follows:

> This component of the RCM review will examine effects that RCM has had on our research and scholarly activity. This review will have two components. One component will be a review of our external research activity based on revenue, mix of research activity by college, mix of funding sources, and number of proposals. The second component is more subjective and will deal with the level of scholarly activity and unfunded research occurring within the faculty. A sense of this will be gathered by reviewing the faculty annual reports and through discussions with Deans and faculty in the general interviews.

Several interesting observations can be made from these two statements. First, they highlight the need to examine the effects of the RCM system on the institution's overall goals in teaching and research. Second, the indicators listed under the heading Quantitative Academic Quality Review are not direct measures of teaching outcomes and thus do not measure academic quality. Similarly, revenues from externally funded research and the number of proposals are not outcomes produced by the university from their research activities. The RCM indicators are thus subject to the same limitations as those usually chosen by institutions to assess their overall performance. Notably absent from either list are indicators relating to the public service mission of the university.

A third observation worth noting is that, putting aside the meaning of these particular indicators, all of them can be affected by a number of factors in addition to the budgeting system. The *ceteris paribus* issue will make it very difficult for the university to determine if RCM has contributed to changes in these indicators. For example, suppose that UNH observes that the graduation rate declines in the years following the adoption of RCM. Without information on all of the other factors that might have also affected graduation rates, as well as an analysis of their impact, the university will not be able to determine if RCM also contributed to the decline. Because the same caveats would apply to the other indicators listed in this section, it is questionable whether the data will be useful for examining the impact of RCM on even these measures. The university recognizes the importance of this issue when the steering committee warned: "It should be noted that a major challenge in this review will be to determine the extent to which any positive or negative trends have a causal or coincidental relationship to RCM." UNH further cautions the university community that: "Trends will not automatically be attributed to RCM."

DISCUSSION

In this chapter, we have provided a rather critical appraisal of whether indicators can be used to evaluate the performance of institutions of higher education and popular initiatives such as RCM. Our review of the performance indicators most frequently used today in higher education shows that while such measures may provide useful information to decisionmakers, to view them as measures of whether an institution is achieving its various goals and objectives from teaching, research, and public service would be very misleading. The discussion highlighted two main reasons why the performance indicator model is more difficult to apply to higher education than it is in the corporate world, and why institutions have struggled in their attempt to define meaningful performance indicators. Without clear measures of institutional outcomes and control over many important factors of production, institutions will have difficulty defining policies based on indicators that will lead to true improvements in their performance.

These limitations, together with the *ceteris paribus* issue, are especially important for institutions with responsibility-centered management budgeting systems to consider when they attempt to define indicators to assess the strengths and weaknesses of the system. These concerns with performance indicators are not meant to imply that RCM budgeting systems are therefore ineffective or detrimental to institutions. It could be true that in many instances, the improvements in budgeting processes that accompany an RCM system are beneficial to institutions, and that the incentive structure induces the type of behavior among units and faculty that are desired. We argue here, however, that regardless of the true utility of an RCM budgeting system, it is very difficult to identify a set of performance indicators that would be appropriate for evaluating the goals associated with the system.

These reasons may be sufficient for some institutions to conclude that the benefits of performance indicator systems in higher education are outweighed by the costs of defining, collecting, and using them for decisionmaking. Other institutions, particularly in the public sector, will still be obligated to implement a performance indicator model in response to pressures from stakeholders to demonstrate that they are providing benefits to society and are using funds wisely. Because of this pressure, colleges and universities are likely to continue collecting information on indicators that are readily available from existing databases, such as graduation rates, average time to degree, and expenditures per student, and establishing targets for them even if they privately question whether such indicators say anything about performance.

Given that the internal and external need to evaluate institutional performance will not go away in the immediate future, how should institutions proceed? First, we need to acknowledge the limitations of most current indicators as measures of performance for IHE, and temper expectations of what can be learned from such measures. The term "performance indicator" implies that the measure being examined is in fact related to an institution's ultimate goals and outcomes, which may or may not be true. Trends in various input, process, and output measures and other statistics, and comparisons of these measures to other institutions, will be helpful to decisionmakers as they try to assess the health of their institution. Unfortunately, it may take years to observe a trend and institutions may not recognize the trend until it is too late. The danger arises when decisionmakers place too much faith in certain measures as indicators of their desired outcomes, and arbitrarily set targets for these measures. As a whole, commonly used indicators can provide information on a variety of aspects of the institution, but offer little constructive guidance as to what specific policies should be implemented to improve institutional performance in terms of achieving the institution's desired goals and objectives. These limitations need to be understood and explained – perhaps repeatedly – to various stakeholders who might have less knowledge about the goals of higher education and, as a result, set unrealistic expectations about the value of applying performance indicator systems to IHE. The most basic purpose of performance indicators is to force institutions to think about how they might improve what they are doing.

Decisionmakers also need to be aware that when they use measures such as graduation rates and reputation scores as institutional targets, these measures can be influenced by a wide range of factors, many of which are difficult for the institution to control and may be changing simultaneously. Other policies that may lead to improvements in some goals could in turn make it more difficult for the institution to achieve other goals. In light of these concerns, performance indicators have some value as supporting information for decisionmaking, especially for measuring financial goals, but not as strict measures of performance. They should be part of the set of information considered by administrators and not a source of easy answers.

Work should continue on developing a better framework for identifying indicators that could be useful for decisionmaking. A number of authors have offered criteria that performance indicators in higher education should satisfy. The National Center for Education Management, for example, suggests that good indicators have policy leverage, are not susceptible to manipulation, are easily understood by lay audiences, embody the interests of multiple constituents, have appropriate benchmarks, are statistically valid, and can be attained at a reasonable cost (Ewell and Jones, 1994). Interestingly, these criteria focus more on the process of measuring of indicators, and on the ability to convey them to various stakeholders, rather than how well the indicators actually measure the desired outcomes of the institution. Likewise, while Banta and Borden (1994, p. 96) argue that "performance indicators should have a clear purpose, be coordinated throughout an organization or system, extend across the entire range of organizational processes, be derived from a variety of coordinated methods, and be used to inform decision making," they also note that of the performance indicator systems they have reviewed, few meet all of these criteria.

At present, it is difficult to see how such a performance indicator system can be devised for IHE. For any set of indicators to yield insight into institutional effectiveness, better measures of "performance" need to be developed that attempt to reflect whether or not an institution is meeting its goals and objectives. Because institutions pursue multiple goals and the outcomes are not easily measurable, it must be acknowledged that any set of measurable outcomes will be incomplete and subject to criticism. However, beginning the process with measures of desired outcomes would be helpful not only for developing policies to improve those outcomes, but also for framing the discussion with internal and external constituencies about the benefits provided by higher education to society and the choices and limitations that they face in achieving these goals. This approach will prove to be more costly, in terms of data collection and time, than one of reporting indicators that are readily available and used by other institutions. However, if the objective behind a performance indicator initiative is to design policies to improve performance, then the definition and measurement of outcomes relating to the goals and objectives of the institution is a necessary first step. The combination of traditional, quantitative measures (often "output" in nature) with more qualitative, outcome-related measures will lead to a more comprehensive, strategic assessment of an institution calibrated to its specific mission.

NOTES

1. Other public colleges and universities that have adopted variations of RCM budgeting systems include the University of California at Los Angeles, the University of Illinois, Purdue University, the University of Oregon, Central Michigan University, and the University of Iowa.

2. Borden and Bottrill (1994) provide an excellent summary of the historical development of performance indicators in higher education. They note that the trend towards evaluating the activities of postsecondary institutions can actually be traced back to the reputational studies that became popular with the work of the American Council on Education (Roose and Anderson, 1970) and the Gourman report (Gourman, 1996).

3. This chapter looks at higher education through an economic or "structural lens"; other lenses through which higher education organizations can be viewed include human resource, political, and symbolic. Moreover, alternative models of how IHE work are numerous (see Peterson, 1986).

4. Professional staff also can be viewed as raw materials to the extent that they produce outputs of value to the institution (such as research), in addition to serving as part of the production process converting faculty and students into outputs.

5. For a review of other early models and theories of higher education, see Witmer (1972).

6. It is not clear whether research and teaching should be viewed as substitute or complementary activities. On the one hand, the fixed time constraint for faculty suggests

that increasing time spent on teaching will decrease time spent on research and ultimately research output. Conversely, it may be argued that research increases the quality of instruction and vice-versa. Empirical evidence, however, suggests that spending more time on teaching decreases research productivity (see Bellas and Toutkoushian, 1999).

7. Perhaps the best comparison from nonacademia would be medical services, where the patient is both an input to production and has some influence on the final outcome by the extent to which he/she follows the doctor's orders.

8. It should be noted, however, that there is no clear evidence of any differentials in an institution's instructional outcomes resulting from the use of regular versus nonregular (e.g., part-time) faculty.

9. One of the authors of this paper is a member of the steering committee at UNH and has participated in the development of the RCM system.

REFERENCES

Astin, Alexander. 1968. Undergraduate achievement and institutional 'excellence.' *Science* 161 (August): 661-668.

Astin, Alexander. 1993. *What matters in college: Four critical years revisited.* San Francisco: Jossey-Bass.

Astin, A., and R. Panos. 1969. *The Educational and Vocational Development of College Students.* Washington, DC: American Council on Education.

Banta, Trudy, and Victor Borden. 1994. Performance indicators for accountability and improvement. *New Directions for Institutional Research*, No. 82 (Summer): 95-106.

Banta, Trudy, E. Warren Lambert, Gary Pike, James Schmidthammer, and Janet Schneider. 1987. Estimated student score gain on the ACT COMP exam: Valid tool for institutional assessment? *Research in Higher Education* 27 (3): 195-217.

Bellas, Marcia, and Robert Toutkoushian. 1999. Faculty time allocations: Gender, race and family effects. *Review of Higher Education* 22 (4): 367-390.

Borden, Victor, and Karen Bottrill. 1994. Performance indicators: History, definitions, and methods. *New Directions for Institutional Research*, No. 82 (Summer): 5-22.

Bowen, Howard. 1980. *The costs of higher education.* San Francisco: Jossey-Bass.

Brinkman, Paul. 1990. Higher education cost functions. In Stephen Hoenack and Eileen Collins, eds., *The economics of American universities: Management, operations, and fiscal environment.* New York: State University of New York Press.

Cave, Martin, Stephen Hanney, and Maurice Kogan. 1991. *The use of performance indicators in higher education: A critical analysis of developing practice.* 2nd ed. London: Jessica Kingsley.

Cohn, Elchanan, Sherrie Rhine, and Maria Santos. 1989. Institutions of higher education as multi-product firms: Economies of scale and scope. *Review of Economics and Statistics* 71 (May): 284-290.

Cullen, Bernard. 1987. Performance indicators in U.K. higher education: Progress and prospects. *International Journal of Institutional Management in Higher Education* 11 (2): 117-139.

Dochy, Filip, Mien Segers, and Wynand Wijnen. 1990. *Management information and performance indicators in higher education: An international issue.* The Netherlands: Van Gorcum.

Dolence, Michael, and Donald Norris. 1994. Using key performance indicators to drive strategic decision making. *New Directions for Institutional Research*, No. 82 (Summer): 63-80.

Ewell, Peter. 1994. Developing statewide performance indicators for higher education: Policy themes and variations. ECS Working paper (draft). Denver: Education Commission of the States.

Ewell, Peter, and Dennis Jones. 1994. Data, indicators, and the National Center for Higher Education Management Systems. *New Directions for Institutional Research*, No. 82 (Summer): 23-35.

Findlay, P. 1990. Developments in the performance indicator debate in the United Kingdom. In L. Goedegebuure, P. Maassen, and D. Westerheijden, eds., *Peer review and performance indicators: Quality assessment in British and Dutch higher education*. Utrecht: Uitgeverij Lemma B.V.

Gaither, Gerald. 1997. Performance indicator systems as instruments for accountability and assessment. *Assessment Update* 9 (1): 1-2, 14-15.

Gaither, Gerald, Brian Nedwek, and John Neal. 1994. *Measuring up: The promises and pitfalls of performance indicators in higher education*. ASHE-ERIC Higher Education Report No. 5. Washington, D.C.: George Washington University.

Gourman, Jack. 1996. *The Gourman report: A rating of graduate and professional programs in American and international universities*, 7th ed. Los Angeles: National Education Standards.

Hirschl, Harry. 1965. *Some economic considerations and a procedure for a university cost study*. Lafayette: Purdue University.

James, Estelle, Nabeel Alsalam, Joseph Conaty, and Duc-Le To. 1989. College quality and future earnings: Where should you send your child to college? *American Economic Review* 79 (2): 247-252.

Kerr, Clark. 1982. 'The uses of the university' two decades later. *Change* 14 (7): 23-31.

Kuh, George, C. Robert Pace, and Nick Vesper. 1997. The development of process indicators to estimate student gains associated with good practices in undergraduate education. *Research in Higher Education* 38 (4): 435-454.

Layzell, Daniel. 1999. Linking performance to funding outcomes at the state level for public institutions of higher education: Past, present, and future. *Research in Higher Education* 40 (2): 233-246.

Lenning, Oscar, Leo Munday, O. Bernard Johnson, Allen VanderWell, and Eldon Brue. 1975. *The many faces of college success and their nonintellective correlates*. Iowa City, IA: American College Testing Program.

Middaugh, Michael. 1990. The nature and scope of institutional research. *New Directions for Institutional Research* 17: 66 (Summer): 35-48.

Middlebrook, William. 1955. *California and western conference cost and statistical study 1954-1955*. Berkeley, CA: University of California.

Mill, John Stuart. 1895. *Principles of political economy*. New York: Appleton.

National Center for Education Statistics. 1996. *Digest of education statistics 1996*. NCES 96-133, by Thomas D. Snyder. Washington, D.C: U.S. Department of Education.

National Center for Public Policy and Higher Education. 2000. In Thad Nodine, ed., *Measuring up 2000*. San Jose, CA: National Center for Public Policy and Higher Education.

Nichols, R.C. 1967. Personality change and the college. *American Educational Research Journal* 4:173-190.

Pascarella, Ernest, and Patrick Terenzini. 1978. Student-faculty informal relationships and freshman year educational outcomes. *Journal of Educational Research* 71: 183-189.

Pascarella, Ernest, and Patrick Terenzini. 1991. *How college affects students.* San Francisco: Jossey-Bass.

Pascarella, Ernest, Patrick Terenzini, and James Hibel. 1978. Student-faculty interactional settings and their relationship to predicted academic performance. *Journal of Higher Education* 49:450-463.

Patterson, Jennifer. 2000. Rank & furor. *Matrix* (June): 88-94.

Paulsen, Michael. 2001. Economic perspectives on rising college tuition: A theoretical and empirical exploration. M. Paulsen and J. Smart, eds., The Finance of Higher Education, p. 193-263. New York: Agathon Press

Paulsen, Michael, and John Smart, eds. 2001. *The finance of higher education: Theory, research, policy & practice.* New York: Agathon Press.

Peterson, Marvin, ed. 1986. *ASHE reader on organization and governance in higher education,* 3rd ed. ASHE Reader Series. Lexington: Ginn Press.

Pike, Gary. 1992. Using mixed-effect structural equation models to study student academic development. *Review of Higher Education* 15 (2): 151-177.

Rock, Donald, John Centra, and Robert Linn. 1970. Relationships between college characteristics and student achievement. *American Educational Research Journal* 7:109-121.

Rock, Donald, Leonard Baird, and Robert Linn. 1972. Interaction between college effects and students' aptitudes. *American Educational Research Journal* 9:149-161.

Roose, Kenneth, and Charles Anderson. 1970. *A rating of graduate programs.* Washington, D.C.: American Council on Higher Education.

Rowley, Daniel. 1997. Using KPIs to anchor strategic choices. Planning for Higher Education 25 (2): 29-32.

Solmon, Lewis, and Paul Wachtel. 1975. The effect on income of type of college attended. *Sociology of Education* 48 (1): 75-90.

Taylor, Barbara, and William Massy. 1996. *Strategic indicators for higher education.* Princeton, NJ: Peterson's.

Terenzini, Patrick, Christos Theophilides, and Wendell Lorang. 1984. Influences on students' perceptions of their academic skill development during college. *Journal of Higher Education* 55 (5): 621-636.

Thompson, Nicholas. 2000. Cooking the school books (yet again). *Slate* (September 14).

Toutkoushian, Robert, and John Smart. 2001. Do institutional characteristics affect student gains? *Review of Higher Education* 25 (1): 39-61.

Wachtel, Paul. 1976. The effect on earnings of school and college investment expenditures. *Review of Economics and Statistics* 58 (3): 326-331.

Winston, Gordon. 1997. Why can't a college be more like a firm? *Change* 29 (5): 33-38.

Witmer, David. 1972. Cost studies in higher education. *Review of Educational Research* 42 (1): 99-127.

CHAPTER 11

INCENTIVE-BASED BUDGETING:
AN EVOLVING APPROACH

Douglas M. Priest

Edward P. St. John

William Tobin

Decline in public support and calls for increased accountability have caused some state institutions to experiment with their budgeting systems. This experimentation has given rise to the application of a number of new budgeting systems. As a result, in recent years, incentive-based budgeting (IBB) has gained some ascendance in the academy. As public universities experience a growing reliance on student tuition and fee revenue, along with the relative decline in importance of state appropriations, they have eyed financial options with increased interest (Whalen, 1996). Yet difficult terrain separates the desire to take advantage of a new budgeting system and actually doing it. Colleges and universities are historically resistant to such wholesale and fundamental changes. Change, when it does arrive, often appears at the margins. Still, there is enormous pressure on academe from the marketplace and various constituents, to follow the lead of industry and government and become leaner and more efficient. Issues of efficiency and effectiveness in financial and other arenas, whether we like it or not, will probably be with us for the foreseeable future.

We suggest that IBB, much like other nonincremental budgeting models, does have attributes that may be useful to many institutions in higher education's current environment. We acknowledge that adoption of any form of budgeting, in higher education, other than incremental budgeting, is at best an uphill proposition. We also note that if one understands the capabilities and limitations of IBB, useful applications of components of IBB may be a more likely proposition than one might think. This may be especially true when these components are linked to aspects of incremental budgeting.

HIGHER EDUCATION BUDGETING

Meisinger (1994) defines budgeting in higher education as an activity focused on the control of financial resources, the evaluation of financial performance, and the facilitation of the institution's mission, and accomplished by calculating and ratifying expectations for revenues and expenditures. Budgeting can also be viewed as an activity that allocates scarce resources in a manner perceived to reflect understood and shared institutional aspirations. There are, of course, other definitions, indicative of the fact that university budgeting is not an exact science and many approaches may flourish simultaneously.

History and Application of Budgeting in Higher Education

The recent history of higher education is replete with examples of various approaches to budgeting that have enjoyed varying levels of implementation in recent years. Historically, universities developed budgets incrementally, with future plans being built on the foundations of historical budgets. Just as new academic units were added to the existing structures of universities as they responded to new conditions, incremental budgeting enabled universities to add incrementally to their plans for acquiring funds and allocating resources to academic units. This incremental budgeting approach worked reasonably well through the 1960s, a period when higher education enrollment expanded exponentially.

However, during the 1960s, colleges and universities, like many states and the federal government, began to experiment with planning, programming, budgeting systems and other cost management methods (Weathersby and Balderston, 1971). These developments set the stage for a new wave of developments in management and budgeting.

During the 1970s, there was substantial expansion of systems approaches to higher budgeting and management in higher education. A number of new cost management methods gained general acceptance (Balderston, 1974). Public agencies and private foundations provided grants to small colleges that encouraged them to adopt management by objectives and other managerial methods (Baldridge and Tierney, 1979; St. John, 1981). By the end of the decade, there had been substantial new developments in management and budget processes in universities. However, there was still an adherence to basic governing values. Academic priorities remained the basis for academic plans, and instructional expenditures increased at about the same rate as administrative expenditure (St. John, 1994).

The 1980s brought new tensions into governance, planning, and budget processes. Almost foretelling the future, Howard Bowen developed the revenue theory of costs, which argued that in the pursuit of excellence, colleges would raise and spend all of the money they could (Bowen, 1980). And, during the decade, there were a number of adaptations to institutional financial strategies.

History suggests that, regardless of the approach taken, budgeting is as much a political and cultural process as it is mechanistic. Green and Monical (1985, p. 48) state, "there are probably as many different ways of allocating resources in institutions of higher education as there are presidents." They suggest that each president has adopted an internal administrative style and method of resource allocation unique to that institution. This is due, in part, to the fact that institutions are funded through a variety of sources, administered through a variety of structures, and function in a variety of environmental settings.

This view, and ones similar to it, could be applied to budgeting approaches such as zero-based budgeting, incremental budgeting and IBB. It is rare for any one approach to budgeting to be applied in a theoretically pristine form. This is an important observation and one that tends to be overlooked when administrators, consultants, advisory groups, and others begin to consider budget reform and advocate specific approaches to budgeting, sometimes in place of more appropriate configurations or permutations based on aspects of institutional profile or culture. Regardless of the mechanism used, it must be integrated with the institution's culture.

The Case for IBB

Why IBB at public institutions? Public higher education during the past 20 years has seen a significant change in the emphasis and direction of public policy. Programs once looked upon as entitlements are now often viewed by policymakers as luxuries, possible to live without, or, at least, in reduced form (Ruppert, 1996). According to Hovey (1999), public institutions have been competing with other state priorities in a climate where states are averse to raising taxes. In the future, it appears that academic goals and agendas at public universities will increasingly have to be achieved within the context of proportionately lowered state financial support. Public institutions will have to fund innovations by reducing expenditures in other areas, or by increasing revenues from sources other than appropriations, such as tuition revenues, grants and contracts, or endowments. However, after many years of tuition increases far outpacing the rate of inflation, colleges and universities are subject to criticism about escalating attendance costs (Honeyman and Bruhn, 1996). This has resulted in many states, while effectively reducing their support, also mandating limits on tuition increases. Indirect cost recovery, a reliable and significant source of income for major research universities, is also threatened as the Federal government begins to run many funded programs through state governments, while reducing the scope of its own involvement in research and development (Slaughter and Leslie, 1997).

In addition to limited state and federal funding, there was the added effect of the economic downturn of the early 1990s (Hovey, 1999). As states struggled to balance budgets, they took their cue from troubled corporations, which successfully shed layers to emerge more efficient. Policymakers wondered why public agencies could not behave in much the same way. A common answer was often the lack of incentives. Outstanding programs and timely innovations were not being rewarded because incremental funding systems treated functional areas in the same way.

Given these external influences, public higher education began looking for ways to exert greater control over its income and expenditures in an effort to potentially smooth out what Hovey (1999) refers to as the disproportionate peaks and valleys in state funding for higher education.

A common assumption of those who develop interest in IBB approaches is that public institutions are increasingly dependent on earned income in place of state support, as they try to fund program enhancements. In this regard, public institutions are becoming more like private institutions, thus more apt to use private institutional approaches to financial and enrollment management. An examination of universities in the Pacific 10 and Big 10 conferences may be instructive. Using the Integrated Postsecondary Education Data System (IPEDS) (NCES, 1998) data for the Big 10, one finds that the proportion of state funding declined by about 7 percent between 1990-1991 and 1996-1997. Analysis of the Pac 10 yields similar, but even more dramatic, results. The average increase in the proportion of tuition fees was about 13 percent with all but two institutions in double digits, although that upward trend has now leveled. The significance of these data in regards to IBB systems is that, while there are several institutional attributes that ought to be present in some measure in order to provide a hospitable environment for IBB, arguably the most useful is an increasing dependence on student fees. This dependence is growing in many areas of the country, and is coupled with an increasing perception of privatization; thus, one may expect to see institutions using financial models that leverage sources of earned income similar to methods used by private institutions. An increasing dependence on this income source may be a catalyst for consideration of IBB. This factor, or catalyst, may become increasingly significant as states find higher priority uses for tax dollars than higher education.

Yet another motivator that could have long-lasting implications, is an unquantified drift toward decentralization in many institutions. This drift may be encouraged by several factors, but one important factor is technology, which allows diffusion of operations and delivery of instruction. This is evidenced by interest in distance education and marketing strategies, which may pull units away from using historic approaches to governance and curricular development. Another factor in this movement might be the perceived desirability of providing economic incentives easily acted upon at the unit or "division" levels. This is consistent with one of the characteristics associated with high performing organizations, which allow decisionmaking at the lowest possible level in the organization. Another influence may be the ever-present competition for state funds and the desire to be seen as efficient as possible, thus embracing at least the trappings of what may be perceived externally as an efficient mode of operation.

Although it is difficult to ascribe weights to any of these factors, it is important to note that in most instances, they will combine to influence whether or not an institution moves toward exploration and possible implementation of incentive-based forms of budgeting. Inescapably, however, environmental pressures or issues can lead to a growing interest in incentive-based budgeting mechanisms in the future.

Implementation

Where might a derived application of IBB flourish? Once campus policymakers understand the theoretical framework of IBB it will become increasingly clear that certain academic environments will be more hospitable for the implementation of IBB than others. Implementation of IBB, and its variants, should be undertaken judiciously, with a thorough understanding of both IBB itself, and the context in which it is to be employed. Since it is fundamentally designed to devolve fiscal authority and decentralize financial operations, it may be that larger institutions will be more likely to consider IBB than smaller ones.

The following outline lists considerations conducive to an implementation of the conceptual model of IBB:

• *The ability to carry cash balances forward from year to year.* This is important for providing incentives to finding savings in operations. If decisionmakers know they will be able to redirect surplus funds beyond the current fiscal year towards emerging priorities they will be able to increasingly plan and adjust for change.

• *Flexibility to set enrollment policies.* The ability to modify enrollment goals to suit current conditions and institutional values is important. The strategic management of enrollments is a critical variable on the revenue side.

• *Sound accounting and fiscal systems.* These are critical for providing decisionmakers with current information about the state of their accounts. The ability to move resources within the current budget requires timely management information. Unforeseen changes in enrollments, for example, necessitate the ability to allocate funds differently than planned.

• *The ability to set tuition and fees.* This is more often characteristic of private colleges and universities, but within certain guidelines, many public institutions also set their fee structures.

• *Campus units empowered with a high degree of control over expenses.*

• *A well-established and credible governance mechanism within campus units.* Deans and financial officers work closely with faculty governance, as a representative of the entire faculty, to create fiscal policy based on academic priorities.

• *Financial savvy, a professional staff, and enough technical capability to manage resources.* Each unit must have the ability to manage its financial affairs.

• *Lack of crisis in the campus environment at the time of implementation.* Incentive budgeting should not be thought of as a panacea for a university in

short- or medium-run financial predicaments. Rather it should be thought of as a method for allowing stable institutions to grow during a period when higher education's share of the public pie is shrinking.
• *Unit deans capable of managing a complex environment.* In the IBB environment, deans must be more than academic leaders, they must lead units in utilizing budgeting systems to assist in the setting of academic goals, priorities, and values. Each unit should be headed by leaders who can balance short and long term academic goals and priorities with prevailing and projected short- and long-term fiscal conditions.
• *A clear understanding of institutional values.* Campus units should be capable of utilizing incentives that match their goals with those of the entire university.
• *A plan for the institution as a whole which guides the units' decisionmaking processes.* Plans must be formulated with a keen awareness and recognition of the institution's values.
• *Flexibility to shift resources.* In an environment of devolving responsibility, the capability to leverage agendas for the common good of the institution is essential to campus planning and institution building.
• *Operational decentralization requires access to useful financial information.* IBB requires an information-rich environment. The availability of institutional and unit data is imperative because conditions often change, and decisionmakers need access to the latest indicators for effective planning. Sharing of information is increasingly easily facilitated by technology.
• *University leadership must retain sufficient funds to leverage shared institutional goals.*
• *Certain services are required for the collective benefit of the university.* There is a need to determine which services are to be treated as public utilities and which are discretionary. Planners must consider which support services (i.e., computing services, library, and registrar) are an integral part of the mission of the academic units and charge accordingly. Libraries may serve as an example of a campus (public) utility. The resources of the library support the teaching and research mission of all the academic units for both students and faculty members. The prestige of the library and resources is also an important quality indicator of the institution overall, and factors strongly in the ability of the university to attract additional resources. It is therefore in the best interests of each individual academic unit to invest in the library – in this example.

This is not an exhaustive list, nor do all the conditions noted exist at many institutions. The considerations allow or permit the opportunity for institutions to consider selective implementation of various components of IBB appropriate to their unique needs and context.

These are points that describe elements of an environment that will make IBB more apt to be successful in a public institution. However, as noted earlier, it is not unreasonable to speculate that incremental budgeting will remain the dominant approach to public institution finance for the foreseeable future. However, given the environmental incentives to incorporate aspects of IBB into an incremental environment, the trick would seem to be an appropriate individualized match between institutional objectives, institutional profile using the criteria noted, and a thorough understanding of institutional culture. This blend will, of necessity, differ from institution to institution but will always benefit from a structural evaluation and implementation.

A conceptual model (Figure 11.1) represents the possible scenarios that would make adaptation of IBB work in an incremental budget. Each environmental condition at the core of the model represents a corresponding component of IBB that could attach itself to the incremental base. Campus decisionmakers should be able to quickly identify the major fiscal conditions that exist within their own context and match it to the appropriate IBB component.

CONCLUSION

The time may be right to explore innovative or adaptive applications of incentive-based budgeting systems for public institutions of higher education. We have known for some time that the IBB concept was viable in the private setting. We now have evidence that, in some measure, IBB is also a viable approach to budgeting in the public sector. It would be helpful if we could better determine the requirements for implementation of components of IBB, with an eye toward developing a matrix that would match institutional characteristics with the charac-

Figure 11.1: Relating Components of Incentive Budgeting to Incremental Budgeting Structures

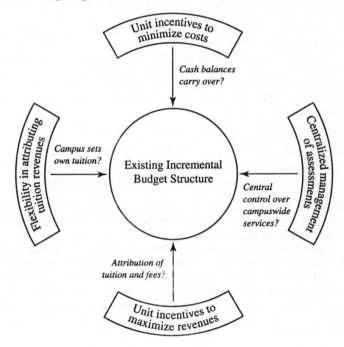

teristics of IBB. It would match the points of commonality with institutional objectives thus conceivably leading to selective applications of IBB, perhaps as a fairly common adjunct to incremental budgeting or other budgeting approaches. Each institution of higher education has characteristics that are familiar to every other institution (i.e., students, faculty, and programs of study). But there are many more characteristics that are unique to the time and place in which that institution resides. IBB is not a panacea for all of higher education's fiscal ills and challenges, nor would a purely capitalistic application of IBB be in the best interest of academe and its many constituents. Any institutional change in budgeting processes and philosophy should be pursued with great care. Even a partial implementation of IBB should not be carried out simply because it fits neatly into an institution's financial system. It should only be accomplished with a thorough understanding of the institution's values, environment, goals, and constituencies.

REFERENCES

American Association of University Professors and Association of Governing Boards. 1966. Statement on governance of colleges and universities. *Academe* 52 (4): 375-379.

Balderston, Frederick E. 1974. *Managing today's university*. San Francisco: Jossey-Bass.

Baldridge, J. Victor, and Michael. L Tierney. 1979. *New approaches to management*. San Francisco: Jossey-Bass.

Bowen, Howard. 1980. *The cost of higher education*. San Francisco: Jossey-Bass.

Cantor, Nancy E., and Paul N. Courant. 1997. Budgets and budgeting at the University of Michigan. A work in progress. *University Record 53* (13), November 26, <http://www.umich.edu/~urecord/9798/Nov26_97/budget.htm >

Green, John L., Jr., and David G. Monical. 1985. Resource allocation in a decentralized environment. *New Directions for Higher Education*, No. 52 (Making the Budget Process Work) 13 (4): 47-63.

Hoenack, Stephen. 1984. *Economic behavior within organizations*. New York: Cambridge University Press.

Honeyman, David S., and M. Bruhn. 1996. The financing of higher education. In David S. Honeyman, James L. Wattenbarger, and Kathleen C. Westbrook, eds., *A struggle to survive: Funding higher education in the next century*. Thousand Oaks, CA: Corwin: 1-28.

Hovey, Harold A. 1999. *State spending for higher education in the next decade: The battle to sustain current support*. Washington, D.C.: The National Center for Public Policy and Higher Education.

Kidwell, Linda J., and William Massy. 1996. Transformation in higher education: Beyond administrative engineering. In Sandra L. Johnson and Jillinda Kidwell, eds., *Reinventing the university: Managing and financing institutions of higher education*. New York: John Wiley & Sons: 3-32.

Meisinger, Richard J., Jr. 1994. Approaches to budgeting. In *College and university budgeting: An introduction for faculty administrators*. Washington, D.C.: NACUBO: 177-188.

National Center for Education Statistics. 1998. *Integrated post-secondary education data system* (IPEDS 98). Washington, D.C.: U.S. Department of Education.

Ruppert, Sandra. 1996. *The politics of remedy: State legislative views on higher education.* Washington, D.C.: National Education Association, April.

St. John, Edward P. 1994. *Prices, productivity, and investment: Assessing financial strategies in higher education.* ASHE/ERIC Higher Education Study, no. 3. Washington, D.C.: George Washington University.

St. John, Edward P. 1981. *Public policy and college management: Title III of the higher education act.* New York: Praeger.

Slaughter, Sheila, and Larry L. Leslie. 1997. *Academic capitalism: Politics, policies, and the entrepreneurial university.* Baltimore: Johns Hopkins University Press.

Weathersby, George B., and Frederick E. Balderston. 1974. PPBS in higher education planning and management: Part 1, an overview. *Higher Education* 1:191-206.

Whalen, Edward L. 1996. Responsibility centered management: An approach to decentralized financial operations. In David S. Honeyman, James L. Wattenbarger, and Kathleen C. Westbrook, eds., *A struggle to survive: Funding higher education in the next century.* Thousand Oaks, CA: Corwin: 127-154.

INDEX